FOUR BROTHERS IN GRAY

by M.A. Hancock

ALFRED NEWTON PROFFIT, SON OF WILLIAM AND MARY "POLLY" WALSH PROFFIT
AND BROTHER OF
WILLIAM HARRISON, ANDREW J. AND CALVIN LUTHER PROFFIT.

Photograph from The Heritage of Wilkes County Vol. I, Ruth Proffit Gregory, Granddaughter

FOUR BROTHERS IN GRAY

by M.A. Hancock
©1975 Wilkes Community College

With
contemporary photographs,
maps, artwork
& transcripts of the Proffit Family letters

Foreword by John Miller

Imaging Specialists, Inc. ★ Sparta, North Carolina

An imprint of Imaging Specialists, Inc.

This edition Copyright ©2013
— Imaging Specialists, Inc. —
Sparta, North Carolina

All rights reserved. No part of this book may be reproduced in any form or by electronic or mechanical means, including information page and retrieval systems, without permission in writing from the publisher.

Part One:
Four Brothers in Gray
by Mary Alice Hancock
Moravian Falls, North Carolina
©1975 Wilkes Community College

Part Two:
The "Connection"
Information on the Proffit Family

Part Three:
Transcripts of
Proffit Family Letters, 1860-1865,
in the Southern Historical Collection,
The Wilson Library,
University of North Carolina at Chapel Hill

Part Four:
Regiments & Battles -
Regimental Histories from the
National Park Service
U.S. Department of the Interior

www.starroutebooks.com

First printing, May 2013

CONTENTS.

LIST OF ILLUSTRATIONS vi

ABOUT THE AUTHOR viii

FOREWORD, *John Horton Miller* ix

FOUR BROTHERS IN GRAY, *M.A. Hancock* 1

THE "CONNECTION" *information on the Proffit Family* 85

PROFFIT FAMILY LETTERS, *Southern Historical Collection* 93

ABBREVIATIONS & DEFINITIONS 96

REGIMENTS & BATTLES 297

HISTORY OF CO. B, FIRST N.C.T., *R. A. Spainhour* . . . 298

RETURN TO THE TENTED FIELD, *Thomas Charles Land* 307

ILLUSTRATIONS.

ALFRED NEWTON PROFFIT, *The Heritage of Wilkes County Vol. I, from Ruth Proffit Gregory* . . ii
JOHN HORTON MILLER ix
FOUR BROTHERS IN GRAY, *Edward O. Wood* x
A PROCLAMATION, *Broadside, U.S. Library of Congress.* 4
A CALL TO ARMS, *Songsheet, U.S. Library of Congress* 4
COLONEL MONTFORT SYDNEY STOKES, *United States Library of Congress* 7
U.S. CAPITOL, *Photographed by Andrew J. Russell, United States Library of Congress* . . . 9
U.S. CAPITOL, *Photographed by Andrew J. Russell, United States Library of Congress* . . . 9
AQUIA CREEK LANDING, VIRGINIA, *Photographed by Alexander Gardner - U.S. Library of Congress.* 10
USA SLOOP-OF-WAR, PENSACOLA, *U.S. National Archives* 11
ROBERT EDWARD LEE, *from The Life Of Gen. Grant, Memorial Edition* 12
JOSEPH EGGLESTON JOHNSTON, *Photographed by Mathew Brady, U.S. National Archives* . . . 13
REBELS LEAVING MECHANICSVILLE, *Drawing by Alfred Rudolf Waud, U.S. Library of Congress* . 14
BATTLE OF GAINES MILL, *War Department, Office of the Chief Signal Officer - U.S. National Archives* . 15
WOUNDED UNION PRISONERS AT SAVAGE STATION, VA, *Photo by James F. Gibson, U.S. LOC* . 15
THADDEUS S.C. LOWE, *Brady-Handy Collection, U.S. Library of Congress* 16
PROFESSOR LOWE'S BALLOON, GAINES MILL, VA, *Photo by Mathew Brady, U.S. LOC* . 16
RICHMOND, VIRGINIA, *Photographed by Andrew J. Russell, United States Library of Congress* . . 17
MAP OF NORTHERN VIRGINIA AND MARYLAND, *Harper's Pictorial History of the Civil War* . 18
LAWRENCE O'BRYAN BRANCH, *Photo by Julian Vannerson, U.S. Library of Congress* . . . 19
AMBROSE P. HILL, *Brady-Handy Collection, U.S. Library of Congress* 20
HARPER'S FERRY, WEST VIRGINIA, *Photo by C.O. Bostwick, U.S. Library of Congress* . . . 21
ANTIETAM BRIDGE, MARYLAND, *Photo by Alexander Gardner, U.S. Library of Congress* . . 22
THOMAS J. JACKSON, *United States Library of Congress* 23
FREDERICKSBURG, VIRGINIA, *Photo by Timothy H. O'Sullivan, United States Library of Congress* . 25
CONFEDERATES AT FREDERICKSBURG, VIRGINIA, *Photo by Mathew Brady, U.S. Nat. Arch.* . 26
THE BOMBARDMENT OF FREDERICKSBURG, *DRAWN BY R.F. ZOGBAUM, U.S. LOC* . . . 27
JAMES HENRY LANE, *Virginia Military Institute Archives.* 31
ROBERT EMMETT RODES, *Virginia Military Institute Archives* 32
THOMAS J. "STONEWALL" JACKSON, *Photographed by Mathew Brady, U.S. Nat. Archives.* . . 35
JAMES EWELL BROWN STUART, *United States Library of Congress* 36
JOHN DECATUR BARRY, *United States Library of Congress* 38
MAP OF THE REGION NEAR CHANCELLORSVILLE, *Harper's Pictorial History of the Civil War* . 39
BATTLE FLAG, 18TH REGIMENT N.C.T., *North Carolina Museum Of History* 42
REBEL PRISONERS CAPTURED AT CHANCELLORSVILLE, *Drawn by Edwin Forbes, U.S. LOC* . 43
RICHARD S. EWELL, *U.S. Library of Congress.* 44
ROBERT HUSTON MILROY, *Brady-Handy Collection, U.S. Library of Congress* 44
GETTYSBURG, PENNSYLVANIA, *Photo by Timothy H. O'Sullivan, United States Library of Congress* . 45
GETTYSBURG, PENNSYLVANIA, *Federal breastworks on Culp's Hill, U.S. LOC* . . 46
GETTYSBURG, PENNSYLVANIA, *Battered trees on Culp's Hill, U.S. LOC* . . . 47
UNION SIGNAL CORPS ON THE RAPIDAN RIVER, *Photo by Mathew Brady, , U.S. Nat. Arch.* . . . 51
TRACKS AT BRISTOW STATION, *Photographed by Timothy H. O'Sullivan, U.S. L.O.C.* . . . 52

COVER— "CONFEDERATE CAMP" DURING THE LATE AMERICAN WAR-
1871 chromolithograph by Louis Zimmer, after a painting by C. W. Chapman, Ordnance Sergeant, 59th Virginia Regiment, Wise's Brigade. U.S. Library of Congress

ILLUSTRATIONS.

BRIDGE ACROSS THE RAPPAHANNOCK, *Photo by Timothy H. O'Sullivan, U.S. L.O.C.* . . . 53
BURNING THE RAPPAHANNOCK RAILWAY BRIDGE, *Drawing by Alfred Waud, U.S. L.O.C.* . . 53
MEMORIAL AT MAPLEWOOD, *Judith Gunnett* 56
ULYSSES SIMPSON GRANT, *by Newton Timothy Hartshorn, United States Library of Congress* . 58
GRANT'S TROOPS CROSSING THE RAPIDAN, *Photo by Timothy H. O'Sullivan, U.S. L.O.C.* . . 60
JAMES LONGSTREET, *Brady-Handy Collection, U.S. Library of Congress* 61
BATTLE OF SPOTSYLVANIA, *From a painting by Thure De Thulstrup - United States Library of Congress.* . 62
CONFEDERATE PRISONERS AT BELLE PLAIN LANDING, VA, *Photo by Mathew Brady, U.S. LOC.* . . 64
GRANT AT COLD HARBOR, *Photo by Edgar Guy Fowx, United States Library of Congress* 64
STAUNTON, VIRGINIA, *From a painting by Edward Beyer, United States National Archives* 65
JUBAL ANDERSON EARLY, *Brady-Handy Collection, U.S. Library of Congress.* 66
WINFIELD S. HANCOCK, *Brady National Photographic Art Gallery, U.S. Library of Congress* . . . 68
FORTIFICATIONS AT PETERSBURG, VIRGINIA, *United States Library of Congress* 70
ROLL OF PRISONERS FROM PT. LOOKOUT, MD, *Civil War Prisoner of War Records, 1861-1865, NARA* . 71
POINT LOOKOUT, MD, *Lith. by E. Sachse & Co., Baltimore, U.S. LOC* 71
CITY OF ATLANTA, GA, *Photo by George N. Barnard, United States Library of Congress* 73
WILLIAM T. SHERMAN, *United States Library of Congress* 73
CONFEDERATE BREASTWORKS AT PETERSBURG, *Photographed by Mathew Brady, U.S. Nat. Archives* . 74
LAST PRISONERS TAKE THE OATH AT PT. LOOKOUT, *The Photographic History of the Civil War* . 76, 77
MAP OF STONEMAN'S NC RAID, *Harper's Pictorial History of the Civil War* 78
GEORGE STONEMAN, JR., *United States Library of Congress* 79
ALFRED NEWTON PROFFIT, *The Heritage of Wilkes County Vol. II, from Ruth Proffit Gregory* . . . 82
THOMAS CHARLES LAND, *The Heritage of Wilkes County Vol. I, from Jessie Parsons Rhyne* . . . 106
COLONEL MONTFORT SYDNEY STOKES, *United States Library of Congress* 109
WINTER QUARTERS AT BRANDY STATION, *by E. Rees for L.N. Rosenthal, Lith., U.S. LOC* . . . 123
MANASSAS, VIRGINIA. CONFEDERATE WINTER QUARTERS. *Photo by George N. Barnard., U.S. LOC* . 123
THE USS MERRIMACK, *United States Library of Congress.* 126
THE CSS VIRGINIA, *Harper's Pictorial History of the Civil War* 126
RICHMOND DAILY DISPATCH, *Boatwright Library, University of Richmond.* 127
MAP OF THE NORTH CAROLINA COAST, *Harper's Pictorial History of the Civil War.* 130
5-CENT CONFEDERATE POSTAGE STAMP, *Smithsonian National Museum* 136
RICHMOND, VA. ARSENAL GROUNDS, *Photo by Alexander Gardner, United States Library of Congress* .148
POTOMAC NEAR HARPER'S FERRY, *drawn by Frances Flora Bond (Fanny) Palmer, U.S. LOC.* . . .152
MAP OF THE SHENANDOAH VALLEY, *Harper's Pictorial History of the Civil War* 156
THE BIBLICAL RECORDER, *Z. Smith Reynolds Library, Wake Forest University* 185
MAP OF THE FIELD OF OPERATIONS OF THE ARMY OF VIRGINIA, *United States Library of Congress* .191
SCENE ON THE U.S. FORD ROAD, *Drawing by Edwin Forbes, United States Library of Congress* . .195
MAP OF THE VICINTY OF RICHMOND, VA., *Harper's Pictorial History of the Civil War.* 197
CHIMBORAZO HOSPITAL IN RICHMOND, VIRGINIA, *United States Library of Congress* 214
DETAIL OF A MAP OF THE SHENANDOAH VALLEY, *Harper's Pictorial History of the Civil War* . .224
JESSE ELIHU LUTHER AND AMELIA MARIEH JAMES LUTHER, *Mike Read.* 246
STEPHEN ARNOLD DOUGLAS, *United States Library of Congress* 248
ZEBULON BAIRD VANCE, *Photographed by Julian Vannerson, United States Library of Congress* . .257
SISTER OF CHARITY, *Drawing, United States Library of Congress* 273

ALL LETTER IMAGES AFTER PAGE 104, *Southern Historical Collection, Wilson Library, University of North Carolina at Chapel Hill*

ABOUT THE AUTHOR.

Mary Alice Hancock was described by Elsie Hamilton in a 1970, *Gastonia Gazette* interview as "a quiet, intelligent, petite bundle of creative talent." At that time, she lived in Mt. Holly, N.C., "quietly with her elderly parents in the home of her sister and brother-in-law."

Ms. Hancock was born in Wisconsin and lived in Missouri, Oklahoma, Ohio, Virginia and Florida before coming to the Blue Ridge Mountains of North Carolina. After two years of college, she served as a Navy WAVE in World War II. She said of her service, "It was the thing to do. Everyone wanted to help."

Ms. Hancock had worked in advertising before she turned to fiction and began writing articles for magazines including the Saturday Evening Post, Sports Illustrated, American Legion Magazine, Progressive Farmer, Catholic Digest and VFW magazine.

She wrote two fictional children's books, *Menace on the Mountain* in 1968 which was eventually made into a two-part, television episode of *The Wonderful World of Disney*. Her second book, in 1969, was a non-fiction novel called *Thundering Prairie* about the Oklahoma Land Rush.

Mary lived in Moravian Falls, Wilkes County, North Carolina when she wrote *Four Brothers in Gray*.

Ms. Hancock passed away in 1999 and was buried at the Western Carolina Veterans Cemetery in Black Mountain. Her marker, there, reads:

MARY ALICE HANCOCK
AERM 3   US NAVY   WORLD WAR II
MARCH 21, 1923
JUNE 19, 1999
OUR WARRIOR FOR WHIMSEY

FOREWORD.

As a youngster growing up our families had many family reunions. Many of our family members were very active in the Civil War; a lot of stories were told. I did not appreciate the history that I was hearing, first hand from people who had been very involved, telling about it.

Four Brothers in Gray is an authentic account of this tragic period in our history. They didn't just read about it. They lived it.

Alfred Proffit was my mother's grandfather. She was married to Reece Miller, whose Great-Grandfather was Captain Horton Doughton who was a hero in the Civil War from Alleghany County.

Other members of the Proffit family, besides my own, who live in Alleghany County are James R. Proffit, Richard P. Proffit, Brady S. Proffit and Rita Proffit Wagoner. The Proffit brothers own and operate NAPCO, one of our leading manufacturing companies in Sparta.

I am very proud to write an introduction to this historic book.

John H. Miller
Mayor of Sparta

ALFRED PROFFIT'S GREAT-GRANDSON
JOHN HORTON MILLER

John Horton Miller, *son of*
Nettie Marie Proffit Miller, *daughter of*
William Albert Proffit, *son of*
Alfred Newton Proffit

Drawing by Edward O. Wood. Original cover art for Four Brothers in Gray ©1975 Wilkes Community College

Part One

Four Brothers in Gray

When the Civil War letters of Andy, Harrison, Alfred and Calvin Proffit recently came to light in the Blue Ridge foothills of North Carolina, they had faded unread, in an ancient tooled-leather chest for nearly a century. The one hundred and twenty-six soldiers' letters tell a hauntingly human story of men embroiled in the birth agonies of a Nation- the personal story of four brothers in gray who fought for the Confederacy in General Lee's Army of Northern Virginia, General Stonewall Jackson's Corps.

And in telling, the Proffit letters dispute- with incontestable documentary proof- two major sources of Civil War history: the U.S. Government printed, *Official records of the Union and Confederate Armies* and *Histories of the Several Regiments and Battalions from North Carolina in the Great War, 1861-'65*, published by the State of North Carolina. The correction to the official records concerns battle action on the bloody, death-filled third day of Chancellorsville- on the morning after Andy Proffit had crouched on the front lines in the dark, tangled woods and breathed the acrid smoke of the Confederate musket volley that struck down, by tragic mistake, General Stonewall Jackson.

And in the telling, too, the Proffit letters paint vivid self-portraits of rank and file Confederate soldiers whose point of view was not represented in the voluminous reminiscences and personal narratives left by the men who fought the war. Many eye-witness accounts were written by generals or other officers, and the few voices from the ranks were those of well-educated and often aristocratic privates who were equipped to communicate their memories. But the common soldier with limited educational opportunities, and unabashed deficiencies in spelling, grammar and punctuation, remained silent in the post-bellum rash of printed reminiscences- most of which was written long after Appomattox, when time had blurred the focus of memory, and the viewpoint of the narrator had changed from brave youth to mature middle age.

In the stark immediacy of letters written from battlefield, camp and bivouac, the Proffit brothers speak for the silent Confederate soldier. Although their hard-earned education- especially Harrison's- was better than average for the times, the very fact of spelling originalities adds a strange, simple eloquence to their words.

They wrote of the scenic wonders of Virginia:

> *"Thare is a young calf in Fredericksburg with 2 heads, 3 years 4 eyes, 4 nose holes & 2 mouths. It sucks with either mouth & its 3rd year is between its heads..."*

And wistful home-thoughts:

> *"How are the mules?... Sis, I am the loansomest chicken you ever saw... Is mustaches fasionable in Wilkes at present? What is the general opinion about peace thare?"*

And war at its grimmest:

> *"I have just passed through another grate battal... I have sean so many horrible things that nothing mutch has any affect on me..."*

Here, in their own words, etched into the war's background of the march from Bull Run to Appomattox, is the story of Andy, Harrison, Calvin and Alfred Proffit. It is told as they wrote the current news to their "Esteemed Parents & Sister" at home; and as William and Mary Proffit- who sent all their sons to war- learned, by mail, how many would come back...

M.A. Hancock

Moravian Falls,
North Carolina

STATE OF NORTH CAROLINA.

A PROCLAMATION,

BY JOHN W. ELLIS,

GOVERNOR OF NORTH CAROLINA

WHEREAS: By Proclamation of Abraham Lincoln, President of the United States, followed by a requisition of Simon Cameron, Secretary of War, I am informed that the said Abraham Lincoln has made a call for 75,000 men to be employed for the invasion of the peaceful homes of the South, and for the violent subversion of the liberties of a free people, constituting a large part of the whole population of the late United States: And, whereas, this high-handed act of tyrannical outrage is not only in violation of all constitutional law, in utter disregard of every sentiment of humanity and Christian civilization, and conceived in a spirit of aggression unparalleled by any act of recorded history, but is a direct step towards the subjugation of the whole South, and the conversion of a free Republic, inherited from our fathers, into a military despotism, to be established by worse than foreign enemies on the ruins of our once glorious Constitution of Equal Rights.

Now, therefore, I, JOHN W. ELLIS, Governor of the State of North-Carolina, for these extraordinary causes, do hereby issue this, my Proclamation, notifying and requesting the Senators and Members of the House of Commons of the General Assembly of North-Carolina, to meet in Special Session at the Capitol, in the City of Raleigh, on Wednesday the first day of May next. And I furthermore exhort all good citizens throughout the State to be mindful that their first allegiance is due to the Sovereignty which protects their homes and dearest interests, as their first service is due for the sacred defence of their hearths, and of the soil which holds the graves of our glorious dead.

United action in defence of the sovereignty of North-Carolina, and of the rights of the South, becomes now the duty of all.

Given under my hand, and attested by the Great Seal of the State. Done at the City of Raleigh, the 17th day of April, A. D., 1861, and in the eighty-fifth year of our Independence,

JOHN. W. ELLIS.

By the Governor,
GRAHAM DAVES, *Private Secretary.*

Broadside. Printed in Raleigh, 1861. United States Library of Congress

NORTH CAROLINA

A CALL TO ARMS!!!

Ye sons of Carolina! awake from your dreaming!
The minions of Lincoln upon us are streaming!
Oh! wait not for argument, call, or persuasion,
To meet at the onset this treach'rous invasion!

Oh! think of the maidens, the wives, and the mothers,
Fly ye to the rescue, sons, husbands and brothers,
And sink in oblivion all party and section,
Your hearthstones are looking to you for protection!

"Her name stands the foremost in Liberty's story,"
Oh! tarnish not now her fame and her glory!
Your fathers to save her their swords bravely yielded.
And she never yet has to tyranny yielded.

The babe in its sweetness—the child in its beauty,
Unconsciously urge you to action and duty!
By all that is sacred, by all to you tender,
Your country adjures, arise and defend her!

"The Star Spangled Banner," dishonored is streaming
O'er bands of fanatics; their swords are now gleaming;
They thirst for the life-blood of those you most cherish
With brave hearts and true, then, arouse! or they perish

Round the flag of the South, oh! in thousands now rally
For the hour's departed when freemen may dally;
Your all is at stake, then go forth, and God speed you!
And onward to glory and victory lead you!

Thompson & Co., Printers, Raleigh, 1861.

Songsheet. Rare Book and Special Collections Division, Library of Congress

In April, 1861, when the bombardment of Fort Sumter lit the fuse of war, the Proffit brothers had shaped their lives to the rugged Blue Ridge foothills of their birth, the Lewis Fork section of Wilkes County, North Carolina. They were tall, rangy men, brown-eyed, dark-haired and with chins as strong as the granite cliffs of home.

Andy, the oldest, was an amiable, twenty-seven-year-old bachelor who farmed, did occasional blacksmithing jobs and taught school in his home hills for "twelve dollars a month and him boarded." Like his brothers', Andy's education had been a hard-bought, piecemeal achievement- with short sessions of schooling sandwiched in between stark necessity of helping his father coax a living from the home farm. In spite of his teaching experience, and, in 1860, his election to church clerk of the Lewis Fork Baptist Church, Andy's grip on the tools of writing slipped.

Harrison, at twenty-two, had also set his sights on the teaching trade, and had outstripped his elder brother in the struggle for learning. Thoughtful, grave-minded Harrison was mature beyond his years, and fiercely dedicated to study and self-improvement, both for himself and his kin. His uncompromising credo was, "Let not a moment pass unimproved!" and he saw teaching as the golden path for his own advancement. When the war reached for Harrison, it found him on the first rung of his career's ladder- assistant teacher in the Beaver Creek School.

The nineteen-year-old twins, Alfred and Calvin, were alternately attending to the farm and going to school. Alfred was a lighthearted, frisky boy with an appreciative eye for the Lewis Fork girls, and his leanings were toward the land instead of the schoolroom. And Calvin, who suffered frequent spells of severe headaches, was torn between the rollicking lead of his twin, and Harrison's stern urgings to hard study and the teaching profession.

For the Proffit brothers, their fifty-eight-year-old parents, William and Mary, and their twenty-four-year-old sister, Louisa, home was a small, hill-rimmed farm near the clear, chuckling waters of Lewis Fork Creek, where William Proffit had reared his young by scratching wheat and corn crops from the stubborn soil and by serving his neighbors as community blacksmith and tooth-puller.

Home was the shaggy mountains, Buck and Chestnut- feminine in the spring with the pink and white of laurel and dogwood, and the air's sweet hint of honeysuckle; but masculine in the fall when nuts, spicewood and cedar scented the hills. Home, too, was community parties at apple-peelings, bean-stringing and sorghum-making time; and the once-a-month preaching meetings at the Lewis Fork Baptist Church, set high enough in the hills to put the awesome feel of Presence to worship, yet- with the cloud-crowned Blue Ridge towering still higher to the west- low enough to breed humility.

A living came hard on the stubborn land of Lewis Fork- starkly harder than on Carolina's rich plantation soil to the east- but there was a quiet pride in the earning of it. Only the highest duty could pull a Lewis Fork man from his hills, and only death could keep him from a homecoming. The duty call came on May 20, 1861, when North Carolina seceded; and the Proffits- a family that had never owned slaves- heard it as the same supreme cause that had sent a former generation of Lewis Forkers to battle the British at King's Mountain- a fight for independence.

Seven days later, on May 27, 1861, Harrison Proffit marched away from Lewis Fork with the Wilkes Valley Guards and recorded his adventures for the home folks:

> *"We crossed the Brushy Mountains... and reached Statesville, where we took the evening train and arrived at Salisbury before night. The Brass Band and many spectators were assembled at the depot. We were escorted through the town in elegant stile, the Brass Band sending forth its most sweet and fascinating notes...*
>
> *"Went from Salisbury to Raleigh... Went from Raleigh to Camp Edwards near Warrenton, N.C.... Very little time spent in idleness as we drill hard almost every day...*
>
> *"You wanted me to inform you how long we had volunteered. We have volunteered 'for the war.' I am well satisfied that I did... Inform me how our mules are doing..."*

CSA COLONEL MONTFORT SYDNEY STOKES

At Camp Edwards the Wilkes Valley Guards were mustered into the 1st North Carolina Regiment as Company B, and the Guard's Captain- M.S. Stokes- was promoted to colonel of the regiment. In a happy interlude between drilling sessions, *a No. 1 dinner was bestowed upon the officers and soldiers of the (1st N.C.) Regiment by the patriotic and noble ladies and gentlemen of Warrenton."*

In late July, 1861- still training at Camp Edwards- Harrison took pen in hand and wrote the Lewis Forkers the latest news that had rumbled down from the Virginia front:

> *"We get the news here every day from Richmond, Petersburg & other points in Va. There are many rumors and reports being circulated and many of them are not reliable...*

> *"I suppose a severe battle was fought... at or near Manassas Junction, General Beauregard commanding the Southern forces, who were victorious..."*

The rumor of a clash near Manassas Junction was fatefully reliable. It was fought on July 21, and called the Battle of Bull Run by the raw Union volunteers who routed the equally raw Confederate troops early in the fight, then later, were themselves routed and panicked back to Washington.

After Bull Run, the war in Virginia sat on its haunches, waiting, for nearly a year- with the Union forces training and strengthening around Washington, and the Confederate troops mobilizing on the south bank of the Potomac River, some within sight of the unfinished Capitol dome.

And to the banks of the Potomac below Washington came Harrison Proffit and the 1st North Carolina Regiment, leaving North Carolina six days after the Confederate victory at Bull Run. Harrison's company was stationed at Acquia Creek, Virginia, to man a battery that overlooked the wide river. From his lofty position as a trained soldier within hearing of the enemy's cannon practice, Harrison wrote slightly patronizing letters to his civilian brothers in August, 1861:

> *"We do not know when we will have a chance to give the Yankees a few balls... but never saw more anxious fellows for a fight than our boys are...*
>
> *"I would be glad to know how you are getting along with your home guard. How many Yankees have you taken? I guess I would like to see you drill once... I recommend you to be certain to attend school without fail."*

Above — Capitol, Washington, D.C., north-east view. Dome and front unfinished.
Photographed by Andrew J. Russell - United States Library of Congress

Below — Capitol, Washington, D.C., south-east view.
Photographed by Andrew J. Russell - United States Library of Congress

AQUIA CREEK LANDING, VIRGINIA. DISTANT VIEW OF FEDERAL SUPPLY DEPOT.
Photographed by Alexander Gardner - United States Library of Congress

By September, Harrison's post had all the earmarks of good duty, with just a touch of excitement:

> *"We spend many of our hours in fishing. We are every one of us living in a house, though they are small, any of them are preferable to tents...*
>
> *"We are situated on Game Point near the Potomac River where we can see any amount of Yankee war steamers sailing up and down the river daily, but they take care to keep near their own shore...*
>
> *"The other day an old steamer happened to sail rather too near our shore, when Battery 2 fired two shots at it, which caused it to halt, and soon after commenced firing at our batteries.*

"They threw some 12 or 15 bombs whizzing through the air at us. Though they fell short of reaching us, yet we could plainly hear them whistle through the air... We felt as brave as little boys, who, with their cornstalk guns, put a score of geese to flight...

"I want you (Andy) to remain teaching school until you have taught at least two or three more sessions... I would be as happy in occupying a seat in that schoolroom as in almost any place I ever saw, for I have spent probably the happiest days of my life in that place...

"I would be glad to know what Alfred's intentions are. I was informed by Calvin that he (Alfred) was riding over the country and taking his pleasure."

In December Harrison's war was still safe and comfortable:

"We have very nearly finished our winter quarters, and they are very comfortable little cabins. Times are quite calm in this part of Virginia, though the sound of cannon is heard here almost continually...

"We have just finished mounting our new pivot cannon. She is a beautiful little gun, weighting about 14,750 lbs...

"I had almost omitted telling you that I think the terms of peace will be agreed upon ere three or four months pass..."

USA
SLOOP-OF-WAR
PENSACOLA

In January, 1862, Harrison's first opportunity to strike a telling blow for the Confederacy ended in frustration, when the Union sloop-of-war, *Pensacola*, sailed within battery range, but ***"our pivot gun became choaked & could not be fired."***

CSA
GENERAL IN CHIEF OF THE ARMIES OF THE CONFEDERATE STATES
ROBERT EDWARD LEE

Image from The Life Of Gen. Grant, Memorial Edition

In February Harrison went home on a twenty-day furlough- a flurry of visits to his Wilkes County friends and kin, which was prolonged by a fourteen-day extension when he informed his regiment of the *"bad state of my health."*

He returned to his regiment in Virginia, then two weeks later, in March, 1862, the 1st North Carolina was ordered back to its home state to meet a threatened enemy advance from the Union-captured port of New Bern, N.C. The attack did not come in North Carolina, but on the western front; the Confederacy fought and lost the bloody battle of Shiloh, Tennessee. And in Virginia, ninety-thousand Union troops landed fifty miles southeast of Richmond and began the siege of Yorktown. Gloom and despair gripped the south.

On May 3, 1862, the Confederate defenders evacuated Yorktown, and retreated slowly up the Peninsula toward Richmond with the Union army in relentless pursuit. On May 10- from his camp near Goldsboro, N.C.- Harrison Proffit wrote spine-stiffening rhetoric to the home folks:

> *"Although our country is apparently enveloped in a dark and portentous cloud of impenetrable apperance, we must recollect that behind this cloud the sun is shining with his undeviating brilliancy and I hope that very soon his genial rays may shine forth upon the people of the Confederate States- firmly united, free, happy and prospering.*
>
> *"Instead of indulging in feelings of despondency, let us compare our situation and cause to those of our illustrious ancestors who achieved the liberties we have ever enjoyed and for which we are now contending..."*

CSA GENERAL JOSEPH EGGLESTON JOHNSTON

Rebels leaving Mechanicsville. Union batteries shelling the Village, May 24, 1862.
Drawing for Harpers Weekly by Alfred Rudolf Waud - United States Library of Congress

In June Harrison's war turned abruptly from words to action. With the Union army within ten miles of the Confederate capital, the 1st North Carolina Regiment was ordered back to Virginia; but arrived in Richmond a few hours too late to take part in the battle of Seven Pines, where Confederate Commander Joseph E. Johnston was wounded and succeeded by a general who had been bitterly attacked in some of the Richmond newspapers for his one previous and unsuccessful field command- Robert E. Lee.

For General Lee, as commander of the Army of Northern Virginia, and for Harrison Proffit, as a soldier, the baptism of fire came on June 26, 1862- at indecisive Mechanicsville, where Harrison's company advanced on the battlefield, as skirmishers, and were exposed to the deadly rattle of enemy musketry and artillery throughout the engagement.

BATTLE OF GAINES MILL, VALLEY OF THE CHICKAHOMINY, VIRGINIA — JUNE 27, 1862.
War Department, Office of the Chief Signal Officer - United States National Archives

WOUNDED UNION PRISONERS AT SAVAGE STATION, VIRGINIA, FIELD HOSPITAL
AFTER THE BATTLE OF GAINES MILL — JUNE 27, 1862.
Photographed by James F. Gibson - United States Library of Congress

Mary Alice Hancock

"One of the most remarkable occurrences of the army has this moment taken place. Park Spring, the telegraph operator, situated in Prof. Lowe's balloon, at an elevation of one thousand feet... is freely and rapidly communicating with the Department at Washington. This is certainly an ingenious and valuable method of giving instantaneous information."
— New York Times, Near the Chickahominy, Thursday, June 5, 1862

USA BALLOON CORPS AERONAUT
THADDEUS S.C. LOWE

Professor Thaddeus S.C. Lowe's hydrogen-filled balloon, the Intrepid, being inflated from the nearby hydrogen gas generators on Dr. Gaines' farm. Lowe made observations over Mechanicsville, Virginia, and the ensuing Battle of Seven Pines- included here as the balloon would surely have been seen by participants in those battles. The Union's "baloon" was mentioned by Alfred in his letter of June 13, 1863, on page 206.
—PUBLISHERS.

Within a week six more battles were fought around Richmond, and after the last- Malvern Hill- the repulsed Union army withdrew from the Richmond area. But the Seven Day's Battles left the 1st North Carolina Regiment shattered with casualties, among them two of the former Wilkes Valley Guards- the Gallant colonel of the regiment, M.S. Stokes, and a Lewis Fork cousin and neighbor of the Proffits, Alfred Walsh. On July 8 Harrison wrote his first letter as battle-tested veteran:

> "I guess you have heard that we have been in several battles during the past few days. Our regiment has sustained a grate loss in the battles. Colonel Stokes was killed. We have lossed all our field officers, at least for a time...
>
> "Four of my company were killed and 20 wounded...
>
> "I was in two battles (Mechanicsville and Gaines's Mill) and escaped uninjured...
>
> "The fatigues of the past few days has almost worn me out. I have never undergone such before...

RICHMOND, VIRGINIA — VIEW OF THE JAMES RIVER.
Photographed by Andrew J. Russell - United States Library of Congress

"The loss of Alfred Walsh was indeed a deplorable one- but such is the horrors of war. A braver soldier couldn't be found. He was much respected by the company and his loss is much regretted by them."

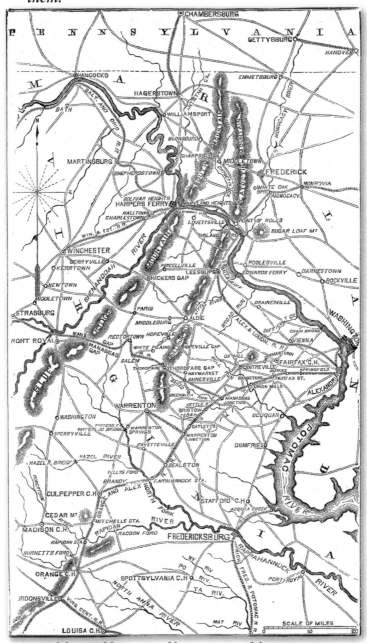

Map of Northern Virginia and Maryland.
from Harper's Pictorial History of the Civil War

After the Seven Days' Battles, Harrison's regiment remained encamped near Richmond for a month. From there, on August 17, he wrote to his younger brother, Calvin:

> *"If the Yankees are making any demonstrations for a renewal of the contest for Richmond, I am unaware of it. "Stonewall" Jackson is keeping their attention directed toward the Valley of Virginia... Large forces are concentrating in the vicinity of Gordonsville, Virginia, and the weasel is expected to pop in a few day...*
>
> *"I understand you are a school teacher. Well, honor your profession and it will honor you... Endeavor to keep always cool and calm, never suffer your passions to rule you. Be ever kind to your students... at the same time let them know that your acquirements must and shall be complied with... Let not an hour pass unimproved. Particularly improve your mode of spelling and hand write..."*

On August 19, Harrison's regiment marched north from Richmond, headed for where the "weasel" would soon "pop" at the Second Battle of Bull Run; but Harrison, himself, collapsed on the march and was hospitalized for the next three months- first at Lynchburg, Virginia, then in the Blue Ridge Mountains of Buchanan, Virginia.

CSA BRIGADIER-GENERAL LAWRENCE O'BRYAN BRANCH

But less than two weeks after Harrison left Richmond, two more Proffit brothers marched into the Confederate capital as recruits for General Lee's army- Andy, twenty-eight then, called from his teaching job at Beaver Creek- and Alfred, the twenty-year-old twin who had been working on the farm and *"riding around the country taking his pleasure."* The raw recruit Proffits had had less than a week of training at Camp Hill, N.C., and were- when Andy wrote home from the Richmond camp on August 29- still without weapons or equipment:

"Our station will be in the 18th N.C. Regiment. I forgot the Col.'s name, but it is Branche's brigade and Jackson's division..."

"Some few of the boys from Wilkes are not well satisfied, but the Stony Fork and Lewis Fork boys are doing finely- waiting for the wagon and anxious to ride..."

And the "wagon" was waiting for them, the bloody-wheeled, corpse-filled wagon called the Maryland Campaign.

CSA LIEUTENANT-GENERAL AMBROSE P. HILL

Three days after Andy wrote his Richmond letter, he and Alfred marched north to join Jackson's men, who had just fought and won Second Bull Run, and were headed, victory-flushed and invasion-minded, toward Union country. On September 9, from the "State of Maryland," Alfred Proffit informed his twin, Calvin, that war- so far- was a dusty hike and a picnic:

"We have had quite a frisky time since we left Richmond. We left thare Monday the 1st of September and hav marched 8 days in succession and cooked our rashions evry night. We waided the Rhappadan and Potomack Rivers...

"I haven't taken off my cloathes since I left home and it will take some rubing to git them clean ...

"I don't know what the intention of Jackson is- he is unwell at this time. When he gits well he will do something..."

Jackson did indeed "do something" when he got well from painful bruises received when a horse fell with him the day after the Potomac crossing. He marched his command to Harper's Ferry to siege and capture the 11,000 man Union garrison, then sped sixteen miles north to rejoin Lee at Sharpsburg, Maryland, where the Battle of Antietam tinged cornfields and creek waters with crimson.

With A.P. Hill's Division- left behind at Harper's Ferry to complete the surrender arrangements- Alfred and Andy Proffit finally received arms: Springfield rifles from the captured Union stores. Then, led by the red-shirted, fiery-eyed Hill, they quick-marched on to Sharpsburg to face the test of fire in the bloodiest single day of the war- September 17, 1862- when Hill's Division arrived on the field just in time to save the broken Confederate lines from certain disaster. On the banks of Antietam Creek the Confederate invasion was turned back, but Lee's Army of Northern Virginia- shattered by 13,000 casualties, but still a potent fighting force- withdrew

HARPER'S FERRY, WEST VIRGINIA. VIEW OF TOWN — RAILROAD BRIDGE IN RUINS.
Photographed by C.O. Bostwick - United States Library of Congress

ANTIETAM BRIDGE, MARYLAND — SEPTEMBER 1862.
Photographed by Alexander Gardner - United States Library of Congress

safely across the Potomac into Virginia, pursued only by two divisions of the Union army, who captured four guns of the Confederate reserve artillery before they were pushed back across the river in the battle of Shepherdstown. On September 22, 1862, Andy Proffit took pen in hand and wrote a jubilant letter to Lewis Fork:

> *"It is with great pleasure that I write you a few lines which will inform you that we are all in the land of the living... We have been gone one month and 2 days, have been in three battles, the 1st at harpers fary where we took about 1,000 prisoners, 2nd in Maryland which was indeed a bloody battle. We did not get to fire ther but was exposed to the fire of the enemy in an open field... Severil of our*

Reg. were killed and wounded. We lay all day next day behind a fense exposed to their sharpshooters.

"That night we crossed back into Va. Althow we ran the enemy from the field, when we left they persued us and crossed day before yesterday. We turned on them and had a bloody engagement. We formed in line of battle about one mile from them and made a generil charge, exposed the hole way to the heaviest bombing said to be by old soldiers that they ever saw, but we routed them and drove them back across the river...

"I suppose we lost a great many but the Yankees lay on the field in heaps and piles... Alfred and I shot as long as we could see a blue coat... The bombs burst round our beads with terrific fury and showers of grape canister fell mingled with limbs of trees thick around us. But God of heaven protected us from their power, which I hope he will ever do. We were much exhausted from the fatigues of the charge that we threw away all our clothes and blankets, only what we have on, but that is all right- we will get more.

CSA LIEUTENANT-GENERAL THOMAS J. JACKSON

"Alfred was slightly struck on the arm with a piece of shell or something. He dropped his gun. I asked him if he was hurt. He said not. He grabed his gun and fought like a hero while the sweat dropped fast from his brow...

"We have not been drilled exceeding 4 hours, but our officers gave us much praise for fighting...

"Pa, I want you to keep Calvin at home, if possible in an honorable way ...for he is not able for such service as is required..."

Thus, in their first month of soldiering, Alfred and Andy Proffit passed most of the tests the war would require of them. And if, during the throat-parching, stomach-queasing moments before their baptism of fire, their most haunting fear was that they might panic to cowardice, they learned the prideful truth in the Maryland Campaign.

After the Battle of Shepherdstown, Jackson's Corps (and Alfred and Andy) camped in the Shenandoah Valley, while the Union army changed commanders and prepared to launch another "On to Richmond" movement. During the three-months lull, the last of the Proffit brothers marched off from Lewis Fork. On November 5, 1862, Pvt. Calvin Proffit, 13th N.C. Regiment, A.P. Hill's Division, Jackson's Corps, joined the family letter writers from Stonewall's camp in the valley:

> *"I write you a few lines to tell you I am moderately well at this time. I have had a very easy time since I have left home, especially for a soldier. I have never stood gard yet. I have not yet received arms... Write me how many bushels they have threashed... and if the mules have minded much..."*

Andy Proffit, too, wrote home from Jackson's Valley camp, gravely concerned about conditions at Lewis Fork:

> *"I am quite sorry Calvin had to come... I do not know how you will go without us all, but there is no other chance now... Take good care of all the money you got for... we have not drawn one cent yet.*
>
> *"Take what you stand in nead of that belongs to me...*
>
> *"Sell my mare, for I know you cannot keep her..."*

In November Harrison Proffit was released from the hospital and rejoined his regiment in time to march with Jackson's "foot Cavalry" (and his three brothers) one hundred and sixty cold, hard miles from the Valley over the Blue Ridge Mountains to Fredericksburg. And on December 12 the Union army crossed the Rappahannock

FREDERICKSBURG, VIRGINIA.
Photographed by Timothy H. O'Sullivan - United States Library of Congress

River; and on December 13 at Fredericksburg, on the red plains below Mary's Heights, lost the battle, but died moving forward- wave after wave of blue charging impregnable defensive positions- with stubborn valor that brought cheers from the Confederate defenders, themselves.

Alfred, Andy and Calvin Proffit fought the battle of Fredericksburg on the front line of Jackson's position, east of the town, where, during a ten-minute period on December 13, about twenty-three of Calvin's regiment died under a Union artillery barrage, and one man froze to death that night. And Alfred and Andy's brigade lost five hundred men when they bore the brunt of a temporarily successful Yankee assault against a gap in Jackson's lines.

Shown here is an amazing photograph from the National Archives - Mathew Brady Collection showing Confederate troops from across the Rappahannock River in Fredericksburg.

They are standing on the remains of a railroad bridge- tracks on the photographer's side are visible in the foreground and belie the actual distance.

The photo was "taken at a distance of one mile." The buildings and shattered bridge are recognizable in the photo on page 25.

—Publishers.

THE BOMBARDMENT OF FREDERICKSBURG — DECEMBER 11, 1862.
Drawn by R.F. Zogbaum, c.1884 - United States Library of Congress

On December 18, after the defeated and demoralized Union army had retired north of the Rappahannock River again, Harrison Proffit wrote the home folks:

> "I will inform you that I have been in the Battle of Fredericksburg, but our division was not actively engaged. We were held in reserve and were only exposed to the fire of artillery.
>
> "The next day after the battle of the 13th, we were sent forward and occupied the front lines. We were near the enemy. We could plainly see three of their lines of battle, and were near enough to have reached them with our small arms.
>
> "We expected every minute to hear the next battle begin- but in the evening the enemy sent in a flag of truce, asking permission to bury their dead. They carried off about half of their dead when the time expired. That night they crossed the river, and when day appeared, the blue lines were not to be seen…
>
> "After the battle was over, I went to the 18th N.C. Regt. and saw Andrew and Alfred. They were in the battle but not hurt. Alfred had seen Calvin a day or two before. He was well and in good spirits."

After Fredericksburg the two opposing armies went into winter quarters, building crude cabins and pitching tents with only the Rapidan and Rappahannock Rivers separating the blue and gray picket outposts, and for five months the war in Virginia hibernated. Camp routine settled into a pattern of drilling, standing guard and- in leisure hours- visiting friends and relations in other regiments. With no battles to be fought, the Proffit brothers found other things to write home about.

In January, 1863, Calvin penned the eternal soldier's lament:

> *"I want to have a letter from home as I have not received a single line in two months... Send me a kneadle and some thread, and let me know how the mules look..."*

Andy reassured his mother:

> *"You seem to be uneasy about our clothing which you kneed not be, for we have plenty of clothing except socks and gloves. I want you to see as little uneasiness about us as you possible can, as it will be no advantage to us but an injury to you. You kneed not think that the government will allow us to starve or go necked, although we get scarce sometimes...*
>
> *"I was sorry you heard I was sick and caused you to be uneasy. There has been but little the matter with me. I had the diarhea and did no deauty, but that is so common here that we hardly call it sickness."*

From Alfred there was advice for his father, who was having a stark struggle to eke a living from the farm:

> *"Do the best you can, Pa, till we come home and then we will help you to do. Bee surtain to keep the mules. Bee sure to set you out an orchid for I see the nead of them. I am paing $3 for apples green and fifty cents a quart for red ones. Send some mulasses and brandy if you can. Send some soap. It is one dollar a pound."*

And from Harrison who was promoted to corporal on February 2, the latest crop of rumors:

> *"The papers give accounts of dissatisfaction and confusion in the North Western states, which are said to be ripe for secession. The Lincoln administration is denounced throughout the whole United States to a grater or less extent. In view of these circumstances and hundreds of other convincing ones, I think a speedy termination of the war may be expected."*

By March, 1863, the twins wrote with pens dipped in homesickness.

From Alfred:

> *"It has been the hardist winter I all most ever saw. It is rain and snow all the time. I want to see you all the worst in the world. I must soon come home and see all the girls in that country or they will forgit me. Give them my love and respecks."*

And from Calvin a wistful reappraisal of tasks that had once been drudgery:

> *"Though I was not vary industrous, I would take delight in assisting you in fixing for a crop. I hope I will get home in time to prepare for a large crop of wheat… I hope I will get to come home to stay and assist in setting an orchard…"*

On March 28, 1863, a week after Calvin dreamed of setting an orchard in his hills, three Proffits wrote letters to Lewis Fork. From Alfred:

> "After my best love and respecks to you, I am thankful to have the good news to write you that I am yet numbered among the liveing while hunards & thousands are dailey deprived of the sweatness of life. This is all the good news I have, but I have the sad and hart brakeing news to write you of the death of our beloved brother, Calvin. He departed this life March the 25. The doctor who attended him in his last hours said it was inflammation of the brain...

> "I have been informed that he died quite easy. Without a word or groan, he closed his eyes and seemed as if he had drooped into a deep sleep..."

From Harrison:

> "Sad as the thought is, it is no worse than thousands have endured since the commencement of this unholy war. I hope you will try to refrain as much as possible from unnecessary grief, as it is a thing of no avail..."

And from Andy:

> "I suppose you would love to know how he was put away. Well, he was washed and clean clothes put on him & his officers buried him with their own hands, a thing I have never seen done before since I have been in service...

> "We buried him in a nice place in an orchard..."

And so died Calvin Luther Proffit, a month before his twenty-first birthday, in a crude winter quarters cabin four hundred miles from Lewis Fork. And as he was buried in the Virginia orchard, the first green whisperings of spring stirred the slumbering armies, a season that promised only new battles and fresh graves during the grim war years.

In April soldiers in the winter camps both north and south of the Rappahannock River wondered at the time and place of that year's spring slaughter- among them, Alfred Proffit:

> *"We are waiting for the Yankees to make a move and then we will give them a cawl. We are strongly fortified from Fredericksburg to Fourt Royal and it is the jeneral opinion of all if they do cross here they will get the worst whipping they ever have got..."*

By May 1, 1863, the troops, blue and gray, knew where and when the green spring would turn red- a few miles south of the Rappahannock near Fredericksburg again, in the tangled woods and thickets surrounding a country mansion named Chancellorsville.

On May Day the armies snapped at each other in small, indecisive skirmishes, but that night General Lee and General Jackson held a fateful campfire conference that early the next morning- sent the three Proffit brothers off on the most famed flanking march in American military history. May 2, 1863, dawned bright and clear over the dense, tangled Virginia countryside aptly called "The Wilderness." The Union line stretched across this wild land with its left flank near Fredericksburg, and its right flank "in the air" a few miles west of the Chancellorsville mansion. With his Confederate troops outnumbered two to one, General Lee made a bold and daring move- dividing his army- and sent Jackson's command to strike the vulnerable Union right. About 8 o'clock on that spring-touched Saturday morning, Harrison Proffit- waiting with his regiment east of Chancellorsville- saw Generals Lee and Jackson for a brief conference, destined to be their last.

CSA BRIGADIER-GENERAL JAMES HENRY LANE

Then Jackson led his command southwestward over woods-concealed country roads that passed along the Union front, with Alfred and Andy Proffit marching in A.P. Hill's Division, Lane's Brigade, and Harrison in Trimble's Division, Colston's Brigade. Late in the evening Jackson's men reached the exposed right flank and rear of the Yankee line, and quietly deployed for the surprise attack. In the second line of assault waited Harrison Proffit. To the rear as reserves stood Alfred and Andy.

About 5:15- an hour and half before sunset- Jackson took out his watch. Under the brim of his cap his eyes glittered with the strange fire of battle that had earned him the name "Old Blue Light." "Are you ready, General Rodes?" he enquired of the commander of the assaulting brigades. "Yes sir," said Rodes. "You can go forward then," said Jackson quietly.

CSA BRIGADIER-GENERAL
ROBERT EMMETT RODES

The gray lines charged eastward, driving panicked deer and rabbits ahead of them in the woods. The Union 11th Corps- unsuspecting and some with their arms stacked while they ate supper- waved their hats and whooped when the terrorized animals bolted through their lines; then with the weird shriek of the rebel yell and the murderous bark of musketry, the gray attackers broke out of the brush and fell on the bluecoats, and smashed them into a panic-stricken mass.

Forward through the dense wilderness the Confederate lines swept, with Harrison Proffit's regiment surging up to the front line early in advance, and by dusk Jackson's men had driven in the union right for two miles. Finally, behind their breastworks at the Chancellor mansion, the Union resistance stiffened, and the two leading divisions of the Confederate attack became broken and disorganized in the baffling darkness of the smoke-hazed woods. The gray advance was halted a few hundred yards west of the Chancellor house to reform its ragged lines.

The moon rode dim and red, and toward the front marched the five regiments of Lane's Brigade- including the 18th N.C.- to relieve the disorganized assaulting brigades. Jackson, too, headed for the front on his sorrel mount, impatient to reconnoiter the advance positions, and set his attack in motion again.

As Jackson rode eastward along the Plank Road that sliced through the Wilderness, a furious Union cannonade forced him to stop and take shelter. Ahead of him, the same enemy barrage compelled the 18th N.C. Regiment to halt its advance to the front and lie down. The heavy shelling cost the 18th several causalities, including its color-sergeant. When the Union fire ceased, Jackson resumed his ride, and the 18th N.C., too, moved forward again. Soon Jackson passed the 18th and rode tensely ahead. Staff officers, couriers and signalmen joined him on his ride, and when he reached the front and moved on beyond the Confederate picket lines, his party had the appearance of a cavalry detachment in the dark-shadowy woods.

Straight ahead into No Man's Land Jackson rode until he heard voices in front of him, and the sharp thwack of Union axes felling trees for breastworks. Hero Jackson drew reign and listened and planned. The attack must be pressed, he decided. With the greatest possible speed, A.P. Hill's Light Division must be thrown against the enemy. Jackson turned his sorrel and rode westward on the dark road, impatient to reach his own lines and order the advance that could make this, already his greatest victory, such a terrible slaughter of Union troops that the war could well end in independence for the Confederacy.

Ahead of Jackson on the Confederate front, Lane's Brigade had moved up and relieved a section of the front lines. The 18th North Carolina was deployed north of the Plank Road, and the 37th North Carolina south of the road. The Tarheels peered nervously into the night that writhed with shadows- a night of confusion for both the Yanks and Rebs. A Union lieutenant-colonel entered the lines of Lane's Brigade under a flag of truce to enquire politely if Lane's men were Union or Confederate troops. And in this tense, black wilderness, where some opposing lines were so close that a man had to ask the color of uniform- and any moment could bring a Union counter-attack, the 18th was informed that there was no one but the enemy in front of them. And toward them- from the direction of the Union lines- rode Jackson and his party.

Suddenly, the 18th N.C. heard a volley of shots burst from the south side of the road.

"Cease firing, cease firing!" a voice shouted.

"Cease firing, you are firing into you own men!" another voice yelled, closer and louder.

Then another voice sounded- louder still- from within the 18th North Carolina's own lines, the familiar voice of a regimental officer. "Who gave that order? It's a lie! Pour it into them, boys!"

And the men of the 18th North Carolina, kneeling in line, fired a volley into the woods to their front, and minie balls from three rifles found targets in the left arm and right hand of Stonewall Jackson, whose horse had swerved to the north side of the Plank Road when the first volley had flashed to the south of the road.

Soon Jackson was carried to the rear with wounds that required an arm amputation that night, and eight days later- a victim of pneumonia- he still muttered battle orders in his last delirium. Then, on the bright Sunday afternoon of May 10, 1863, the mumbled commands ceased; and quietly, lucidly and cheerfully, Jackson said, "Let us cross over the river, and rest under the shade of the trees."

And with this strange, peaceful vision lighting his face, he died.

CSA
LIEUTENANT-GENERAL OF THE ARMIES OF THE CONFEDERATE STATES
THOMAS J. "STONEWALL" JACKSON

Portrait, by Matthew Brady, taken at a Spotsylvania County farm on April 26, 1863, seven days before he was wounded at the Battle of Chancellorsville. - United States National Archives

But mercifully, on the night of May 2, the 18th North Carolina did not know that their volley had struck down their beloved commander. They knew only that there were Yanks and death in the black, wilderness woods, and battles to be fought.

Before midnight, the Union artillery opened fire on the Confederate lines, blasting several causalities among the Tarheels. General A.P. Hill, who had succeeded to Corps command after Jackson fell, was himself disabled with leg wounds, and a cavalryman was summoned to command the troops in the wilderness- the dashing Jeb Stuart, who had never before directed an infantry attack.

The spine-prickling night crawled toward the dawn, but twice, in the blackness, Union troops charged the 18th North Carolina's front; and the Tarheel's stout repulse of the advances brought commendation from General Robert E. Lee in his report of the Chancellorsville Campaign. Wrote Lee:

CSA MAJOR-GENERAL
JAMES EWELL BROWN STUART

"At this time the right of Hill's Division was attacked by a column of the enemy... This attack was gallantly met and repulsed by the Eighteenth and Twenty-eighth and a portion of the Thirty-third North Carolina Regiments, Lane's Brigade..."

Then came the dawn of May 3rd- a warm, pleasant Sunday with mist on the high ground, and Jeb Stuart ordered a general assault against the Union lines. The 18th North Carolina (and Andy Proffit) charged through the brush, carried the Union's first line of breastworks, then swept on to within a few yards of the second Yank line of defenses. There, reported the lieutenant-colonel of the 18th North Carolina:

"The enemy opened on us a most terrific and galling fire of grape, shell and Minie balls. We held our ground, suffering very severely for about half an hour, when the enemy... turned the right of our line, leaving our right flank exposed. We were then ordered to fall back... and the regiment acted as skirmishers for most of the time until the battle ended."

And in the general assault, the 1st North Carolina Regiment and Harrison Proffit advanced also, ordered to support the 18th North Carolina's division and press the assault straight to the Chancellor mansion.

"We soon occupied the (first) line of (enemy) breastworks," reported the regimental commander of the 1st North Carolina Regiment. "Here the enemy made a stubborn resistance... and many brave officers and men fought their last battle... We assisted in the capture of the enemy's works... in the vicinity of the Chancellor house... We continued to advance under one of the most destructive fires from the enemy's field guns and small arms, till a portion of the command on our right was checked... We were taken back to the vicinity of the Chancellor house, where we remained..."

By the night of May 3, the battle of Chancellorsville was over for the 1st and 18th North Carolina Regiments; and on May 5, it passed into history as the Union army withdrew across the Rappahannock River and went into camp on the north bank.

Chancellorsville's terrible toll of casualties gashed deep into both armies- for the Union, 11,000 killed and wounded; and for the victorious Confederacy, more than 10,000, with Jackson- the irreplaceable- among them. Throughout the land, north and south, the word sped of another great battle fought near the Rappahannock; then the home folks waited the long, anguished days for the mail that would tell whether the victory or the defeat had been at personal cost to them. To the hills of Lewis Fork the first word finally came- from Harrison, who had been promoted to sergeant-major on May 2, and wrote to the home folks on May 8:

"I have just passed through one of the bloodiest battles of the war. We have had another desperate battle on the Rappahannock, but I am glad to inform you that victory is ours. Our regiment was in the hardest part of the battle and suffered severely. I received a wound in the jaw on Sunday evening (May 3), and have since been at a hospital... near the battlefield where the wounded were carried during the fight...

"About 30 of our company are killed and wounded... I have not received any correct news from our connections in other Regts..."

And a letter written on May 15 brought news of Alfred

"(Alfred) gave out on the march to the battlefield and was sent to the rear. He had had nothing to eat for a day or so and marched hard which made him sick. Nothing but fatigue and hunger was the matter with him..."

Finally to Lewis Fork came word of Andy Proffit- in accordance with Brigadier-General H. Heth's report in *Official Records of the Union and Confederate Armies, Series 1, Vol, 25, Part 1, Page 893* dated May 21, 1863:

The Eighteenth North Carolina Regiment- In regard to the loss of the flag of this regiment, Col. John D. Barry (then Major Barry) makes the following report: "On Saturday night (the 2nd instant), while marching by the flank upon the Plank road under the severe shelling of the enemy, Color Sergeant (J.E.) Richardson was severely wounded and sent to the rear. Corporal (A.J.) Prophet, (sic) of the color guard, then seized the flag, and at the beginning of the action the 3rd he bore it.

CSA COLONEL JOHN DECATUR BARRY

"During the action he was killed... and Corporal Eakins... was intrusted with it... and bore it through the first charge upon the enemy's entrenched position until orders were received to fall back... He had gone but a few feet when, he, too, was killed...

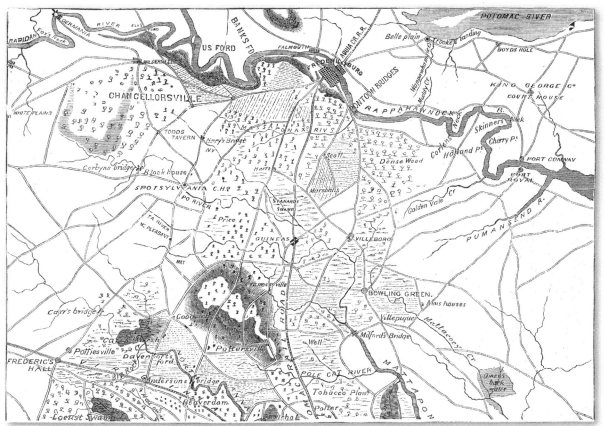

MAP OF THE REGION NEAR CHANCELLORSVILLE.
from Harper's Pictorial History of the Civil War

and (the enemy) entering the line we had fallen back from... the position in which the colors had fallen made it impossible to recover them; at least very unwise to attempt it."

In *Histories of the Several Regiments and Battalions from North Carolina in the Great War, 1861-'65, Vol. 2, Page 40,* the historian of the 18th North Carolina corroborated the "Official Records" in his comments on the Battle of Chancellorsville: *"Color Bearer Richardson, of the Eighteenth, was wounded in the night fighting, and Prophet and Edwards were killed, successively, at the second breastworks next morning."*

And in agreement with both reports, William and Mary Proffit were notified that Andrew J. Proffit was killed in action- the second of their sons to die within two months period.

But on May 15- about the same time that Colonel Barry was penning his report on the loss of the 18th North Carolina's regimental flag- another eyewitness version of the incident was written in Camp Lee, near Richmond. It was an unofficial report, a corporal disputing a colonel, yet with an unassailable claim to authenticity- documentation in the hand of the "dead man" himself, Andy J. Proffit:

"Dear father, I take this kind opportunity of writing you a few lines which will inform you that I am again on southern soil, well and doing finely. I am sorry to inform you that I unfortunately fell into the hands of the enemy on Sunday, the 3rd inst. I will now try to tell you how it happened.

"As we are on the march to the battlefield, I with another Corporal were appointed to guard the flag, one of the most dangerous positions in battle. On Saturday night there fell a bomb in my company and exploded in 4 or 5 feet of me and wounded the flag bearer and 5 or 6 of my company, taking off one man's leg and wounded my lieutenant. When the flag of my country fell to the earth, I grabed it with my own hands. My colonel told me to throw down my gun and hold on to the flag which I did.

"That night the Yankees charged on us but we soon repulsed them. Next morning we made a charge on them, routed them from their first breastworks and proceeded to the second. Was ordered to charge them (the second breastworks) which part of us did. I carried the flag to the breastworks. We routed a long line of them and held our position, but the 28th N.C. Reg. on our right failed to charge them. The enemy commenced fireing upon our lines, and gave them a chance to retake their works again which give us no chance to escape. I lay there with two lines of battle cross fireing at me a short distance and three batteries throwing grape at me not more than 3 or 4 hundred yards distant. The first I knew the Yanks were (within) five steps (of me was

when) two jumped over the breastworks and grabed the flag out of my hand and said to me fall in, john, ha. ha. ha. John fell in, but he did not like to do it...

"They took us to Washington and kept us about 13 days... treated us with great respect, give us plenty to eat...

"My colonel was killed and my lieut. col. wounded (in the battle) and the great Gen. Jackson was mortally wounded by his own men and is now dead...

"Father, I am getting used to all kinds of hardships in warfare and though I say it myself, I know nothing of cowardice, and God forbid that I ever should..."

And so in the midst of mourning at Lewis Fork, the mourned wrote a letter that brought him back from the grave. Andrew J. Proffit was not killed in action at Chancellorsville; and as to the other points of conflict between his and Colonel Barry's reports, there is no reason to doubt the reliability of Andy's version. It is probable that Colonel Barry based his report on fragments of information gleaned from survivors who, in the wild turmoil of battle, could see very little of what went on in the smoke-obscured thickets. Colonel Barry, a major when Jeb Stuart ordered the May 3rd advance, succeeded to command of the 18th North Carolina during the battle when the colonel was killed and the lieutenant-colonel wounded- a battle which cost the 18th North Carolina's brigade nearly one-third of the entire 2,500 man command. And captured with Andy Proffit near the second line of Union breastworks were 300 prisoners, and four other Confederate regimental flags.

And perhaps, too, in writing his report of the regimental flag's loss, Colonel Barry- a gallant officer who was later promoted to temporary brigadier-general- was distracted by haunting, anguished self-accusations. According to his brigade commander, General Lane, it was

Colonel Barry who had shouted, "Who gave that order? It's a lie! Pour it into them, boys!" when the 18th North Carolina fired the volley that struck down Jackson.

But for Andy Proffit, there was gnawing remorse that he might have had a hand in the wounding of his beloved commander. None of the three fateful minie balls could have been triggered by him. Before he arrived at the front on that night of May 2, he had already carried out his colonel's order to *"throw down my gun and hold on to the flag."*

The battle flag carried by the 18th Regiment North Carolina Troops at Chancellorsville, Virginia, and captured by Colonel W.J. Sewell's 5th New Jersey Infantry. According to NC Museum of History, the "...flag has two unusual features. In late 1862, the five regiments in the North Carolina Branch-Lane Brigade received new battle flags. Unlike other flags issued to North Carolina regiments, these flags not only had white battle honors, instead of the usual blue or black, but the honors were painted on both sides of the flag."

Image Courtesy North Carolina Museum Of History

FOUR BROTHERS IN GRAY

REBEL PRISONERS AND BATTLE FLAGS CAPTURED AT CHANCELLORSVILLE,
BEING TAKEN TO THE REAR BY CAVALRY AND INFANTRY GUARDS.
Drawn by Edwin Forbes, May 3, 1863 - United States Library of Congress

With the Battle of Chancellorsville, the war was only half over. On June 5, 1863- one month after Chancellorsville- Harrison Proffit's division received marching orders; and less than two weeks later, Andy and Alfred Proffit trudged north with A.P. Hill's Corps. The army of Northern Virginia was headed for Union country, and a small Pennsylvania village named Gettysburg.

But on June 24, Alfred wrote a letter to Lewis Fork from the hospital at Gordonsville, Virginia:

> *"I with many others give out (on the march) and could not go on. Andy went on with the regiment, but he was very tired."*

And also written on June 24- from a private home in northern Virginia, near the Maryland border- was a letter from Andy:

> *"I am at an old gentleman's house by the name of James Sealock. We have had another hard march from Fredericksburg toward Winchester. The march was so hard and the weather was so hot that hundreds gave out. I marched three days until I could go no more. They halled me one day, but the ambulances were so crowded that they broke part of them down, so the doctors gave me a pass to shift for myself. There is nothing the matter with me more than I am broken down. My feet worn out & my head pains me right smartly. It was said that many marched until they fell dead on this march."*

CSA LIEUTENANT-GENERAL RICHARD S. EWELL

But Harrison, who had formerly "given out" on two other marches was still on his feet, and on June 18 wrote jubilantly from Shepherdstown, Virginia- where he was bivouacked with the command of General Ewell, who had replaced Jackson at the head of the Second Corps:

> *"We have been marching 13 days. We went from Fredericksburg to Winchester and whipped Genl. Gilroy's forces and captured from 3 to 5,000 prisoners. I am now in the best of health... except I am very much wearied & have sore feet..."*

USA BRIGADIER-GENERAL ROBERT HUSTON MILROY

On June 22, writing from near Sharpsburg, Maryland, Harrison elaborated on the Second Corp's victory at Winchester:

> *"Our brigade was formed quickly in line of battle... (The Yankees) raised a most hideous yell and came at us... Our boys lay low and kept cool... Almost deadly fire was poured into (the Yanks) which caused them to change their direction quickly. They made two other charges, with like results... then surrendered. After the battle was over & the captured horses collected, our regiment was mounted and went into full chase after the Yankees who escaped. Our boys enjoyed the sport very much...*
>
> *"I know nothing of the movements of our army. It is said that our cavalry is in Pennsylvania. I suppose it is so, as about 700 fine cattle passed here yesterday from that direction going to the rear of our army...*
>
> *"We are faring finely and if no bad luck I think we will continue to do so..."*

GETTYSBURG, PENNSYLVANIA.
Photographed by Timothy H. O'Sullivan, c.1863 - United States Library of Congress

But there was "bad luck" ahead for the 1st North Carolina Regiment- nine days and one hundred thirty marched miles after Harrison wrote the letter from Sharpsburg. On the evening of July 2 his brigade- Stuart's- fought its way up the slope of Gettysburg's Culp's Hill, captured a section of the first line of Union breastworks and was the only brigade in the whole left wing of the Confederate army to hold throughout the night the position it had stormed.

GETTYSBURG, PENNSYLVANIA - FEDERAL BREASTWORKS IN THE WOODS ON CULP'S HILL.
United States Library of Congress

On the morning of July 3- still clinging to its foothold despite a furious dawn bombardment from Union artillery- Stuart's Brigade was ordered to storm the crest of the hill. With fixed bayonets, the men of the brigade surged toward the heights, but were broken and turned back by the withering fire of the Union defenders Stuart's troops withdrew to their former position, and with their retreat, the battle on the Confederate left wing died down.

GETTYSBURG, PENNSYLVANIA - BATTERED TREES ON CULP'S HILL.
United States Library of Congress

But as the 1st North Carolina Regiment stumbled down Culp's Hill– leaving thirty-eight of its dead on the bloody slope– another Confederate advance was shaping up on the right center of General Lee's Line– Pickett's charge. In the early afternoon Pickett's Virginians, and Pettigrew's and Trimble's North Carolinians- 15,000 strong- swept gallantly forward against the bluecoat defenders of Cemetery Hill and were turned back, a shattered remnant, by the equally valiant Union lines; and the Battle of Gettysburg was over.

On July 4 the decimated Army of Northern Virginia began its long, hard retreat toward southern soil, and on July 13 crossed the Potomac into Virginia. On July 9- from bivouac near Hagerstown, Maryland- Harrison Proffit wrote a letter to Lewis Fork:

"Since I last had an opportunity of writing you... I have passed through a variety of scenes, which I think could not fail of being interesting to you...

"The Corps to which we belong went within a few miles of Harrisburg, which is the capital of Penn., and I have very little doubt that we could have taken the city had we not been ordered to rejoin the main army... The Yankee army was compelled to retire from Virginia... The two armies met at a town called Gettysburg in Penn.

"The fight continued for three days and closed without either army being routed or driven back. The enemy secured an elevated position and fortified it well, which saved them from their usual fate...

"It is said the Yankee papers admit a loss of Forty two thousand, and say it is the gratest defeat they ever sustained... Two of our company were killed, and 7 were wounded. I was not hurt..."

The Union and Confederate armies suffered about equally in the nearly 50,000 casualties of the Gettysburg Campaign; and the two shattered forces again went into camp on the opposite sides of Virginia's Rappahannock and Rapidan Rivers. By August, Harrison Proffit (and the Confederacy) had painfully reappraised Gettysburg from "the gratest defeat the Yankees ever sustained" to a Union victory. And there was defeat for the Stars and Bars on the Western front, too, where Vicksburg, the Confederacy's last stronghold on the Mississippi, fell to a tenacious Union general named Grant on the day after Pickett's futile charge at Gettysburg. On August 10- from camp near Orange Court House, Virginia- Harrison wrote to his sister, Louisa:

> *"We are enjoying most of the comforts of a quiet camp... I have heard no word concerning Andrew and Alfred... and am becoming uneasy.*
>
> *"Our late reverses are no cause for submitting to our enemies, to accomplish what we first began...*
>
> *"My health is good..."*

On August 28, Harrison wrote to Lewis Fork again, angry at the ever-growing number of desertions from the Confederate army:

> *"There is little news afloat in the camp. All the soldiers are enjoying rest and quietude, except those who are either deserting or contemplating how to escape.*
>
> *"I supose that I would be as glad to see my parents and relatives & friends as almost any man, but if there is never an opportunity offered for me to visit them honorable, I have no idea of ever seeing them again.*
>
> *"Thank God there are many who have not and will not desert...*
>
> *"My health is good, except that I have pains in my limbs a good deal like rheumatism..."*

In the meantime- after a two months silence from the two Proffits who had "given out" on the march to Gettysburg- there was word from Alfred, written on August 20 from the hospital at Staunton, Virginia:

> "I am yet in the hospital. Since I last wrote you I have had a vary savear attact of disintary, which weakened me very mutch, but I am now over it and tolerable stout...
>
> "Sis, I am the loansomest chicken you ever saw... I walk the streets of these long eavenings by myself with no person to communicate my thoughts to...
>
> "This day 12 months ago I taken my leaf of home... The time has passed fast but I have seen hard times since I saw you...
>
> "I think I will git a furlough this fawl..."

And written on August 19 was a shaky-handed letter from Andy:

> "I am very low & weak yet. I am still at Mr. Sealock's. The fever fell in my feet and legs so that I could not walk, nor get off of my bed for some time. I was not out of the house for seven weeks, and no one who saw me thought that there was any chance for me to live, but the God who rules and governs all things saw fit in his tender mercies to raise me up again, for which I shall ever feel grateful...
>
> "I think if I was at a Richmond hospital, I could git a furlow, but I can't git there until I git able to walk. It is about 80 miles to the railroad & the Yanks is all around us here..."

On September 29, camp near the Rapidan River, Harrison Proffit again took pen in hand:

> "We have just returned from the banks of the Rapidan where we have been performing our part of the picket duty. The Yankees picket the west side of the River with cavalry...
>
> "I received a letter from Andrew a few days ago, under the date of September 16th- he said he was quite weak, but his health was improving very fast. He said he was still at Mr. Sealock's, but expected to start to his regiment that day (16th)...

> *"Since I last wrote you I saw Alfred. He was with his company and in fine health…*
>
> *"They are giving a few furloughs now. I think if I live till the later part of the winter, it will be my time…"*

On October 8 Andy Proffit wrote welcome news to Lewis Fork:

> *"This note is to inform you that I am with my regiment enjoying a resonable portion of health… Alfred is here- quite stout & looks finely…*
>
> *"As soon as this comes to hand, write and give me all the news, how you are getting along & how your crop is about to turn out…*
>
> *"We have been cooking three days rations today in order for a march, but to what place I am unable to say…"*

UNION SIGNAL CORPS ON THE RAPIDAN RIVER, VIRGINIA.
Photographed by Mathew Brady - United States National Archives

The march was north, on October 9, as General Lee maneuvered to drive the Union army back to the Potomac for the winter. But after the two armies made brief contact at Bristoe Station- about thirty miles southeast of Washington, near Manassas Junction- the Army of Northern Virginia marched south again, clashed with Union forces at Rappahannock Bridge; then- on November 10- withdrew south of the Rapidan River and built winter quarters.

TRACKS OF THE ORANGE & ALEXANDRIA RAILROAD, DESTROYED BY THE CONFEDERATES BETWEEN BRISTOE (OR BRISTOW) STATION AND THE RAPPAHANNOCK.
RAILS WERE HEATED RED-HOT OVER BONFIRES OF CROSS-TIES RENDERING THEM USELESS.

Photographed by Timothy H. O'Sullivan, October, 1863 - United States Library of Congress

ABOVE — BRIDGE ACROSS THE RAPPAHANNOCK RIVER, VIRGINIA. AUGUST 19, 1862.
Photographed by Timothy H. O'Sullivan - United States Library of Congress

BELOW — BURNING THE RAPPAHANNOCK RAILWAY BRIDGE. OCTOBER 13, 1863.
Drawing for Harpers Weekly by Alfred Rudolf Waud - United States Library of Congress

On October 27, while the Confederate army was still north of the Rapidan near Culpepper, Andy Proffit wrote ominous news to the home folks:

> "I saw D. M. Carlton the other day. He informed me that Harrison was gone to the hospitle. He had been unwell for some time & give out on our late march toward Manassas.
>
> "I held out to get there & it was a severe fight though my brigade was not engaged, neither was Harrison's..."

Three weeks later, camped south of the Rapidan again, Alfred and Andy shared a single piece of stationery, dated November 17:

From Alfred:

> "Times are good in camp. Cince I last wrote you... We run the Yankees to Manasses... then fell back to our old camp where we first started from. We have put up some fine houses and are fixen to live at home... They have stoped deseartion in the army by shooting a few. I have seen as many men shot as I wish to..."

And from Andy:

> "I have seen 10 men shot for desertion, which is a shocking scene, but I have seen so many horrible things that nothing has mutch affect on me...
>
> "Father, I am quite sorry that you will have to sell one of your mules... All I can say is do the best you can & try to keep plenty to eat... We have not heared form Harrison since he went to the hospital. I am quite uneasy about him..."

F̲our days later- on November 21- another hand wrote a letter to Lewis Fork. The script was delicate, flowing, and unfamiliar:

> *"The occasion upon which I address you, I am sorry to say, is one of deep mortification to the writer as well as the person addressed... It has become my lot to be the communicator of the sad fate my own affectionate and highly esteemed friend as well as your beloved son, Seargt. W. Harrison Proffit who died in the hospital at Gordonville, Va. on the 25 of last month, the disease not known.*
>
> *"He left the company on the 18th (October) while on the march near Manassas, and we never heard anything form him until this morning and alas by Surgeon's Certificate to Lt. Curtis, he was reported dead.*
>
> *"I am sorry that I cannot state the full particulars of his death..."*

And so from William Witherspoon of the 1st North Carolina Regiment, William and Mary Proffit learned that the second of their sons was dead; and this time, the tragic news was no mistake. After fighting and surviving the Seven Day's Battles, Fredericksburg, Chancellorsville, Winchester and Gettysburg, Harrison Proffit succumbed at twenty-four to a "disease not known" (possibly rheumatic fever), and was buried in Virginia soil with his brother, Calvin. And mourned in Lewis Fork was the fiercely dedicated teacher who had, in fact, "spent the happiest days of my life in that (Beaver Creek) schoolroom."

The letters in the tooled leather chest add no more details to Harrison's death.

Harrison Proffit is listed in the records of the "Receiving Hospital" in Gordonsville, Virginia as: William H. Proffitt- Co. B, 1st North Carolina- October, 1863, at: www.hgiexchange.org (another site correctly lists him as a musician and to have died of Typhoid fever.)

Information from The Civil War Museum at the Exchange Hotel: Before the Civil War, the Exchange Hotel with its high ceiling parlors and grand veranda welcomed passengers from the Virginia Central & the Alexandria Railroads. When the war began, troops, supplies and wounded were transported on these railroads to Gordonsville. The Exchange Hotel became the Gordonsville Receiving Hospital which provided care for 70,000 soldiers, both Confederate and Union.

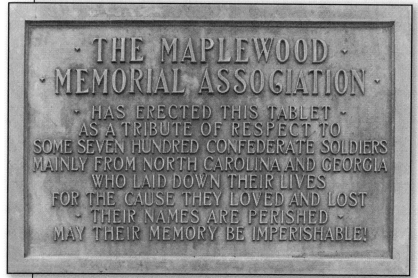

As the United States healed and the railroads boomed, this graceful building returned to its role of hotel. Now fully restored, the hotel is a Town History and Civil War Medical Museum.

The building is the only Receiving Hospital still standing in Virginia. The location of specific graves is not known. Probably all of the Union casualties were moved to the national cemetery in Culpepper. The Confederate dead, initially buried near the hospital, were moved to the Maplewood cemetery.

Photos of the monument at Maplewood were made by Judith Gunnett who graciously gave her permission to include them here. —Publishers.

The next word from Alfred or Andy- after two months of winter quarters inactivity, broken from November 28 to December 2 by a bitterly cold march and entrenchment at Mine Run, where Union forces had advanced south of the Rapidan and threatened attack– was dated January 24, 1864, from Alfred:

> "We are stout and fat and we hope you are too. Andy and I taken a tripp down to the 53rd (N.C. Regiment). We found all the buoys well and harty... with very good winter quarters. Wm. and Whig (cousins of the Proffits) came home with us... and you may guess we had a very good time telling old tailes and jokes...
>
> "We furlow one man for every eight men in a Co. I think Andy and I will git furlows in about 18 or 20 days... if the Yanks don't come up on us..."

The Yankees stayed north of the Rapidan in their own winter quarters, and in February Alfred and Andy Proffit spent a furlough in Lewis Fork. On March 9, 1864, Alfred wrote the home folks of what must have been a fairly happy trip back to camp:

> "Myself with Andy returned to camp yesterday. We drank all our brandy before we got camp. We drank the last in cite of camp. I found my house in bad order. It looked to me like it had not been swept cince I left. Altho they said it had. I guess I gave it a good brush this morning..."

And on March 10 Andy wrote:

> "There has been but little done since we left camp. The Yankee cavalry made a raid on Richmond, got whipped & left. There is nothing of interest going on at this time... I feel much better satisfied since I have seen you all."

But the day before Andy penned the note on this new-found peace of mind- a new Union general came east to command all the Federal armies- the stubborn conqueror of Confederate forces at Fort Donelson, Shiloh, Vicksburg and Chattanooga: U.S. Grant.

USA
LIEUTENANT GENERAL, GENERAL IN CHIEF, OVERLAND CAMPAIGN
ULYSSES SIMPSON GRANT

Original by Newton Timothy Hartshorn - United States Library of Congress

But for two months- while Grant planned, and strengthened his troops north of the Rapidan- things remained quiet in the tents and cabins south of the river. On April 2 Alfred Proffit commented on conditions in camp:

> *"We have the worst rain and snow I ever saw... As for rations, what we draw and what we by, we make it do... I guess we make the wilde onions git up and git...*
>
> *"We fish a good part of our time... a very good traid..."*

On April 30 Andy wrote of the great religious revival in the Confederate camps, and one of the practical fruits thereof:

> *"I can inform you that a great many soldiers have joined the church here of late. The officers join the Presbyterians and the privates join the Mudheads (Primitive Baptists). There has been a good many of my Co. joined, and they have not stoled any of my rations since & I am in hopes that they will not ever be guilty of such a trick again, for they know that it is rong..."*

Alfred wrote home on April 30, too, and took a stab at anticipating General Grant's strategy:

> *"We are still in camp... but we expect an early attack some whare between hear and Fredericksburg soon..."*

And he was right. Five days later- on May 4, 1864- Grant led 118,000 Union soldiers across the Rapidan River, and in the terrible tangle of "The Wilderness," near the Chancellorsville battleground of the year before, Lee and Grant clashed for the first time.

Grant's troops crossing Germanna Ford Rapidan River, Virginia — May 4, 1864.
Photographed by Timothy H. O'Sullivan - United States Library of Congress

With Wilcox's Division of A.P. Hill's Corps, Alfred and Andy Proffit and the 18th North Carolina fought off furious attacks on the afternoon and evening of May 5, then lay in the woods on the Confederate front all night- disorganized brigades who waited, exhausted and without entrenching, to be relieved on the front line by the expected arrival of Longstreet's Corps.

By the dawn of May 6, Longstreet's Corps was still three miles from the battlefield, and when the Union troops launched an overwhelming attack on the scattered brigades of the Confederate front, the gray lines wavered under the onslaught. With the other regiments of Heth's and Wilcox's Divisions the 18th North Carolina fell back, fighting as best it could; but the confused retreat put the center of the confederate line perilously close to penetration and rout. Then- in the nick of time- Gregg's Texans of Longstreet's Corps ran on the field and checked the Union advance with a furious counter-attack.

Later in the morning, troops of Longstreet's Corps attacked the exposed left flank of the Union line, rolled it up and threw it back; but- as had happened at Chancellorsville when the Confederate army stood on the threshold of a glorious triumph– the gray advance stalled when the Corps commander was shot by his own troops by mistake. Unlike Jackson, Longstreet did not die of his wounds, but was lost to the army for five decisive months.

Late in the evening, part of Ewell's Corps struck the Union right flank in an initially successful attack that was halted by darkness, and the battle of the Wilderness was over. But in the woods- flames in many places with brush fires ignited by the flash of musketry- lay more that 2,200 Union dead, and about half as many in Confederate.

Again, the home folks in Lewis Fork waited fearfully for the mail. Written on May 8, there was word from Alfred:

> "We left camp Wednesday. We reached the field in time to go into it the next day. There was hard fighting all day. The Yankees held their position vary well. The next day (when) it was light enough to see, they fired a signal gun they then charged and the first fire the infernal rascals fired, they put it to me. I was struck just above the right eye. It split me to the skull about three inches... When it gits well I will fight them again...
>
> "I left Andy thare. I have not heard from him cince... I am now at the hospittal at Orange (Court House)..."

CSA LIEUTENANT-GENERAL JAMES LONGSTREET

For Andy Proffit there was no time for writing letters. After the Union's bloody repulse in the Wilderness, Grant broke the pattern of former Federal commanders. Instead of retreating north of the river to lick his wounds, he sidled his army south toward Richmond. But General Lee's men, too, hurried from the Wilderness- southeast twelve miles to Spotsylvania- and again stood between Grant and the Confederate capital.

With the 18th North Carolina, Andy Proffit arrived at the Confederate Spotsylvania line on May 10; and after spending a day constructing breastworks, moved forward to man a position on the right of a horseshoe shaped front dubbed the "Mule Shoe" by the Confederate soldiers- but would later be renamed "The Bloody Angle."

BATTLE OF SPOTSYLVANIA.
From a painting by Thure De Thulstrup - United States Library of Congress

Before dawn on May 12, a furious Union attack broke through the left of the "Mule Shoe" salient, surged through the rear of the Confederate defenders on the right of the line and surrounded and captured virtually an entire gray division- including two Confederate generals and 3,000 men, among them, one-half of the 18th North Carolina re-formed and charged with Lane's Brigade to halt the Union advance on the right.

After the furious, bloody, hand-to-hand fighting of the terrible twelfth of May, the two armies lay entrenched and stalemated on the Spotsylvania line for a week; then Grant moved southeast again.

But the cost of Spotsylvania in killed, wounded and captured was nearly 20,000 for the Union and about one-third as many for the Confederacy. From Andy Proffit, himself, the home folks received no word; but finally- written on June 2, from the hospital in Staunton, Virginia- there was news of Andy, from Alfred:

> *"I am in good health and a nurse in (this) hospital. I have a heap to do. We have a heap of bad wounded and lots of them are dying...*
>
> *"I wrote to Andy a few days ago, but when it was answered, it came from the Sergt. of my Co., informing me that about half of our Regt. was taken prisoners cince I left- Andy with the rest... Thare is but six of my Co. left. I shall have a small Co. when I git back...*
>
> *"Our forces are still in line of battle near Richmond, but not mutch fighting going on..."*

And so Andy Proffit- prisoner of war, captured at Spotsylvania's "Bloody Angle" on the misty pre-dawn of May 12- was sent north for imprisonment. There would be no prisoner exchanges in this crucial summer of 1864; negotiations had failed and further exchanges of prisoners suspended. And in prisons- both north and south- men would wait in over-crowded misery; and from hunger, cold, disease and desperation, many would die.

CONFEDERATE PRISONERS AT BELLE PLAIN LANDING, VA., CAPTURED WITH JOHNSON'S DIVISION — MAY 12, 1864.
Photographed by Mathew Brady - United States National Archives

And Alfred Proffit- recuperating casualty of the Wilderness- nursed the wounded and dying in a hospital one hundred miles northwest of the blue and gray battle lines near Richmond. But of *"not much fighting going on"* in his letter of June 2, Alfred was wrong. From Spotsylvania, Grant had marched his bluecoats to within ten miles of Richmond; and there- at Cold Harbor- General Lee's men again entrenched between Grant and the Confederate capital. From June 1 to 3, Grant hurled his men futilely against the gray lines; then lay entrenched on the Cold Harbor line for eleven days– to count the terrible toll of more than 10,000 Union casualties, and to decide where to hammer next.

GENERAL U.S. GRANT AT HIS COLD HARBOR, VIRGINIA, HEADQUARTERS.
Photographed by Edgar Guy Fowx - United States Library of Congress

Meanwhile in the Shenandoah Valley near Staunton, another Union army was on the move. On June 5, blue troops under General Hunter defeated a Confederate force in the Battle of Piedmont, and on June 6, the victorious bluecoats occupied Staunton.

From Alfred Proffit, temporary nurse in the Staunton Hospital, there was word written on June 12, from Lynchburg, Virginia- fifty miles south of Staunton:

> *"I am sorry to say (that) the Yanks run us away from Staunton. They whiped our forces out and taken the place, but all that could walk got away We had a long, hard march through the mountains. We all came to Lynchburg. It is said the Yanks are going to try this place soon..."*

The Union attack on Petersburg reported by Alfred Proffit was repulsed on June 9, a half-hearted try by Yankee troops who had moved on Richmond from the

BIRD'S-EYE VIEW OF STAUNTON, VIRGINIA.
From a painting by Edward Beyer c.1857 - United States National Archives

southeast- up the James River- at the same time that Grant was battering his way from the north. But the bluecoats would try again. Petersburg, only twenty miles southwest of Richmond, and with the other Confederate states, was Grant's target.

On June 12 Grant began moving his troops from the Cold Harbor line, crossed the James River, and approached Petersburg and Richmond from the south. From June 15 to 19, Union forces attacked Petersburg again; but again failed to pierce the fiercely stubborn Confederate defense. And with General Lee's Army of Northern Virginia again blocking Grant's road to Richmond, the Union commander changed his tactics from assault to siege. In ever-lengthening lines, the two armies entrenched along the front before Petersburg- a line that would stretch for thirty-five miles and would be manned by blue and gray for nine long months.

But in the Shenandoah Valley, Hunter's Union army was still on the move. Re-enforced at Staunton, the blue columns marched on Lynchburg, where Alfred Proffit was again caring for the sick and wounded in the hospital. But the Confederate defenders, too, were re-enforced, by men of the crack Second Corps by Jubal Early who left the Cold Harbor Line June 13, and reached Lynchburg June 17, to find the Union troops within three miles of the vital railroad center. Hunter launched a few small-scale attacks on Lynchburg that were repulsed by the gray defenders. Then the Union commander turned his troops and retreated with Early's men in pursuit.

CSA LIEUTENANT-GENERAL JUBAL ANDERSON EARLY

On July 3 Alfred Proffit wrote again from the Lynchburg hospital:

> "I am still at the hospital, assisting in cooking for the sick and wounded... The Yankees has made a raid on this place cince I came hear. They came vary near taking it but we got troops in time to give them a nice thrashing. They had to leave all their wounded in our hands. We have about one hundred in this hospital. They are the worst wounded men I ever saw. A good many have died..."

On July 10 Alfred wrote from Lynchburg again:

> "I want you to give me a full account of our affairs at home, the small grain, the corn crop, the fruit... and how those trees don that I holpe set out...

> "We have women hear in the hospital attend to the men who call themselves Sisters of Charity belonging to the Catholick Church. They dress in a different way from any other woman... Their bonnets... remind me of some great fowl with its wings spread in the air to sore aloft in the skies..."

> "I have heard... nothing... of Andy, only that he was captured..."

Less than three weeks later, on July 29, Alfred wrote from a new address- the Petersburg line, ten miles below Richmond:

> "I have returned to my command safe and sound... The brigade was ingaged in a contacked with the enemy when I got in hearen of them. We drove them back some distance, but in the charge our line got scattered so that we had to fall back and the Yankes held the field- loss small on boath sides...

> "P. Walsh (a Lewis Fork cousin) received a slight wound in the side, but not cerious. It broosed more than anything...

> "Thare is skirmishing and canonadeing along the lines evry day..."

By August 3, things were quieter on Alfred's section of the Petersburg front:

> "We are now on the line injoying ourselves fine. We draw plenty to eat and have nuthing to do but cook and eat...
>
> "My Co. consists of about 12 men and the rest of them (the 18th N.C. Regiment) are as bad or worse... Write soon... as I have not got a letter cince April..."

On August 24-25 Alfred and the 18th North Carolina moved out of the trenches and into action in the Battle of Reams Station, fought west of Petersburg, where Union troops had captured the vital Weldon Railroad. Against the Union Two Corps, commanded by Federal General Hancock, the 18th North Carolina advanced with Lane's Brigade in the Confederate attack that routed the bluecoats and took over 2,000 Union prisoners.

USA MAJOR-GENERAL WINFIELD S. HANCOCK

Although the victory at Reams Station did not recover the Weldon Railroad for the Confederacy, it was sweet revenge for Alfred Proffit and his regiment. The captured Yanks were of the same Union Corps that had- on May 12- surged into Spotsylvania's "Bloody Angle" and made prisoners of Andy Proffit and half the 18th North Carolina.

By September 1, Alfred Proffit was back in the trenches, had finally received some letters form home, and- in his spare time- made presents for the Lewis Fork girls:

> "We are now in our breastworks ten miles southwest of Peetersburg.
>
> "There are no Yanks in our front nearer than one mile and a half, but the picket duty is vary hard as our brigade is vary small.
>
> "I would love to be thare to help you eat some vegitables as they are so dear here, I can hardly by them. I will give you the prices of a few artickles.

Butter, $15 per lb. Small loves of bread $2.00 a lof Milch $4.00 per quart... I am glad to hear of your good prospect for potatoes, for I have just paid out one dollar for four little things ...

"Sis, I send Julyan Miller a wring... Give it to her as soon as you can. If it is two small, tell her to give it to one of the rest... of the girls and I will make her another..."

On September 16 Alfred wrote again:

"We are still in the trenches around Petersburg... Skirmishing and shelling is going on all the time...

"We ar drawing flower all the time now and it dont hold out so well as cornmeal...

"Tell P. Walsh to hurry back (from furlough in Lewis Fork) for I am vary loansome- nobody to talk with but dadburn Sandlappers who has been raised on yam potatoes...

"No news from Andy..."

But other news came to the thin, gray lines at Petersburg- grim, ominous news for the Confederacy. On September 2, Atlanta had fallen to Sherman; on September 19, Sheridan's bluecoats defeated Early's Second Corps in the Battle of Winchester and drove the gray remnants up the Shenandoah Valley; and when Alfred wrote home on September 26, Grant's tightening noose around the Petersburg-Richmond supply lines had sent a silent enemy stalking the men in the gray trenches- hunger:

"Our bread rations are not vary good and the buoys of the 18th flank anything they run up with. We take corn, pumpkins, shugar cane or anything we can eat, anywhere we find it...

"Sis, I think the war will close soon. In what way I dread not say. I leave that for you to guess at...

"I am vary glad to hear from Andy. I hope he is all right at Point Lookout..."

And so to Lewis Fork finally came news of Andy Proffit. He was in one of the largest of Union prisons, Point Lookout, Maryland, located on a low peninsula where the Potomac River joined the Chesapeake Bay. At Point Lookout, prisoners were housed in tents instead of barracks, the climate was damp, food was scant, disease was ever-present and the imprisoned considered that they had a better chance for their lives fighting in the army.

Back on the Petersburg line, Alfred Proffit and the 18th North Carolina fought skirmishes with Union troops on September 30 and October 1; and on October 14 Alfred wrote of another silent enemy that had joined hunger in the Confederate trenches:

> *"We have but little wood and the wind begins to blow pretty cool. It looks like we would suffer with coaled this winter. No prospect of going into winter quarters this winter...*
>
> *"I fear we will haft to stay in the ditches...*
>
> *"Sis, last night I dreamed of you and many others of my friends whom I would to see, but can't say when I shall, but soon, I hope..."*

FORTIFICATIONS AT PETERSBURG, VIRGINIA.
United States Library of Congresss

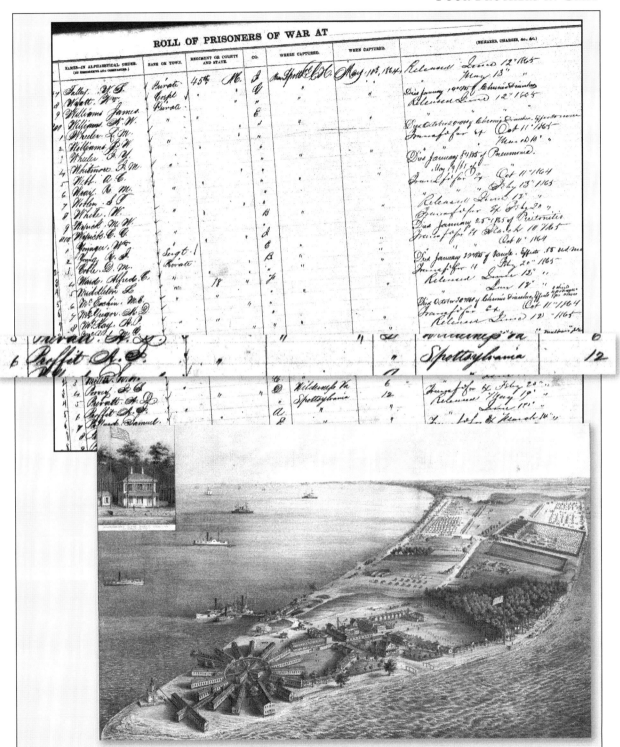

Above- Roll of Prisoners from the Union Prison in Pt. Lookout, Maryland, showing A.J. Proffit captured May 12, Spotsylvania, Virginia, and "transferred-or-exch" February 20, 1865.
Below- View of Hammond General Hospital (lower-left) & U.S. Depot for POWs (upper-right, dark edged field).

By November 20 Alfred's morale had improved:

> "We are still on the line three miles west of Petersburg. We don't anticipate another ingagment with the Yankees soon for we have been building winter quarters... just in rear of our works...

> "We have just drawn a full suit of clothing... If you can send me my overcoat, I would bee glad..."

On November 27 his morale rose oven higher, then plummeted as a visitor brought him tragic and ominous news while he was writing the letter:

> "(I am in) fine health and very good spirits for I have my house entirly done. I have splendid chimney and but two besides (me) to enjoy its nourishing comforts, if sutch a thin camp life as comfort...

> "P. Walsh has just left here, He toled me the painful news of the Death of our mutch esteemed and beloved (cousin) William Walsh, who is said to have died Point Lookout in prison... We all have the same troubles to bear, yet I hope his folks bear it with fortitude."

On December 17 Alfred wrote again:

> "Cinse I last wrote you I have been nearly to N.C. A party of Yankeys made a raid down the Weldon Railroad about the Nottoway River. It hit just right for the cold spell of weather that come a few dayes ago. It rained, snowed, hailed, and the wind blew hard and the way it was cold you dont know. It was hard to take just out of good warm winter quarters...

> "We are now in our same quarters. Cinse I commenst this letter I have taken a harty brakefast pease and potatoes. The buoys of Co. "D" have lately got some boxes from home and I taken some with them...

> "Christmas is near at hand and the prospect for a good dinner is bad, but I hope times will change before the day comes..."

CITY OF ATLANTA, GEORGIA.
Photographed by George N. Barnard c. 1866 - United States Library of Congresss

Times changed; but for the Confederacy, from grim to desperate. On December 16 the Confederate Army of Tennessee was defeated, decimated and routed in the Battle of Nashville; and on December 21 Sherman occupied Savannah, Georgia, after his "March to the Sea" from Atlanta.

New Year, 1865 dawned, and with it, sunset for the Confederacy.

USA
MAJOR-
GENERAL
WILLIAM T.
SHERMAN

On January 1, Alfred Proffit wrote a bleak letter from the Petersburg trenches:

> *"There is snow on the ground and the wind is vary sharp... Christmas has past and vary near in cilence hear, no fun, and but little to eat. We have not drawn but dayes rations of meat for five or six and one of them was spoilt so I could not eat it, but I don't wish to disharton or make you uneasy...*
>
> *"Tell mother and father I am not starving, but would love to have something good from home... Perhaps you could send me a box..."*

CONFEDERATE BREASTWORKS IN FRONT OF PETERSBURG, VIRGINIA, 1865.

Photographed by Matthew Brady - United States National Archives

On February 15, still in the ever-thinning gray line at Petersburg- Alfred wrote of what hunger, doubt and hopelessness could do to some men who had on other days and other battlefields fought bravely, long and well:

> *"The soldiers are going home and to the Yankes steady. Some go almost evry night... (some) went a few dayes ago to the Yankes that rather surprised me. I did not think of sutch a thing, but lots go that you would not think of...*
>
> *"I hardly think I shall go, but if I ever run away from the Army... I would not pertend to come home. Thare are things that would make me go, but it is not worthwhile to say what those things are at present..."*

On March 4 Alfred wrote again. He had received a box of food from home; and if "the things that would make me go" had happened, they had not- in the last moment of decision- driven him to desertion:

> *"We are still in our ditches doing the best we can, altho our duty is vary hard. We have lots of picket duty to do, and what makes it worse is so many desearting, the like has never been known. I dont know which takes the day- the Yanks or the woods. Thay are going to the Yankes evry night. We lost 16 out of the 18th (N.C. Regiment) a few nites ago...*
>
> *"My box has gone up the spout, but it done me a lot of good... I am in hopes Andy will get home before long as our prisnors are being parolled. I rather think Andy... will get home this spring...*
>
> *"Pop, I want you to write me a long letter... I have not had a letter from home by mail for near three months..."*

This letter of March 4, 1865, was Alfred Proffit's last soldier's letter to Lewis Fork. As he wrote it, Sherman's bluecoats were marching irresistibly, north toward the Petersburg trenches, and after sweeping through Georgia and South Carolina, reached Fayetteville, North Carolina, on March 10, and on the Petersburg-Richmond front, Grant's ever-lengthening, ever-strengthening blue lines had stretched the Confederate defensive lines almost to the breaking point. In these last, desperate days of the Confederacy a soldier manning the gray ditches had neither the time nor heart for writing letters.

But dated March 15, 1865, was word from Andy Proffit, returned from Point Lookout as an exchanged prisoner of war. The letter was written from Richmond in a shaky, almost unrecognizable script:

THE LAST CONFEDERATE PRISONERS TAKE THE OATH AT POINT LOOKOUT.

"I drop you a short note which will inform you that I am in Howard's Grove Hospittle. My health is quite bad, though I do not think I am dangerous, for I am improving.

"I can get a furlough to come home if I was able to come, though I do not know when that will be.

"I have been sick so long, ever since the middle of Nov. I can walk about the yard and set up a little. I hope to be at home in a few weeks. Tell mother that I shall want some fine beer & a great many nice little things to eat such as eggs, pickles, &c. If there is any brandy in the country, I want you to try to procure me a little as I am quite weak…"

Review of Reviews Company, 1911, From The Photographic History of the Civil War

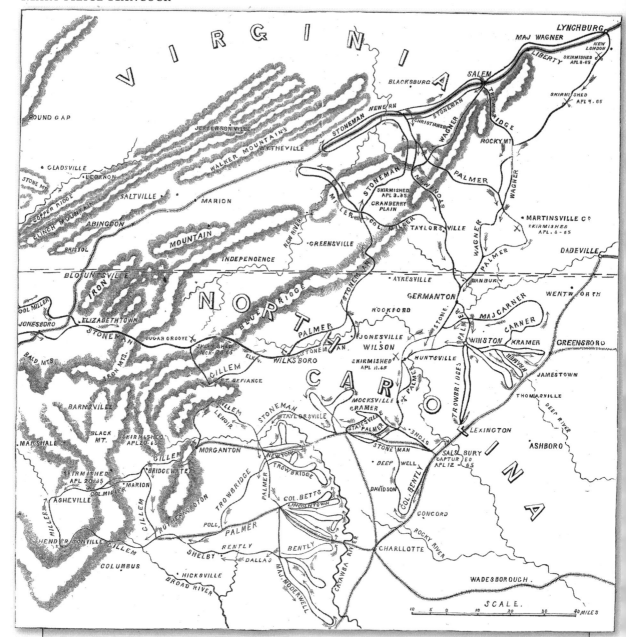

MAP OF STONEMAN'S NORTH CAROLINA RAID.

"Stoneman moved with three brigades- Brown's, Miller's and Palmer's- commanded by General Gillem, through Bull's Gap, and thence eastward up the Watauga River, and across Iron Mountain to Boone, in North Carolina, where, on the 18th of April, he had a slight skirmish with some horseguards. Continuing his advance to Wilkesborough, he then moved into southeastern [southwestern] Virginia. By the main column and detachments from it, Christiansburg, Wytheville and Salem were captured, and the railroad was destroyed from near Lynchburg to Wytheville."

Harper's Pictorial History of the Civil War

Two weeks after Andy wrote this letter- on March 28- the war galloped into the Lewis Fork Hills, as General Stoneman led his Union cavalry through Wilkes County on his way to raid the heart of North Carolina's communications. Although Stoneman had given strict orders against looting, the blue troops took, as they passed the Proffit farm, the last of the brothers' beloved mules.

And back on the Petersburg line, doom stalked the men in gray. On March 19 to 21- in the Battle of Bentonville, North Carolina- Sherman brushed aside the remnants of the Confederate Army of Tennessee, and nothing but a march stood between Sherman and junction with Grant at Petersburg.

And as Sherman's blue legions closed in from the south, Lee's army failed, on March 25, in its last, desperate breakthrough attempt at Petersburg when Union forces beat off a gray assault on the Fort Steadman front. And on April 1 Sheridan's bluecoats overwhelmed and defeated Pickett's Confederate command ten miles southwest of Petersburg at Five Forks.

The loss of Pickett's 10,000 men stretched the hairbreadth Confederate lines even finer, and on the front held by Lane's Brigade, the men of the 18th North Carolina were posted some twenty feet apart in defense of their trenches.

Before dawn on April 2, doom crouched and sprang. In a general assault on Petersburg front, Grant's blue waves charged the gray defenders, and overwhelmed and captured the first line of Confederate entrenchments. Lee managed to stabilize his shattered line in the Petersburg suburbs, and hold the town until nightfall; then withdrew his troops from the Richmond-Petersburg front for

USA MAJOR-GENERAL GEORGE STONEMAN, JR.

a westward march that Lee hoped would lead to junction with the Army of Tennessee, but was destined to end seven days later at Appomattox Courthouse.

Among the exhausted, half-starved gray soldiers who trudged the agonizing route from Petersburg to Appomattox were the survivors of the 18th North Carolina- less than one hundred men of a regiment that once numbered eleven hundred. The 18th suffered further losses on the march- in engagements with pursuing Federal troops near Jetersville and High Bridge- and was again formed in line of battle when General Lee surrendered his surrounded and starving army under the spring-touched Appomattox sky of April 9, 1865.

During the late afternoon of April 9, the 18th North Carolina and many more of General Lee's men received their first adequate meal in several days- from Union commissary wagons sent to the Confederate camps by General Grant. And to some ravenous Confederates food came even earlier, from blue troops who were themselves tired and hungry from the long, fatiguing pursuit from Petersburg, but gave their own individual rations to their hungrier former enemies.

And on April 9, too, the, men of the 18th North Carolina wept unashamed as General Lee rode down their lines for the last time.

They wept from the boundless anguish of defeat for themselves and their lost cause, but perhaps most of all, they wept for the beloved commander, himself- for it was only personal loyalty to Lee that had kept many of them fighting during the last terrible months.

On April 11 the 18th North Carolina stood in a dazed, heartbroken line to receive the parole certificates that permitted the bearer "to go to his home and there remain undisturbed." And on April 12 they marched with the Army to Northern Virginia in its last parade- to stack arms and battle flags in formal surrender.

As the dismal gray columns trudged onto the muddy fields, the Union divisions assigned to receive the surrender snapped to "carry arms" salute to the valiant remnants of the once-invincible Army of Northern Virginia; and receive, in return, an answering salute from the men in gray. Silently, the Confederate column marched on to stack weapons and regimental colors; then shuffled back to camp to hear General Lee's farewell message to his troops read to them. Again, they wept, but from a pride that was the beginning of healing- the badge of honor that Lee's words had given to each of them.

"You will take with you satisfaction that proceeds from the consciousness of duty faithfully performed," Lee wrote, "I bid you all an affectionate farewell."

It was over. Soldiers- blue and gray- went home to mend the gash in the land.

To William and Mary Proffit, waiting in Lewis Fork, only one son came back. With peace only days away, Andy Proffit died in the Richmond hospital- sickened by his imprisonment, then further and fatally weakened by the meager rations of the besieged Confederate capital.

Only Alfred Proffit saw and felt the agonies of Appomattox, and came home to his hills- a lank, bony twenty-three- to farm the land, and, as part time blacksmith, to point his neighbors' plows for twenty-five cents, and to shoe their mules all around for fifty cents. In 1870 he married Sarah McNeil, one of the girls he had once sent his "respecks" to and fathered seven sons- the first one named Robert Lee- and three daughters.

Until the late 1880s Alfred Proffit was plagued by throbbing headaches, which were cured abruptly one day when he sneezed violently and blew from his sinus the wandering piece of lead that had, at the Battle of the Wilderness, *"struck me just above my right eye and split me to the skull about three inches."* This minie ball is still in the possession of the family.

In 1929 Alfred Proffit died, an eighty-six-year-old, white bearded patriarch with thirty-one grandchildren; and was buried in the graveyard of the Lewis Fork Baptist Church- a peaceful green rise rimmed by an amphitheater of hills.

ALFRED NEWTON PROFFIT

Photograph from The Heritage of Wilkes County Vol. II, Ruth Proffit Gregory, Granddaughter

Harrison, Calvin, and Andy Proffit lie in unknown, unmarked Virginia graves. But in their soldier's letters to Lewis Fork, the four brothers in gray wrote their own epitaphs:

- Harrison Proffit -
"Our late reverses are no cause for submitting, but should cause us to make the more determined and vigorous efforts to accomplish what we first began"

W. H. Proffit

- Andy Proffit -
"Though I say it myself, I know nothing of cowardice, and God forbid that I ever should"

A. J. Proffit

- Calvin Proffit -
"He had gained the respect of all his officers by being a brave and obedient soldier- They said they had never heared of his murmuring at any deauty which he had to do- and they buried him with their own hands"

C. L. Proffit

To their own tumultuous times that swept men's destinies from their grasps, the Proffit brothers answered by stretching to the full heights of their individual courage. A man could do no more. And thus they rest in peace.

END.

Part Two

The "Connection"

The Proffit Family

William Morgan Proffit, Jr. was the son of William Morgan Proffit & Elizabeth Elmore, both of Goochland County, Virginia
   William, Jr. was born- June 4, 1803, and died- April 21, 1888

Mary Ann "Polly" Walsh was the daughter of Andrew Master Walsh from Ireland & Rhoda Poteat of Loudon County, Virginia
   Mary was born- September 7, 1805, and died- July 9, 1884

Children of William Morgan Proffit, Jr. and Mary Ann "Polly" Walsh:

1. **Elizabeth Proffit** (1829-1879)
   Married- Jesse Miller on November 18, 1850
     Jesse Miller (b. 1824), enlisted on April 30, 1862
     Co. K, 53rd N.C. Infantry Regiment

2. **Rhoda Proffit** (1831-1909)
   Married- Linville Land on August 14, 1849
     Linville Land (1822-1881) Reverend and carpenter
   Both are buried- Mount Pleasant Baptist Church Cemetery at Wilkesboro, N.C.

3. **Andrew J. Proffit** (Andy or A.J. in the letters)
   Born- January 8, 1834, at Lewis Fork, N.C.
   Enlisted- August 22, 1862, at Camp Hill, N.C.
     Co. D, 18th N.C. Infantry Regiment
   Captured- May 2, 1863, at the Battle of Chancellorsville
     Released Abt. May 15, 1863
   Captured- May 12, 1864, at the Battle of Spotsylvania
     Released February 20, 1865, from Pt. Lookout Prison, Maryland
   Died- March 27, 1865, in Richmond, Virginia
     Howard's Grove Hospital
   Buried- Probably at Oakwood Cemetery in Richmond, Virginia

4. **Rachel Louisa Proffit** (1836-1918) (R.L. in the letters)
   Married- George Jackson Ball on November 3, 1866
     George Jackson "Captain" Ball (1836-1926)
     Second Lieutenant, Co. E, 22nd Texas Infantry (Hubbard's) Regiment
   Both are buried- McGirk Cemetery, Hamilton County, Texas

5. **William Harrison Proffit** (Harrison or W.H. in the letters)
   Born- June 11, 1839, at Lewis Fork, N.C.
   Enlisted- May 27, 1861, at Camp Edwards, N.C.
     Co. B, 1st N.C. Infantry Regiment, Musician, Wilkes Valley Guards
   Died- October 23, 1863, in Gordonsville, Virginia, at Gordonsville Receiving Hospital, of Typhoid Fever
   Buried- Probably at Maplewood Cemetery in Gordonsville, Virginia

6. **Calvin Luther Proffit** (Calvin or C.L. in the letters, twin to Alfred)
   Born- April 27, 1842, at Lewis Fork, N.C.
   Enlisted- September 27, 1862, at Wake County, N.C.
     Co. H, 3rd N.C. Infantry Regiment
   Died- March 25, 1863, at Camp Gregg, Virginia, of Brain Fever
   Buried- Unknown site at Camp Gregg, Virginia

7. **Alfred Newton Proffit** (Alfred or A.N. in the letters, twin to Calvin)
   Born- April 27, 1842, at Lewis Fork, N.C.
   Enlisted- August 22, 1862, at Camp Hill, N.C.
     Co. D, 18th N.C. Infantry Regiment
   Married- **Sarah Anne McNeil** (1849-1921) on May 2, 1863
   Died- August 3, 1929, at Lewis Fork, N.C.
   Both are buried - Lewis Fork Baptist Church Cemetery at Purlear, N.C.

The Proffit Family

The Proffit brothers had many double-first cousins as three of their father's sisters married three of their mother's brothers.

The following pages give information on the three Walsh brothers, Kalip McAlpin, Thomas and Samuel who married Proffit sisters and their families as well as extended family members mentioned in the Proffit family letters.

Kalip McAlpin Walsh was the son of Andrew Master Walsh
  from Ireland & Rhoda Poteat of Loudon County, Virginia
  Kalip McAlpin was born- 1801, and died- After 1880
Rebecca Caroline Proffit was the daughter of William Morgan Proffit
  & Elizabeth Elmore, both of Goochland County, Virginia
  Rebecca Caroline was born- 1835, and died- November 6, 1918

Children of Kalip McAlpin Walsh and Rebecca Caroline Proffit:

1. **Mary Walsh** (1835-1918)

2. **William Walsh** (1837-1862)
   Enlisted- May 31, 1861, Co. B, 1st N.C. Infantry Regiment, Wilkes County
   Died- September 30, 1862, in Aquia Creek, Virginia, of disease

3. **Margaret Ann Walsh** (1838-1918)
   Married- John Wesley Church

4. **Thomas Walsh** (1842-1863)
   Enlisted- September 27, 1862, Co. H, 13th N.C. Infantry Regiment
   Died- October 14, 1863, at Hospital in Charlottesville, Virginia

5. **Rebecca Walsh** (1843-1903)
   Married- Asa Henderson Hamby

6. **Martha Matilda Walsh** (1846-1915)
   Married- John Ivey Stikeleather

7. **James McAlpin Walsh** (1853-1922)
   Married- Sarah Elizabeth Wolfe

8. **Rhoda Clara Walsh** (b. 1854)
   Married- George Hamilton Dyer

Thomas Walsh was the son of Andrew Master Walsh
> from Ireland & Rhoda Poteat of Loudon County, Virginia
> Thomas was born- 1798

Nancy Elizabeth Proffit was the daughter of William Morgan Proffit &
> Elizabeth Elmore, both of Goochland County, Virginia
> Nancy Elizabeth was born- August 1, 1784, and died- 1863

Children of Thomas Walsh and Nancy Elizabeth Proffit:

1. **Polly Walsh** (b. 1829)

2. **Elizabeth Walsh** (1831-1929)
   Married- Jacob M. Eller

3. **Matilda Walsh** (1834-1896)

4. **Thomas Finley Walsh** (1836-1887)
   Married- Malinda Cardwell on February 2, 1868
   Enlisted- March 14, 1864, Co. F, 13th N.C. Infantry Regiment,
     Wilkes County

5. **Phillip Walsh** (1837-1911)
   Married- Anna Belle Eller on August 20, 1865
   Enlisted- November 20, 1861, Co. F, 37th N.C. Infantry,
   Promoted- January 1, 1864, to Full Sergeant

6. **Amanda Walsh** (b. 1837)

7. **William Leander Walsh** (1839-1877)
   Married- Rebecca McGhee on November 11, 1858
   Enlisted- March 29, 1862, Co. K, 53rd N.C. Infantry Regiment,
     Wilkes County
   Wounded- Gettysburg
   Buried- Mount Pleasant Baptist Church Cemetery

8. **Henderson Walsh** (1860-1928)
   Married- Laura Jane Marky

The Proffit Family

Sanford Samuel Walsh was the son of Andrew Master Walsh
> from Ireland & Rhoda Poteat of Loudon County, Virginia
> Sanford Samuel was born- 1794

Mary Rhoda Proffit was the daughter of William Morgan Proffit &
> Elizabeth Elmore, both of Goochland County, Virginia
> Mary Rhoda was born- September 10, 1791, and died- May 9, 1888

Children of Sanford Samuel Walsh and Mary Rhoda Proffit:

1. **Harvey Walsh** (1825-1864)
   Married- Elizabeth Holman on August 10, 1852
   Enlisted- March 23, 1863, Co. K, 53rd N.C. Infantry Regiment
   Died- September 18, 1864, POW, Elmira, New York

2. **Turner Calvin Walsh** (1827-1863)
   Married- Frances "Fanny" L. Norris on September 10, 1855
   T.C. is still at home according to Harrison's letter dated Aug. 17, 1861 (p.110), but is with A.J. by Sept. 8, 1862 (p.146). Harrison mentions hearing of the death of T.C. Walsh in a letter dated Dec. 18, 1862 (p. 159)
   T.C. Walsh doesn't show up in official war records but Y.C. Walsh is listed with information below.
   Enlisted- Aug. 14, 1862, Co. G, 18th N.C. Inf. Reg't. in Iredell Co.
   Died- November 22, 1862, of disease
   The letters "T" and "Y" are beside each other on standard configuration keyboards (qwerty) invented around 1870, and the Rosters of North Carolina Troops were printed in 1882, so it's possible that there was simply an error in transcription, and that Y.C. was T.C. Walsh.

3. **Larkin Walsh** (1830-1863)
   Married- Mary Philipps on December 3, 1859
   Enlisted- April 29, 1862, Sergeant, Co. B, 55th N.C. Inf. Reg't.
   Died- April 23, 1863, at Suffolk, Virginia

4. **Nancy Walsh**

5. **Elizabeth Walsh**

6. **Martha Walsh**

7. **Alfred Walsh** (1841-1862)
   Enlisted- May 31, 1861, Co. B, 1st N.C. Infantry Regiment
   Died- killed at Malvern Hill, July 1, 1862

8. **Mary Walsh**

9. **Samuel Walsh** (1845-1865)
   Enlisted- October 12, 1863, Co. K, 53rd N.C. Infantry Regiment
   Died- February 28, 1865
   Buried- Pt. Lookout Prison, MD.

T.C. Land (1828-1912, brother of Linville Land)
    Married- Jane Dula in 1878
    Enlisted- Co. B, 1st N.C. Infantry Regiment, Wilkes County
    Promoted- 3rd Lieut. of the 53rd Regiment, Co. K

William Chapman Proffit (1843-1862)
    Son of Thornton Proffit (brother of William Proffit, Jr.)
    Born- May 21, 1843
    Enlisted- August 18, 1862, in Co. I, 58th N.C. Infantry Regiment
    Died- November 19, 1862
    Buried- Mt. Jackson, Virginia cemetery

The Proffit Family

Alfred Newton Proffit was the son of William Morgan Proffit
    & Mary Ann "Polly" Walsh, both of Wilkes County, North Carolina
    Alfred was born- April 27, 1842, and died- August 3, 1929

Sarah Anne McNeil
    Sarah Anne was born- November 1, 1849, and died- May 7, 1921

Children of Alfred Newton Proffit and Sarah Anne McNeil:

1. **Robert Lee Proffit** (1871-1952)
2. **Benjamin Franklin Proffit** (1872-1944)
3. **Augustus Judson Proffit** (1874-1937)
4. **Lougerta Lenora Proffit** (1874-1953)
5. **Wade Hampton Proffit** (1876-1915)
6. **George Hamilton Proffit** (1878-1957)
7. **William Albert Proffit** (1880-1954)
8. **John Triplett Proffit** (b.1882)
9. **Mary Lavisa Proffit** (1885-1929)
10. **Sarah Elizabeth Proffit** (1887-1977)

William Albert Proffit, #7 above (1880-1954) married
    Mary Lou Walsh (1884-1974)

Children of William Albert Proffit and Mary Lou Walsh:

1. **Nettie Marie Proffit** (1905-1989)
2. **Wayne Thomas Proffit** (1906-1978)
3. **Ray Hamilton Proffit** (1908-1970)
4. **Ruth Dare Proffit** (1910-2001)
5. **Seth Alfred Proffit** (1913-1986)
6. **Jewel Proffit** (1918-1919)
7. **James Paul Proffit** (1921-1961)
8. **William Albert Proffit** (b.1924)
9. **Howard Van Proffit** (b.1927)

Part Three

Proffit Family Letters

A NOTE ABOUT THE PROFFIT FAMILY LETTERS.

Letters included in this edition of *Four Brothers in Gray* are from the Southern Historical Collection in the Wilson Library of the University of North Carolina at Chapel Hill.

Our original idea was to include images of actual correspondences but faint pencil or faded, 150-year-old ink on a variety of original paper sizes, colors and textures, printed in black and white at our limited page size, proved mostly illegible.

We, then, decided to transcribe the information, faithfully reproducing punctuation, capitalization and formatting. But the informal, handwritten script of the writers- while generally quite readable- because of a lack of punctuation and formatting looked inappropriate or even childlike when it was rendered in a standard font.

So, the final product is a compromise- our own interpretation of the texts rather than an exact transcription. While we've kept the writer's original words and spelling (the best we could read them), we have added capitalization and punctuation to enhance the reader's understanding.

We worked to preserve sentence formulation, the cadence and the invented spelling that actually describes for us pronunciation and accents of the period.

These personal correspondences, related in the common vernacular of the time and place are no more incorrect than any dialect of any language and are a beautiful part of our Western Carolina heritage.

Out of respect for persons and their descendants, names mentioned in a disrespectful or dishonorable way have been omitted.

—PUBLISHERS.

Abbreviations & Definitions.

&c - etc. or et cetera a Latin phrase translated as "and so on," or, "and so forth." The ampersand is "et" or "and" and is a stylized version of the letters.

AS WELL AS COMMON - feeling "average," or "about as well as can be expected."

BEG - to want or pray for.

CONNECTION - relatives or kinfolk including extended family.

INST. - abbreviation for instant meaning, in 19th century usage, "of the current month" thus "the 15th inst." means the 15th of this month.

FLANK - (Military) to the side. It also appears to be a slangy synonym for filching or stealing.

GRAPE OR CANISTER SHOT - (Military) Fired from canons, Grape shot consisted of balls held together between steel plates. Canister shot consisted of balls in a cylindrical steel tube. Both broke apart into shrapnel, when fired, and were used against personnel. Solid shot, like a non-explosive canon ball, was used, primarily, for destruction of material, fortifications or ships. (See page 148.)

LEWIS FORK - William and Mary Proffit lived near Lewis Fork Post Office, Wilkes County, North Carolina.

MILITARY ORGANIZATIONS - In ascending order of size, units were: company, regiment, brigade, division, corps. Theoretically, company contained 100 men; a regiment, 1,000; a brigade, 4,000; and a division, 12,000.
- INFANTRY REGIMENTS were usually composed of 10 companies. These companies were lettered in alphabetical order, with the letter "J" omitted.
- BRIGADES generally consisted of 4-6 regiments.
- DIVISIONS were the second largest unit. There were 3 or 4 brigades to a division.

- Corps were composed of 2 or more divisions. Corps were numbered in the Confederate army but were often referred to by the name of their commander. Thus, the II Corps in the East was called Jackson's Corps, even after he was killed.
- Armies were the largest of the organizations. The Union followed a general policy of naming their armies for the rivers near which they operated as in *The Army of the Potomac*; the Confederates named theirs from the states or regions in which they were active as in *The Army of Northern Virginia.*

Minie Ball - The first conical lead bullets invented by Captain Claude-Etienne Minie of France. Minie balls were more accurate and faster to load than round ammunition for rifles.

Mudhead Baptist - From *The Chautauquan* Volume XVI. - New Series, Volume VII. - Editor's Notebook on the Eleventh Census: "Several bodies of varying beliefs have reported themselves simply as "Brethren." Separating from parent Baptists come their well-known offshoot, the Seventh Day Baptists, followed by Six Principle Baptists, Mudhead Baptists, Free-Will, Primitive, General, General Free-Will Baptists, and the River Brethren."

N.B. - Nota bene - means "Special note."

N.C.T. - North Carolina Troops.

On the goose - alright or well off.

Rapidan River - The largest tributary of the Rappahannock. Named for Queen Anne of England, the name was combined with the word rapids and was originally known as the "Rapid Anne River."

Rappahannock River - a de facto border between Union and Confederate forces in Virginia during the Civil War. The river runs from the Blue Ridge around Front Royal in Northern Virginia to the Chesapeake Bay.

Stony Fork, Lewis Fork and Naked Creek - all tributaries of the Yadkin River in Wilkes County, North Carolina.

Tellico, Tenn.
April the 12th 1860
Mr. A.J. Proffit

Dear Friend,

It is with no small degree of pleasure that I embrace the present opportunity of dropping you a few lines in answer to your very kind letter which come to hand a few days since, which gratified me much by informing me you were well. I was gratified to learn that you had (on the 14th February) drawn such a delightful companion. I wish you great success in your present undertaking and hope that you will never find cause to repent of your choice. I have seen the lady myself; but did not fancy her much; but perhaps it is because I had had but little acquaintance with her for you know that I am of rather a timid disposition among strangers, especially among the fair sex, but since you have gotten her, I hope you will use her well, and I have no doubt she will use you well; for I have always heard that she was very kind & obliging. And I am quite sure that the more attention you pay to her, the more delightful she will appear to you.

I would be happy in having such a companion myself but owning to my timid disposition, I have concluded to win the affections of another "fair one" which has been recommended to me. Her name is either Chemistry, Botany or Rhetoric (perhaps all.) The reason why I have concluded to take one of these is, they are said to be excellent companions, and more easily to be gotten acquainted with and you know this sort of folks suit me to a demonstration of exactness.

Whilst reading your letter, where you spoke of the many hours of social enjoyment we had had together, it brought forcibly to my mind the old "Blacksmith Shop," the "Coal pit" and many other places where we used to spend our time so aggreeably. When I meditate upon those delightful scenes of by gone days, I long for the time to roll round when I shall have the pleasure of seeing you and enjoying your company as in days past & gone. for there is nothing on earth that gratifies me more than to be with friends, "For," as has been well said, "without a friend, this world is but a wilderness." I never knew how tru that copy was till I come to this State; but I was not long without friends, and I am proud to say that I now have many friends in this section, who are very kind to me. My session closed on Friday the 6th of this inst. and you can better imagine my feelings on that occasion, than I can describe them to you; for when I first came here, all were strange but in a few short months, I had become acquainted with them, they were kind to me and each seemed to try to make my new home as agreeable as possible. And when the hour rolled round in which we had to part, it caused an aching void to cling around my heart.

> *To think my friends in Tennessee*
> *Would soon be left behind by me.*

I had an examination at the close of my session and was highly pleased with the manner in which my students answered the many questions put to them.

There are a great many natural curiosties in this section, among which are the "basins" and "mounds." The former are places which are below the general surface and of different depths and sizes. Some of which contain water, while others do not. The latter are portions of earth elevated above the general surface. I visited one yesterday, which covers about an acre of land. It is about 25 or 30 feet above the general surface gradually sloping inward from the base to the summit which is about 60 yds in circumference. There are human bones, beads, old coins, silver branches, musket balls, &c, &c, to be found about these mounds. And it is quite reasonable to suppose that these mounds are situated near where there have been battles fought by some human beings, but it is unknown to us who they were, whether white or black, yellow or red... And what seems to be a stronger proof that they are situated on batte grounds is, there are almost aways sure to be two mounds in a short distance of each other, and by each containing human bones, it is supposed they were used as repositories for those slain in battle.

There are also great many caves or caverns in this country, some of which are very large. There is one near my present residence which I expect to visit and explore next Saturday. If I do, I will try to give you a history of it when I return to old North Carolina.

I expect to start for N.C. next week if I do not conclude to teach another session. If I do, I will write you again soon. If I do not, I wish you to answer me at Elkville, N.C.

These lines have me well, greatly hoping they will reach & find you enjoying the same blessing. Give my respects to your Father & family, and all enquiring friends.

Hoping to see or hear from you soon, I subscribe myself Respectfully yours &c.

T.C. Land
To Mr. A.J. Proffit
Parleir's Creek, N.C.

P.S. I think your views on the subject of the "hard shell" Baptists are correct.   T.

P.P.S. O. I forgot to tell you about the girls. We have some out here who are as neat girls as you ever saw, but they cant beat the N.C. girls- only in one respect. That is in wearing big hoops. But that's no odds so as it suits them and I think it's right for them to wear hoops any how, for the Scriptures say that woman is the weaker vessell. So it requires a great deal of hooping to make her equal to man. I'll tell you all, when I see you.

T.C.L.

A.J.P.

Texas
Wood County
Dec. the 18th 1860
A.J. Proffit, Esq.

My Dear friend & schollmate,

Through the mercies of almighty God I [am] once more blessed with an opportunity of writing to you, in answer to your very kind and interesting letter, which came to hand a few weeks since. Sir, it was a sorce of much sadisfaction to me to read from you again and learn of the good health you friends & relatives were blessed with. Sir, your letter found me well, and my health is tolerable good this eavening. My soul's desire is that these lines may find you and all our friends and people blessed with a reasonable portion of health.

Well A.J., I must acknowledge that I have no nuse to enterest you with at this time. Health is very good in this country, and times is very hard. Money is as scarce hear as I ever saw it in any country- everything high, though not so high as what it was a few weeks ago. Flower & pork has come down considerable- flower is worth 3 cts at Jefferson, 65 miles from hear, pork from 4 1/2 to 6 cts. per lb., beef 3 & 4 corn 100 & 125, wheet $175 & 225, oat 75 & one dollar, sweet potatoes 4 bits, Irish potatoes $4.00 per bushell &c.

Well A.J., there is a great excitement in this country about the way the election terminated. Hear is a number of people that is in favor of disunion or of a southern confederacy & if they cannot have that, they say they will have a lone confederacy. I went to Vanzandt Co [Van Zandt County, Texas] last week & returned to Wood [County] yesterday. I saw a great many people with the lone star a sticking on ther hats & flags in Quitman & Canton reared to the height of 112 feet. I only thought it to be a cowardly sign. There is no preparations a making for ware but thare is a great deal of talk about fighting.

I must soon close as I have named above I went to Vanzandt last week & found relatives- Fosters &c. Wile I went to collect the money that was dew me thare, I had very good luck in getting my money. I lef Cousin Mary Foster's last Sunday morning- only stayed thear 3 days. During the time that I was thare, there was a [wed day?] came off in 2 hundred yards of cousin's.

I seen a great may of the Vanzandt girls. They was as handsom as ever if not more so.

I had the pleasure of enjoying myself in company of as fine a one as travails the Texas paths. She was only 16 years of age and just as pretty as a monny [morning?] rose. I did not tell here how pretty I thought she was- neither did I tell her how she had wne [won] my affection. The reason I did not was I intended to have an excuse to visit her again. Well excuse foolishness & bad writing, spelling, &c.

I have been making some money this fall, & doubtless will make more after while. I am a going to start to school the 1st monday in Jan. I will go some 4 or 5 months.

I will close give my respects to all the ladies in your country,

Yours respectfully Geo. J. Ball

Write soon & often. Direct to: Webster P.O.

1861.
July the 14th.

Dear Cosin,

It is with grate pleasure I take this oppertunity of wrighting you a few lines to let you know that I am well and all my friends in camp and to answer your letter which came to hand in good time dated the 8 of this mo.

I was vry anxious to hear from you all as I had not heard any thing from you- only J.H. Speinbower told us you were all well. I had no news of importance to communicate at you that would interest you.

If I could see you I could tell you a bout our travil which would interest you. May [Many] others things I could tell you which I have not time to wright we have 2 or 3 showers rain evry week but thank the ruler of events it has fard off [faired off] and halv a boutiful clear sky above and we are in fine spirits and anxious for a fight which I sincerely trust we will hare [hear] of in a few days. Then we will deal out to thouse black villains their just deserts. We show them what Suthern men is and what Suthern stel [steel?] was made for. Ther are battles beng [being] fought evry day on the soil of Virgina and the dark and ominous clouds may rise and threten to [illegible] sweep us off with great odds. We will persist in conkering or dying in the attempt. Our troops halv met with success in evry attempt. The time is coming on when we must either fall and wither under the iron of despotism or rise to the proud emminence [illegible] which thare is no dout but what we will. Oftimes I of the pleasurebul hours we halv all spent together living together as we ware. When our cuntry maid a call, her cal I had [listened?] to obey.

We seperated now tho I hope the day is close at hand when we all shal meat and in joy our selfs as we always halve done. I must close my letter. I hope you will excuse my bad composition for camp is the worst place to write [I ever?] saw.

Write me as soon as you get this. Give me a long letter. Give my respects to all my friends &c.

From A. Walsh[1] to A.J. Proffit

---

1 *Alfred Walsh, Co. B, 1st N.C. Infantry, Wilkes County, killed at Malvern Hill, July 1, 1862.*

Well A.J.,

I wold have been happy in writing you a long letter, but my friend A. Walsh has taken up so much room having his portrait drawn, that he has not left me but little room. His motto is liberty or death and I think he is about half right, for who on all this green Earth is there that had not rather die on the field of battle than to suffer old Abe and his hireling crew to subjugate and rule over us.

Well, nothing on Earth would gratify me more than seeing you, but since that cannot be at present, write to me, and I will give you just as good an answer as I am able to put up. I must close lest I crowd on this beauty, and if I were to do that, then there would be another fracas in camp.

So take a good look at him also look at his musket with which he is going to gain his liberty. Please write me soon and give me all the news. Yours &c.

T.C.L.

Liberty or Death

Just look at his leg.

He's a well muscled man ain't he?
But he's a soldier for all that, so he is.

Change bayonet. Shoulder Arms. Double quick march. Eyes right.

Write to me when this you see,
Though far away from thee I be.

Alf drew this portrait himself.

T.C.L. was Thomas Charles Land- brother of Linville Land who married Rhoda Proffit, sister of our four brothers.

—Publishers.

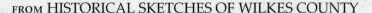

FROM HISTORICAL SKETCHES OF WILKES COUNTY

Published in Wilkesboro, N.C.
by John Crouch in 1902:

"Thomas C. Land is one of the landmarks of the county. He was born March 18, 1828, and was raised on a farm, attending the old field schools a few weeks for a part of the winters. He attended old Beaver Creek Academy for a short time while Hugh Stokes was principal. At the outbreak of the war he joined Col. Sidney Stokes' company [Co. B, 1st N.C. Infantry] as a private and served during the war in over 65 major battles.

"He was appointed commissary and later corporal. In the Seven Days Fight around Richmond he was wounded and was allowed to come home on furlough.

CSA LIEUTENANT THOMAS CHARLES LAND

"During his absence from the army he was appointed 3rd Lieut. of the 53rd Regiment, Co. K which position he assumed on his return to the army. He was wounded at the battle of Winchester and a number of other times but not seriously.

"After the war, Thomas Land returned to Wilkes and engaged in teaching school and farming. In 1870 he went to Oregon and took up land and lived there until 1884 when he returned to Wilkes. In 1891 he again went to Oregon and lived there until 1898 when he returned to Wilkes and where he has lived since. While in the West he engaged in farming, teaching and mining.

"Thomas Land has considerable literary talent and is the author of the popular ballad, "The Death of Laura Foster" [Made famous in the 1950's song *Tom Dooley* by the Kingston Trio. Thomas C. Dula served as a private in Co. K in the 42nd N.C. Infantry] and a number of other poems.

"Thomas Land[1] has been fond of hunting and while in the West he had quite a little experience in hunting deer, bear and elk. He has the horns of a large elk that he killed which he prizes very highly. Thomas Land is at present a member of the county Board of Education, the only office he ever held."

1 See Mr. Land's poem, "Return to the Tented Field" on page 307

Camp Edwards, N.C.
July 14, 1861
A.J. & G.L. Proffit:

I recieved your letters yesterday evening which gave me much satisfaction by informing me that you were all well &c. &c. I can inform you that I am enjoying fine health hoping they may find you all well. I have no reliable news of interest about the war to write you.

You wanted me to inform you how long we had volunteered. We have volunteered "for the war."

I am well satisfied that I did. I almost know it better for me- I have not time to explain myself on that subject now but will refur it till I come up which I expect to do shortly. I am coming on a visit if nothing happens before long.

I can accept that appointment if I choose I & think I will do so. I will write more shortly.

W.H. Proffit

From W.H. Proffit to A.N. and R.L. Proffit:

I received a few lines from R.L. but none from A.N. I was glad to learn that you were all well. I have nothing of interest to write you. There will be preaching at camp shortly, therefore I cannot write much I will come up on visit before long I think. I wish I could have been in that hunt for huckelbunes [huckleberries].

A.N. inform me how our mules are doing, &c.

Write me soon

W.H. Proffit

Camp Edwards, N.C.
July 20th 1861
Jesse Miller

Dear Brother:

Having been stationed here for sometime, I ask your pardon for not writing you sooner. The reason why I did not was because I had nothing much importance to write. It is the same way, yet. I suppose you have not heard from our company frequently.

After arriving at Raleigh we ascertained that Capt. Stokes had already been elected to service honorable positions in other Regiments which he declined to keep; because he could not get his company in those Regiments (as they were full). Then he was offered the office of Col. in the 1st Regiment of State Troops "for the war" which, after consulting his own men and majority agreeing to join, he accepted. After we remained at Raleigh 12 or 13 days we started for Warren Depot[1] and encamped about 2 miles from there.

And now the Regiment is almost complete. I suppose you heard of some of our company going back from Raleigh; I think that the men who have families are justifiable and did perfectly right, but those young men who were free from enthrallments, I think, disgraced themselves. The regular service is the place for young men and when it is absolutely necessary men of families can volunteer for a short time & return agan to their families. I would be extremely glad to see you all, and I think if times get no worse I will have an opportunity of coming home occassionally.

We get the news here every day from Richmond, Petersburg & other points in Va. There are many rumors and reports being circulated and many of them are not reliable. I suppose a severe battle was fought two or three days ago at or near Manasses Junction- General Bauregard commanding the Southern forces, who were victorious.

I have nothing reliable concerning the war to write you at present. The "State Journal" will give you more reliable news than you can

---

1 *Warren Plains Depot?*

obtain from other sources. When anything of an extraordinary character occurs I will write you when I am well assured of the particulars. We had a grand time in Warrenton the 4th of July. I cannot give you an account of it now. I would be glad to see Elizabeth and the children and all our old friends and neighbors on Lewis Fork.

Give them my love and best respects I will write a few lines to Mathias Eller- please hand it to him. T.C. Miller, William Walsh and your friends at camp send their respects to you they want you to write them.

These lines leave us enjoying good health, hoping they may find you all in the enjoyments of good health. I ever remain yours &c.

W.H. Proffit

(Write me very soon)

CSA COLONEL MONTFORT SYDNEY STOKES

Accokeek, Stafford Co., Va.
August 17, 1861
Alfred N. Proffit

Dear Brother:

These lines will inform you that I am enjoying good health at present, hoping they will find you all well.

I will inform you that we left Richmond a few days ago and came to this place which is a short distance from Fredricksburg. We are encamped in a broken, hilly portion of the country which affords good water & from the appearance I think it to be quite a healthy country. There are, at present, quite a number of our company in the Hospital at Richmond who are sick with the measles. The company are generally well except those who are sick with that disease.

We are encamped within 4 or 5 miles of the Potamac (I suppose it is not farther). We do not know when we will have a chance to give the Yankees a few N.C. balls; but I should not be surprised if we do not go to them, if it would be some time before we will get to chance at them, but you never saw more anxious fellows for a fight than our boys are. William and Alfred Walsh are enjoying fine health, and are doing finely. Also T.C. Land, T.C. Miller,[1] D.M. Carlton,[2] &c &c.

I would be glad to see you all or at least to hear from you I suppose there are quite a number of letters for me at Warrenton, NC. which I will get in a few days, I suppose.

I suppose you will be apt to hear from us by Col. Stokes as he and a number of the boys of our Co. are now absent on a visit to Wilkes. I would be glad to know what you and C.L. are doing and in what occupation you will be employed this fall and winter, however I suppose you will be at school, or at least I recommend you to be certain to attend school without any fail.

I would be happy in seeing A.J. and knowing how he is getting

---

1 *Thomas C. Miller, Co. B, 1st N.C. Infantry &, later, Co. K, 53rd N.C. Infantry - Married Elizabeth Land, Niece of T.C. Land*

2 *Daniel M. Carlton, Co. B, 1st N.C. Infantry, w. at Malvern Hill, Chancellorsville & Spotsylvania Court House, d. May 15, 1864*

along with his school at Beaver Creek, but I doubt not that he is doing finely. I am quite confident that he will do well there and I want him to remain there. Tell Father and Mother and Sis that I would be happy in seeing them and that I expected to have come home before this time, but on account of our removing from Warrenton N.C. so soon as we did, I did not have an opportunity of coming but when Col. Stokes comes back and things become quiet again I have no doubt but I can get an opportunity of coming.

Please give my respects to Unkle Samuel and McAlpin Walsh and their families, Jesse Miller, Wm J. Miller, T.C. Walsh, Larkin Walsh and all my relatives and friends.

I would be glad to know how you are getting glong with your home guard; how many yankees or Black Republicans you have taken &c &c. I guess I would like to see you drill once. Please write me soon and direct you letters thus

>W.H. Proffit,
>Accokeek Po.
>Stafford Co., Va.
>Care of Col. Stokes
>1st Reg N.C. State Troops

I would be glad to know if you have been over to Unkle Thomson's or not and, if so, how they are getting along. Please infom me who are the School Teachers on Lewis Fork and Naked Creek- what J.W. Triplett is doin &c- also whether H.M. Stokes is teaching or not and if he is, where he is teaching? Give them my love & respects.

Tell Martha and Margaret & Lilly & all the girls that I am becoming quite impatient in looking for letters from them. Tell them to write us frequently & give us the news &c. &c. &c. &c.

>I ever remain yours &c
>
>W.H. Proffit

Camp Bee
Sept the 8th 1861
Mr. A.N. Proffit

Dear Cozin,

It is with grate pleasure I take this oppurtunity of writing you a few lines to let you know that I am well, hoping when these lines comes to hand they may find you all well. I halvent any news of importance to write to you more than our Co. is drilling in a battry and I expect we will take charge of a battry.

All of your friends are well in camp except a few cases of the measels. All of our boys that hav them are geting well. W.H. and Wm. are as fat as a bar. They look better than i evry saw them. I am fatter than I halv bin in [ten or two] years we get plenty of fresh beef to eat. You wrote me when I was at Warington. You said that C.L. and Thomas had bin corting [courting]. I want you to tell them for me that I want them to put that cin [sin] back if they pleas. I would not allow it when I was there.

I want to see you all very bad. I thought I would come home at Christmas if times was still. The girls wrote me they were drying fruit to make pies I told them to fix a pockut in my over coat- a bigon behind and fill any with apples tarts and I would come after it. We are glad to hear our folks any time. Nothing on Earth could give me grater satisfaction, than to be with you all. I tell you more than you evry heard of all kind of news. I want you to write to me soon as you get this. Giv my respects to all in quiring friends and except for youself I must close by saying I remain yours truly

A. Walsh

Resolved that the flag of Suthern independence stand wavern [waving] high over every acre of Suthern soil. Resolved that she may evry flote [float or flutter] as she had at Manasses and Bethel.

A Walsh

One day after date I promise, Lewis Fork, Wilkes County
Lewis Fork N. Carolina

Aquia Creek, Va.
September 20th 1861
A.J. Proffit

Dear Brother:

Your very kind and interesting letter of the 6th inst. is at hand to which I hastend to reply. Your letter gave me much satisfaction by informing me you were all well, and that times were tolerably good, &c., &c. I have very little interesting news to write you at this time that will be of much interest to you, more than to inform you I, with the rest of your relatives and friends, in camp, are all well, hoping when you receive these lines you will all be enjoying health and prosperity.

I suppose you are aware of our company's being at the mouth of Aquia Creek, and having charge of a Battery at that place. We have been here near a week and are far better accommodated here than we have been since we have been in camp. I cannot say that we are encamped at this time for we are every one of us living in a house. Though some of them are small, any of them are preferable to tents. This is the prettiest place I ever saw; the river at this place is said to be five miles wide and the creek one. When we go to the spring we get in a boat and cross the creek, as the spring from which we get our water is on the opposite side of the the creek to where we are stationed.

We spend many of our leisure hours in fishing, which at this place is not an uninteresting business. You may suppose T.C.L. makes the fishing business pay. You can see ships, boats and schooners at almost any time. Some are sailing up and down the River while others are motionless.

We are improving our fortifications at this place which will be very soon sufficiently strong or, however, we think it will be. We have been in no fights yet, neither am I able to tell you when we will. There has been heavy firing heard in the direction of Washingtonton City both yesterday and today; we have not heard the result, but there is no doubt that there is a dreadful battle being fought near that place.

I was happy in receiving a full account of your school which indeed is one that is worthy of your time and attention, and I felt quite confident that the citizens of Beaver Creek will continue to furnish you with a good school as long as you wish to teach, and I recommend you to remain there until you have taught at least two or three sessions. I was informed by C.L.P. that he did not know whether or not he would have the opportunity of returning to school with you; if his opportunities are bad at present, I want him to remain there with you during the winter. He informed me that he was requested by E.K. Walsh to teach a school in his district. I think it would be a good idea for him to teach a few months sometime in the Winter, but not to neglect going too long on account of doing so. He wrote me a few weeks ago concerning his intention to volunteering in Mr. Barber's company. I would be glad for Mr. Barber to succeed in getting up a good company, but if C.L. wishes to volunteer, if he will wait until I come home he can come back with me and join this company. I would prefer that all my relations and particular friends should be with us.

I would be glad to receive a letter from A.N. and know what his intentions are. I was informed by C.L. that he was riding over the country and taking his pleasure. I would be happy in hearing of his going to school this Winter, but I know it is impossible for you all to be gone from home long at time.

I would be glad to know if R.L.P.[1] is going to school any this fall or not. I was glad to hear that Father's crop was so good and that his and Mother's health is as good as usual.

You said in your letter that you would be glad if I could take charge of your school so that you could accomplish some valuable piece of work at home. I will assure you that I would be as happy in occupying a seat in that school soon as in almost any place I ever saw, for I have spent, probably, the happiest days of my life at that place.

As I commenced your letter on yesterday and did not have one opportunity of finishing it, I have received some acct. of the battle near Washington city. I heard this morning that news was brought on the 12 o'clock train of last night that General Beauregard had taken Arlington heights with the loss of an immense number of men, perhaps 14 or 15,000, the above is a mere report, and I am unwilling to vouch for the truth of the same, though we are unable to give you the particulars, it is unnecessary to doubt that a tremendous battle has been fought, for we heard the report of cannon a large part two days. About sunset last night four or five large guns were fired a few miles down the river- over heard the report distinctly and saw the smoke ascend and some say they saw the place where the balls struck the

---
1 William Harrison's sister, Rachel Louisa Proffit

water. I am unable to inform you why the guns were fired. I will very soon close by asking you to write me soon after the reception of this letter and give me the news. Please direct your address to

Fredericksburg, Va.,
Care of Capt Brown
1st Reg N.C. State Troops

T.C. Land, D.M. Carlton, Wm. and Alfred Walsh, T.W. Laston, Wm. H. Witherspoon, and your relatives and friends in camp are well and doing finely. Please give my love and respects to all enquiring friends, particularly to A.M. Foster, and family, to all your students &c. Tell John J. Foster that I was glad to hear that Mr. West's drum was as good as it was when we last saw it and that there is great nead of Mr. West and his drum in the army. Give (J.J.F.) my best respects, and tell him "it is all right on the Goose."

I hope to see you all very soon and tell you some good jokes and then it will "all be right on the Goose." You said Wm. and Alfred's likenesses had reached home and that they were a very exact resemblance of them. You said you would be glad to have mine, I will send it to you as I have an opportunity of sending it to you. I think I will go to Fredericksburg very soon and have one taken.

Write me soon.

I remain now as ever yours &c.

W.H. Proffit

P.S. Please inform me when your sessions will close and if you are going to have an exhibiton, &c.

W.H.P.

N.B. I caught quite a number of fish last night I wish you could be here to assist me in fishing, &c.

W.H.P.

Tell C.L.P. and John H. Foster I will write them soon.
H.

Tell me when you write whether or not it is all right on the Goose.
H.

Game Point, Va.
Dec. 3, 1861
Mr. A.J. Proffit

Dear Brother:

These lines will inform you that I received your kind letter on yesterday, bearing date of Nov. 28. You stated that you had not received a line from any of us since the 21st of Oct., and you also seemed to have concluded that the reason why, was that perhaps we have no paper. Had your expectations been true, that would, indeed, have been an excellent reason, but let me assure you, that the reverse is the fact. We have plenty of paper, envelopes, and stamps, and we also make good use of the same, in writing you. I am extremely sorry you do not get my letters. I and the other boys write you every few days, we also answer all your letters immediately after their reception, therefore, if they fail to reach you, most assuredly, you have no just grounds for blaming us.

We receive letters from you frequently and hope to do so hereafter, and we will write you often and perhpaps you will receive one occassionally. D.M. Carlton sends his best respects to you: he says he wrote you long since and received no answer. He requests you to write him agan soon. A. Walsh has also been expecting a letter from you, but has not yet received one- also T.C. Land. William Walsh has gone home on a furlough. Therefore, it is unnecessary for me to attempt writing you any War news, as he will be able to give you more information concerning the war questions than I could write in a month.

I will, however, inform you that we heard this morning that the 1st Reg. N.C. Cavalry, or at least a skirmishing party of that Reg. have had a slight skirmish with about 180 of Lincoln's cavalry; it is said to have been a glorious affair on the side of the Confederates: our boys killed a number of them- took others prisoners; some fine horses, &c. &c. Maj. Gordon participated in the exercise. You said when you heard from me agan, you would write to me long letter containing the news of the day, well, I hope these lines may reach you, and soon after you receive them, you will do accordingly.

These lines leave me and your friends generally well hoping they may find you all well.

Please give my respects to Mr. Foster and family, and your students with all enquiring friends.

I remain, as ever, yours
W.H. Proffit

P.S. Excuse bad writing as I wrote in great haste but perhaps I will do better next time.

W.H.P.

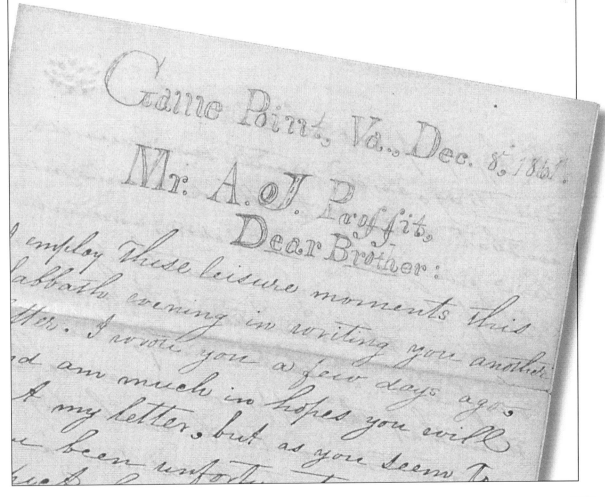

Game Point, Va.
Dec. 8, 1861
Mr. A.J. Proffit

Dear Brother:

I employ these leisure moments this Sabbath evening in writing you another letter. I wrote you a few days ago and am much in hopes you will get my letter, but as you seem to have been unfortunate in that respect, heretofore, I will, perhaps, write you more frequently in the future. I have nothing of a new or interesting character to write you at this time, therefore, I will not attempt writing you a long letter at the present.

Times are very calm, at present, in this vicinity, so far as I know. We have been quite busily engaged for the past week or two in building Cabbins (I believe that's what they call em) I guess we will have them finished by Christmas, and if we do, some of the boys proposes that we have a quilting, and invite our friends in that vicinity to attend. I will just here give you an invitation; and in behalf of the company authorize you to extend the invitation to the rest of our friends in that vicinity, assuring them that their appearance on such an occation would be in the highest degree satisfactory to us. As an encouragement, you can inform them that Esq. Land says we will kill that old gobbler, and manufacture a large chicken pie.

I will cease writing such nonsense. Well, as this is Sunday evening & the 1st Sunday in December, I guess you have all returned from Church at Lewis Fork, and are now enjoying yourselves finely and I guess I would like very much to be with you, but as I cannot enjoy such priviliges at present I remain tolerably well satisfied where I am and with such company as I have in Camp. I guess William Walsh is now with you, he can tell you many things that will, no doubt, be of much interest to you.

I very much regret to announce to you the death of our much esteemed Orderly Sergeant, B.C. Cilreath[1]: his death is supposed to have been occasioned by a fall from the train when in motion. It is

---

1 Burrel C. Gilreath, 1st Sergeant, Co. B, 1st N.C. Infantry, d. Dec. 5, 1861, at Fredericksburg, Virginia.

also with the deepest regret that I inform you of the death of Cousin Thomas Miller[1] of Watauga: he died at Manassas Junction from relapse on the measels. The health of our company is tolerably good at present, there a few who are complaining of the chills, but I think there will be but few cases of chills when the weather becomes cold.

I am anxious to hear from cousin William- to know whether or not he reached home safely- and how his health is at present. I must soon close, these lines leave me well, with the exception of a cold, cough, &c. greatly hoping they will find you all well.

Please write me every opportunity and give me the news for I am at any and all times glad to receive a letter from you.

I remain yours, till death,

W.H. Proffit

P.S. A. Walsh says he lis looking for an answer to a letter he wrote you some time since.

W.H.P.

N.B. I had almost omitted telling you that I think terms of peace will be agreed upon ere [once] three or four more months pass. I guess if it is it will all be right.

W.H.P.

---

1 *Thomas J. Miller, Co. D, 1st N.C. Cavalry Regiment, d. at Centreville, Virginia. Thomas's grandfather (and namesake), Thomas Proffit, was brother to William Proffit.*

Game Point, Va.
Dec. the 10th/61
Mr. A.J. Proffit

Dear Cousin,

I take the prasent opportunity of writing you a few lines which will inform you that I am well. As my friends in camp and I do truly hope when these lines come to hand thay may find you and your friends all well.

I halv but little news to write you at this time. Maj. J.C. Gordon had bin in a churmish [skirmish] with the yankees and routed them.

He and his force made a charge and killed three or four and took 19 prisners and about $4,000 worth of property, that is all write on the goos. The other news- W.H. had in formed you of. When you get this short letter you must be shore to write. I rote you along letter and halv got no answer.

A.J. I often think of you and wont to see you. I think I shal come home shortly if opportunity will offer its self. You will pleas ecuse this bad wrote, spelt and composed letter for I halv had not brekfast this morning. So I must close. Giv my respects to all inquiring frends &c. Write without fail and give and all the news so I remain yours truly &c.

A. Walsh

[back of letter]

Lewis fork, N.C.
Lewis fork N Carolina, L. Walsh

> Game Point, Va.
> Dec the 19th/61
> Mr. A. J. Proffit

Dear Cosin

I this morning take my pen in hand in order to drop you a few lines which will in form you that I am well hoping when this short note comes to hand it will find you well.

I halv no news to communicate to you at this time I can inform you that I way [weigh] [illegible] lbs. I can out run, out-jump, whip, thro down any cousin that I halv got- none execpted. That is all rite on the goos, ant it?

A.J. I want you to write me soon as get this for I halv wrote two letters to you and got no answers. I must come to a close for the trane is here and Hareson [Harrison] wantd to send his letter.

Write soon bee shore- so no more at present but ever remains yours with respect &c.

A. Walsh

giv my respects to all my friends &c. A. W.

Game Point, Va.
Dec. 19, 1861
A.J. Proffit, Esq.

Dear Brother:

These lines will inform you that I received your kind letter, of December 8th, a few days ago. I will just here inform you that news is scarce in this vicinity, therefore, you may expect a short and uninteresting scroll. I will, however, inform you that we have just finished mounting our new pivot cannon. She is a beautiful little gun, weighing about 14,750 lbs. Since she has been mounted, a vessel passed down the River, and we fired upon her two or three times: I tell you they were excellent shots, considering the immense distance. The ball, or shell, weighs 100 lbs.

Times are quite calm in this part of Va. so far I know, but I guess if you were here, you would think they were quite stormy, as the sound of cannon is heard here almost continually. The sound of cannon is as familiar as the sound of the dinner-horn because we hear it much more frequently.

We have very nearly finished our Winter quarters and they are very comfortable little cabbins. Capt. Brown[1] and a number of others have gone home on furlough, and others are expecting to start soon; I guess some two or three will start today. I guess my time will roll around before long I have not yet made application for a fulough but will when I see a chance to get one. I was glad to hear that William Walsh had arrived safely at home, but I was sorry to hear that his health was so very bad.

I guess from what information I have concerning his health, that he will not be able to return to the Army in less than two or three months. You said you were not going to continue at Beaver Creek. I would like to know what occupation you expect to engage in, but you can tell me about those things when I come home. These lines leave me well, hoping they will find you all well. Write me every opportunity and I will likewise.

I remain your affectionate brother

W.H. Proffit

---

1 Hamilton A. Brown, Captain, Co. B, 1st N.C. Infantry, promoted to Full Colonel on Dec. 14, 1863.

WINTER QUARTERS BUILT BY THE REBELS, NEAR BRANDY STATION, OCCUPIED BY FEDERAL TROOPS.
by E. Rees for L.N. Rosenthal, Lith. - United States Library of Congress

MANASSAS, VIRGINIA.
CONFEDERATE WINTER QUARTERS.
Photo by George N. Barnard

Game Point, Va.
Jan. 1, 1862
Mr. A.J. Proffit,

Dear Brother:

These lines will inform you that yours of the 23 December was gladly recieved on yesterday morning; and I hasten to reply.

I had been expecting to have recived letters from you or some of my friends on Lewis Fork for two or three weaks but as I did not receive any, I wrote A.N. a few days ago which I hope he will get. I am unable to interest you on the War question, as there is but little news in this part of Virginia. We seldom get an opportunity of firing upon the Yankee steamers, but when one approaches within 3 or 4 miles of our Battery, we are shure to give them a sign by which they may know that we are yet living and wide awake. I would have been glad to have taken Christmas with you, but as some 12 or 15 of the company had gone home on sick furlough I made no application for a furlough, but I thought I would content myself until those who were absent returned.

The manner in which we spent the Christmas Holidays, compared with former ones, presented a contrast that is more easily imagined than described; but we spent the day or at least a portion of it quite agreeably, particularly while seated at the dinner-table partaking of an excellent chicken pie, &c., &c., which had been prepared by **mess no 5**.

On yesterday morning one of my messmates and I took a small row-boat and went up Aquia Creek about four miles, where we called at a private house and took dinner and bought some articles for the mess and returned to camp a little before night, I tell you we enjoyed our trip very much, as we have not, until lately, been allowed such priveliges, since we have been stationed at this point. I would have been glad if you could have been here to have taken a New Year's dinner with us, as we dined upon a fat Turkey well baked and other delicaces, but I would advise you to stay on Lewis fork, at least till next spring.

I was glad to hear that those East Tennesseeans were being compelled to walk up to the chalk. The only thing to be regretted concerning those traitors, is that they had not been hanged long since. Tell Mother that I received her letter long since, and answered it immediately after its arrival.

I will soon close for the present by informing you that I am quite well at present, hoping these lines will find you all well.

Please give my compliments to all enquiring friends.

T.C. Land and T.C. Miller say they would have written you along since, had they rcd. ans. to the ones they sent you: They say they are not due you a letter as you supposed.

I remain &c. W.H. Proffit

PROCLAMATION.
HEADQUARTERS,
Greeneville, East Tenn., November 30, 1861.

To THE CITIZENS OF EAST TENNESSEE:

So long as the question of Union or disunion was debatable so long you did well to debate it and vote on it. You had a clear right to vote for the Union but when secession was established by the voice of the people you did ill to distract the country by angry words and insurrectionary tumult. In doing this you commit the highest crime known to the laws.

Out of the Southern Confederacy no people possess such elements of prosperity and happiness as those of East Tennessee. The Southern market which you have hitherto enjoyed only in competition with a host of eager Northern rivals will now be shared with a few States of the Confederacy equally fortunate politically and geographically. Every product of your agriculture and workshops will now find a prompt sale at high prices and so long as cotton grows on Confederate soil so long will the money which it brings flow from the South through all your channels of trade.

At this moment you might be at war with the United States or any foreign nation and yet not suffer a tenth part of the evils which pursue you in this domestic strife. No man's life or property is safe, no woman or child can sleep in quiet. You are deluded by selfish demagogues who take care for their own personal safety. You are citizens of Tennessee and your State one of the Confederate States.

So long as you are up in arms against these States can you look for anything but the invasion of your homes and the wasting of your substance. This condition of things must be ended. The Government commands the peace and sends troops to enforce the order. I proclaim that every man who comes in promptly and delivers up his arms will be pardoned on taking the oath of allegiance. All men taken in arms against the Government will be transported to the military prison at Tuscaloosa and be confined there during the war.

Bridge-burners and destroyers of railroad tracks are excepted from among those pardonable. They will be tried by drum-head court-martial and be hung on the spot.

D. LEADBETTER,
Colonel, Commanding.

From: A Compilation Of The Official Records Of The Union And Confederate Armies- Series II, Vol I. Chapter 5

The USS Merrimack, above, and the reworked CSS Virginia, below. Scuttled by the Union, the steamship was reconstructed as a casemate ironclad by the Confederates after they captured the shipyard at Portsmouth, Va. The renamed, Virginia, sank the USS Cumberland, and destroyed the USS Congress on March 8, 1862, before it clashed with the Yankee's Monitor the next day at the Battle of Hampton Roads. —Publishers.

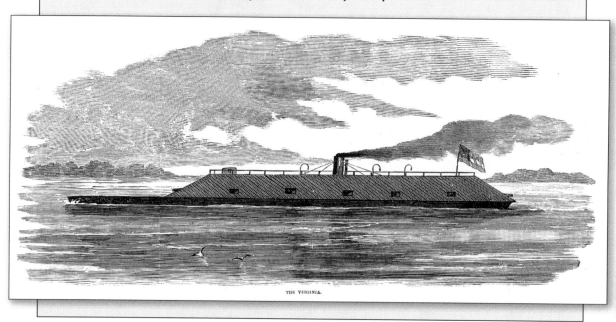

[This undated letter was included here because Harrison mentions the Virginia in battle with, presumably, the USS Cumberland and the USS Congress.]

Late yesterday evening, we received news to the effect that another tremendrous battle had been fought in Mississippi by Gen. Beauregard, resulting in an entire defeat of the federals. We also received intelligence that those large battles which had been pending in Va. had been fought. Gens. Johnson, Jackson, Magruder & others com'g Confederates. The Confederates are said to have gained glorious victories! Also that two or three Federal Gun Boats which had passed our Battery and ascended the James River to some distance had been totally destroyed by the Confederate Steamer, Virginia!

Who ever heard more good news! Should one half be true it is all right. I cannot vouch for these reports, I am inclined to believe the most of them.

Respectfully, WHP

A. Walsh and I have ordered the "Richmond Dispatch" to you it will come to Maple Springs directed to Samuel Walsh, Esq. but it is intended for you all. Please send us the date of the first one that arrives.

Give my compliments to cousin William Walsh tell him I received his letter and will answer it soon.

Tell A.N. that a note from him would be gladly received.

Yours, W.H.P.
To A.J. or C.L.P.

Camp McIntosh, N.C.
May 10th 1862

A.J. Proffit, Esq.,

I received yours of the 6 Inst. last evening, to which I hasten to reply. I was glad to hear that the family and neighbors were well, &c., &c., but sorry to learn that the prospect for farming was so very bad, but hope we may yet be favored with a good season, and that the labor of what few are farming be crowned with luxurient crops.

I will here inform you that the "conscription bill" has become a law- and all the able bodied men between the age of 18 and 35 are subject to enrollment and to be brought into service whenever called for by the Gov. There are, however, a few exceptions. I am of the opinion that this law will, but seldom, if ever, be rigedly enforced over the entire Confederacy- particularly in N.C. However they may occsionally take a few of the nearest to the army as necessity requires.

This being my opinion- I cannot do otherwise than recommend you to press on with your crop, and if the worst comes- let it come! All intelligent men know that something must be made to sustain those who are helpless and unable to sustain themselves as well as those who are in the service.

Although our country is apparently enveloped in a dark and portentous cloud of impenetrable appearance- we must recollect that behind this cloud the sun is shining wht his undeviating brilliancy and I hope that very soon his genial rays may shine forth upon the people of the Confederate States- firmly united, free, happy and prosperous. Instead of indulging in feelings of despondency let us compare our situation and cause to those of our illustrious ancestors who acieved the liberties we have ever enjoyed and for which we are now contending.

When you write me agan, inform me if you accepted that mary [mare?] as a part of your pay in our trade and how much more I am owing be certain to give me a plain, satisfactory answer and make any proposals you wish concerning any property I have.

How did you swap horses? I hope you have done well but fear you did badly.

Give my love to the family and friends, particularly my sister, Mrs. Miller & family.

As ever, your brother
W.H.P.

Goldesboro, N.C.
May 11, 1862
Mr. C.L. Proffit

Dear Causin,

After my best respects to you, I seat myself for the purpose of writing you a few lines in ans. to yours, which come to hand a few days ago. I was very glad to learn that you had got diverted so well at that forked litng [lightning] rod, als[o] several others things. You said you had the best jolk to tell me if so you will pleas write it in your next letter for I shal not get to see you for 2 or 3 weeks and mayby not for a month.

We are geting a long the best kind. I havent stood gard but twice cince I came from home for we halv no gard around our camp. We are not exposed any at all.

You said to tell you when I thought peace would be maid- I halv my privet opinion. I think it will bee maid in a short time, for they are whiped if thay knew it. The latist from Eurpoe say that thay are going to recognise the gulf stats and leave the border stats to go back to the union and force peace in America. I say if thay undertake to do that thay will halv a happy time if thay don't recognize the fool [full] Confedracy. They must ly [lie] low and keep dark and thay will see one of the damdest bar fits [fights] thay ever saw. If thay don't thay will feel same as the bar fite if thay interfear in soth [such] a time as this. The general oppinion is that the two pending battels will bee be the turminating battles- one at Richmond the other at Corinth.

So you must write soon and give my best respects to all inqurin friends &c.

Yours truly, A. Walsh

P.S. W.H. lost his hat on the cars as we moved to Goldsboro.

Proffit Family Letters

Map of the North Carolina Coast.

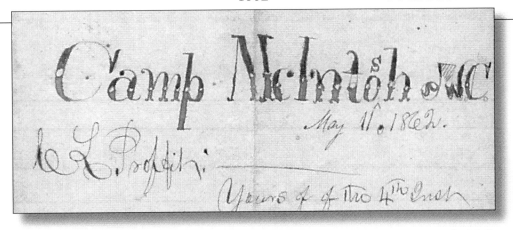

Camp McIntosh, N.C.
May 11, 1862

C.L. Proffit:

Yours of of the 4th Inst. came safely to hand a short time since, which was the first letter I received from Wilkes since I left there, but I can now very easily account for it.

We have such a variety of reports here that it is unnecessary for me to write any of them. There has been some fighting recently on the Peninsula, which resulted in favor of the Confederates. There is nothing of interest from the Coast of N.C. I cannot tell you how long we will remain here or where our next destination will be, but I hope we will not be removed from North Carolina I heard from our friends at Kinston N.C. yesterday- Messrs. David Hall[1] and Jesse Triplett[2]- I suppose Wm. Blankenship[3] is dead. The others were well.

You ought to be more industrious this summer than usual, as the demand for the products will, no doubt, be greater than formerly. Inform me in your next how [the] wheat crop looks - the prospect for fruit &c.

Has Dr. Lynn succeded? Who clubbed Jackson? Were the times good at John Blackburn's wedding? When did you last hear from Unkle Thornton's folks? When did you hear from Unkle [Albrs] folks? Who is Capt. of the Rifle Company? What is the general opinion about peace there? Had Alfred Ball returned home? Why? Who attends the saw-mill now? Is mustaches fasionable at present? Give A. Walsh information on these questions. My love to the family and connection

Your brother W.H.P.

{We are well hoping you th same.}

---

1 *David Hall, Corporal, Co. C, 26th N.C. Infantry*
2 *Jesse Triplett, Sergeant, Co. C, 26th N.C. Infantry*
3 *William Blankenship, Co. C, 26th N.C. Infantry, d. April 13, 1862, at Kinston, North Carolina*

Goldesboro, N.C.
May 20/62
C.L. Proffit

Dear Cousin,

It is withe the gratist of plasure that I seat my self for the purpose of droping you a few lines in answer to yours wich I resieved the 17th inst.

I found 50cts inclosed- in direction what to do with it, I sent to Goldesboro to day for stamps which I'll resieve in a short time by the time I get this brown paper wrote over. News is scarce, rumors are plenty.

I would bee quite happy in seeing you and hearing the good jolks that halve transpired since I left. When you write a gain, give the fool [full] purticulars of the boys success on that spree you spoke of &c. We are at camp McIntosh, yet. Do not expect a fite hear soon- if ever. Ever thing on the cost [coast] is quite [quiet]. Thay are [expecting a] fite at Richmond daily. I entertain no dout about [the] result.

Write to me and tell [what] the prospect for farming is- how wheat is geting along &c. [Since] I comenced writing I [have] heard the News from Raleigh. Calaway[1] is Lieut Col. of the [55th] Reg. T.C. Miller[2] was offered the {s?} of Maj. but would not [accept?] so it is all rite on the goos must close thes lines [leave]s me well W.H. is well [Giv]e my best respects to [all] my frends &c.

Yours truly

A. Walsh

I inclose 50 cts worth of stamp[s] in hear

---

1 Abner S. Calloway, Sergeant, Co. B, 1st N.C. Infantry, Promoted to Full Captain of Co. B, 55th N.C. Troops on Mar. 27, 1862.
2 Thomas C. Miller Co. B, 1st N.C. Infantry, Promoted to Full 2nd Lieutenant on Mar. 25, 1862.

Richmond, Va.
Jun the 11th, 1862

Dare Cousin,

It is with much pleser I take my pen in han to rite you a fue lines to let you no that I am well at this tim an I hop[e] when this letr come to you[r] hand hit will find you well with all the rest.

I hav no nuse to rite to you at this time- only we hav binn in another fite at Hanover. We hav binn marchin so I cod not have no chanch to rite. We lost 22 men out of our coumpny kill[ed], wounded an taken. I can't tell you all about the fite. I sent a paper home an I think you can go over an see hit an my likeness- if they gote thare. I woud like to see you an all the rest, but I can't see you yet, but I hope the time is comin when we will meat an enjoy our selvs together again. Tell Unkill an Ant I wante to see them an all the rest of my conneck. I want them an you not to forget me. I no that you can rite to me if you will I can say to you that hit is a [hard?] chance to get paper, heare.

I oftimes think of the time that we hav had together in the gardin with the rest. Tell the boys to rite to me. I woud rite to all them, if I can stay in a place long anouth [enough]. We have binn marchin day an nit of some time. We are shellin in three miles of Richmon. I supose that Cournl Stokes is about thar somewhere.

I want you to tell the [illegible] folks to rite to me an all so the [illegible] gal to rite to me. I want you to hav a [quilting?] when I come home an wey will hav a fine time. I think the ware will stop befo[re] long. I hop[e] so.

I must soon close my leter. Tell [list of illegible names] all to rite to me. I will close my leter. Rite soon an direck your leter to [illegible]

James Holim is well an sends you his respek. I will come home as soon as I can. Rite soon. So no more at this time but I remain you[r] frend till deth.

To R.L. Profitt From Philip Walsh

Richmond, Va.
June 11, 1862
C.L. Proffit

Dear Brother,

 This will inform you that I received a letter from you a few days ago which gratidfied me much by informing me that you were well &c. &c.

 I suppose you have been informed of our leaving North Carolina and returning to Virginia. We encamped a few days at Petersburg, during which time we wrote you, but have received no answers to our letters. I also had my Type [tintype] taken and [sended?] to you which I hope will be received. I guess you have heard of the recent fight near Richmond, and how our boys <u>licked</u> the yankees, I am not prepared to communicate any particulars of the battle.

 It will suffice to say that the Federals were repulsed with fearful loss- driven from their camps &c. It is said the <u>Old North State</u> [North Carolina] stands first in honor of the battle. We are encamped near the city of Richmond and are getting along finely. The health of the Regiment is good at present and a spirit of unyielding resistance prevails among our soldiers. I had forgotten to tell you that the 1st Regt. was ordered from Petersburg to the scene of action in the late battle and arrived upon the field just as the battle of Sunday closed. As I was unwell, having had another slight attack of chills, I did not accompany them, but rejoined them a few days after. My health is now very good. Our Regiment was on picket guard, day before yesterday, and if I could see you, I could recite several instances relative to it- that would perhaps interest you; at least it was interesting to me as it was the first time I had ever been on picket duty. Several shots were exchanged between our pickets and those of the enemy with what effect I am unable to say so far as regards the yankees, but none of our boys were hurt. The yankees were assured of our superior gunnery by the hideous yells of a large spotted dog that iminated from the woods near the place where the enemy pickets were concealed, it als[o] served to inform the owner that his appearance would be treated in like manner.

A. Walsh is in fine health and getting along nobly, also T.C. Land,[1] D.M. Carlton,[2] T.W. Laxton[3] and your friends generally.

The weather remains quite rainy and during the past few days has been very cool.

The most intelligent men with whom I have conversed lately, express the belief that the war will continue, but a few more months. I hope it may be so, and I believe it will.

Give my compliments to the family and neighbors.

Tell A.J. that I have been looking in vain, a long time for a letter from him, tell A.N. that his are few and far between.

I shall expect to hear from you frequently. I would like for you to be a little more communicative in the future.

Tell cousin William Walsh I would like to hear from him more frequently. Try to make good crops for they will be needed.

Yours, till death,
W.H. Proffit

---

1 *Thomas C. Land, Co. B, 1st N.C. Infantry*
2 *Daniel M. Carlton, Co. B, 1st N.C. Infantry*
3 *Thomas W. Laxton, Co. B, 1st N.C. Infantry*

Richmond, Va.
June 12, 1862
Mr.'s C.L. & A.N. Proffit

Dear Cousines,

 I seat myself for the purpose of writing you a few lines in answer to yours, which reached me this ev[ening]. You of corce love to hear from our army at every point, but I can not give you a strate account of them- only at somes points. The army is all rite hear and our army in Western Va. is rite there. Old Stonewall Jackson had whiped out the yankees thare and got lots of prisners also lots of amunitions, comisaries stored and munitions of ware [war], camp equipage &c. &c.

 Our forses halve falen [fallen] back from Corinth. The yankees are reported to halve falen back hear. There [is] fiting going on at Charlstown S.C. This is the news in today's dispach- it is rumered hear that our Reg. is orderd away from hear. I do not know and I don't care if it is, for the strong limestone warter is not good for no 1. We halv plenty to eat and ware but our rashones of whiskey is quite small. We got a dram the other morning is the second drop I have had since I saw you- only a little in Salisbury.

 I think peace will be maid shortly. It is the oppnion of pretty near all the people and the yankees to those who halv bin taken prisners there is not one soldier that would care how quick.

 I had the plasure of seeing our noble president some few days ago. I nead not try to gave you a discription of him if you will look at a postedg [postage] stamp, he is fully picturd thare- also Gen. Lee & Longstreet, Gen. Hill of N.C., Homes & Cobb. These generals make a booly [bully] apearance. I had like to halv forgoten to ask you if you got them postedg stamps I sent you or not. Pleas write soon, excuse bad spelling, writing, &c.

 Write soon and gave all the news & no more at present but ever remens your true friend

A. Walsh

 Mr. A Walsh, Esq- yours of the 12 June is at hand which did not fail to giv a resonable quantity of pleasure.

 Your folks are all write on the goose

Camp [Land?] [illegible] County
Ju[n]e the 18th 1862
Mr. A. J. Proffit

Dear Friend,

I write you a fiw lines which will inform you that I am tobille [tolerable] well. Though not able for duty- I have had the mumps which has left me reather week [Tod] has the fever. Right back, &c. I hop[e] these lines will find you all well.

I have nothing new to write you, the helth of the Company is good. Some of them have the mumps. I think we ar located in a tolrible [Hlsty] plac for this country if we could ever get over the mumps Measles, &.c. I have no news from this cruel war to write you. I see no prospect for pice untill it starvs out which I think will done in 8 or 12 months. McClelan's army is falling back at Richmond. Consequently, no moore fighting is expected thar at presant- only with the out posts.

The yankes war repulsed at Charleston, the prospect is much moore favorable for the south now than it has been if [they?] will follow up thir victorees.

We ar situated whar we get fish and some other vegetables, but we pay for them, bacon 27c , whiskey $10.00 per gallon. If you or any other good man will bring me 15 or 20 stout men, I will give you the offic of 2nd Lieut. &c. I hop[e] you will except [accept].

You will far[e] as well her as any whar in the army. Tell the conscrips, to[o], to come her[e], or some of them.

Sur as nobody else will write to me I hop[e] you will condecend to give me a letter containing the general items to which I will amediatly corespond, giving you the same in return from my pos. & &c.

Tell my folks I am nearly well, and have not got any letter from them yet. Write me. How crops of all kinds appear to be. How the friends are getting along in general. Tell me how uncal Ben's folks is, uncal John, Goforths, Nancy-all.

Write me how uncal Jo Handson is getting as I know you and uncal Jo to be quite intimate. Tell Alf. to informe whether Tom. Hamby has split my [rails] or not. Tell me whether Wm. Walsh has got well or not, and w[r]ite how my folks ar, &c. In short, give me all the news you think would serve to interest me, and any thing from that county will do that.

The males [mails] hav come. I must quit. [all?] by [r ct]

Salisbury, 53rd Regiment, NC Troops
A.J. Proffit

Wm. J Miller[1]

---

1 *William J. Miller, Captain, 53rd Regiment, N.C. Infantry*

Camp, Near Weldon, N. Carolina
June 25th 1862

Dear Fothe & Mothe & Friends,

I take the oportunity of droping you a few lines to let you know that I am well at this time, hoping when these few lines reaches you, that they will find you all enjoying the same blessing.

I have nothing of intrust to write to you at this time, more than I am well and have been. We are now stationed at or near Weldon N.C. guarding the bridges. I canot tell how long we will stay here but not long I don't suppose.

They are expecting a fight at Richmond every day and J.B. says he expects they began yesterday. Well I must close for John B. is in a hurry to start. Write soon and direct to

Garysburg, N.C.
53rd Reg. N.C.T.
Care of Capt. Miller
No mor at present but remains, yours, &c.

Jesse Miller

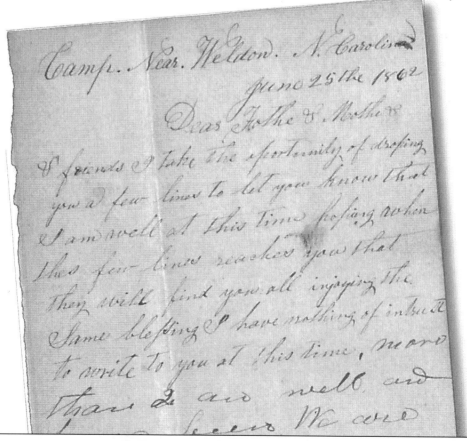

Camp near Weldon Bridge N.C.
July the 4th 1862
Mr. A.J. Proffit

Dear Brother,

I, for the first time, have taken my pen for the purpose of writing you a few lines which will infom you that I am very well at this time, and have been mostly all the time, since I left home, and I hope these lines will find you enjoying good health.

Well you have no doubt, ere this, heard of the great Battle,[1] which has been raging for the last eight days at Richmond and is yet continuing I heard today that W.H. Proffit, T.C. Land, D.M. Cartlow [Carlton] and several others of our friends who were in Capt Brown's Com. were wounded. Also Col. Stokes[2] is badly wound and is expected not to live. Col. Lee's[3] boddy passed here yesterday, a corps[e]. It has no doubt been the hardest battle, ever fought on the American continant or elsewhere but we, if all accounts be true, have gained the greatest victory ever gained over any [thing], and I think it will be a considerable cause towards making pease. I must stop. It is now dress parade and I want you to write to me and Direct to

Garysburg, N.C.
53rd Reg. N.C.T.
Care Capt. Miller

Your brother,
Jesse Miller

---

1 *The Seven Days' Battles*
2 *Montford Sidney Stokes, Colonel, 1 N.C. Infantry, d. July 3rd from wounds on received in the Battle of Mechanicsville (2nd of the Seven Days) on June 26, 1862, at Richmond, Virginia.*
3 *Charles Cochrane Lee, Lieutenant Colonel of the 1st N.C. Volunteer Infantry, Colonel, 37th N.C. Infantry, killed on June 30, 1862, at Fraysers Farm, Virginia. (5th of the Seven Days' Battles)*

Camp 16 miles East of Richmond, Va.
July 8th 1862
A.J. Proffit

Dear Brother,

Although the chance is bad for writing, I will try to drop you a few lines. I guess you have heard that we have been in several battles during the past few days. Our Reg. has sustained a grate loss in the battles. We have lossed all our field officers, at least for a time. Our Major, a brave and gallant officer, was killed in the first battle we were engaged in. Col. Stokes was badly wounded in the leg, which has since been amputated. I learned today there were not much hopes of his living.

The Lieut. Col. & adjutant will, perhaps, soon recover. Several company officers & many privates were either killed or wounded.

I was in two battles and escaped uninjured. Being unwell and much exhausted from hard marching, I was unable to continue the march with the Reg. on the 1st of July and was not in the battle that day. It was in that battle that we lossed about 28 in killed & wounded. Alfred Walsh,[1] Thomas Hamby, [a]nd John E. Hendren[2] were killed I will not now give you a list of the wounded: T.C. Land & D.M. [Cartrow], also D. Eller was among the wounded. I suppose they have gone home they can doubtless give you more infrormation than I can write.

I have been unwell for a few days but have recovered again and am now in tolerably good health- however the fatiques of the past days [have] almost worn me out. I have never undergone such before but I am glad to inform you that the enemy have been completely routed and driven with severe loss about 20 miles. They are now aboard of their gunboats and I suppose are not making much demonstrations of another attack.

The loss of Alfred Walsh is indeed a deplorable one, but such as the horror of war. A finer soldier could not be found. He was much respected by the company and his loss is much regretted by them.

We are now about 20 miles from our camp (ie- where our tents are, &c.) When we go back I will try to write you a better letter. I rec'd. letters from you a few days ago.

Write me every mail & I will write every chance. Yours, as ever,

W.H. Proffit

---

1 *Alfred Walsh, son of Samuel Walsh and 1st cousin to W.H. Proffit, Co. B, 1st N.C. Infantry*
2 *John Evan Hendren, Co. B, 1st N.C. Infantry, killed at Malvern Hill (6th of the Seven Days' Battles)*

Camp near Richmond, Va.
August 7, 1862
C.L. Proffit

Dear Brother.

I write you a few lines to inform you that my health is much improved and am now almost as well as I have been for several months. I am a little astonished at not receiving any letters from you in more than a month.

The dates of the last letters I rec'd. from home was the 30th June. I received one from Unkle Saml. Walsh a few days ago which informed me you were all well.

Please continue to write me and give your letters the proper direction and I will be apt to receve some of them at least. There is no very important news in this vicinity.

Samuel Ginning, Joseph W. Peden, Lieut W.W. Vannoy, John Perkins and 2 privates of Co. F who were taken prisoner on 15th June and taken to Fort Delaware, returned to camp on yesterday evening. We were glad to see them & much interested in their conversation. There [is] continuing to be much sickness here and the weather is intensely hot. We learned this morning that the Confederates have taken Baton Rouge, La.

I must soon close.

Give my love to the family and neighbors, and be certain to write me frequently.

Yours till death,

W.H. Proffit

P.S. There is thought to be a good prospect for a speedy termination of the war.

W.H.P.

Camp near Richmond, Va.
Aug. 17/62
C.L. Proffit

Dear Brother:

I use this as the first opportunity of responding to yours of Aug. 2d which came to hand in due time. I left camp on the 8th inst. with a detachment to work on the breastworks which are being constructed for the safety of Richmond. During the time of my absence from camp, my health has improved rapidly, as we have had the advantages of good water, &c. We are going to return this evening for the purpose of completing the part of the fortifications assigned us. I am unable to give you much information relative to the movements of the Armies before Richmond. If the Yankees are making any demonstrations of a renewal of the contest for Richmond I am not aware of it. In my opinion Richmond is in no danger of another attack at least for several months, and I would rather add, for ever.

"Stonewall" Jackson is keeping their attention directed toward the Valley of Virginia. He attacked the advance of Pope's army a few days since and gave them as good a licking as could have been during the time they would stand and take it, but they soon grew weary of the sport and ran off, however, upward of 400 remained with him 29 com'd [command] officers [and] one Brigadier Genl.

Large forces are concentrating in the vicinity of Gordonsville, Va., and the weasle is expected to pop in a few days. The weather is remarkabley cool and pleasant for this season of the year, and is thought the health of the soldiers is improving.

H.M. Stokes visited us a few days ago, we were much pleased at seeing him. He will visit you when he returns.

I understand you are a school teacher. Well, honor your profession, and it will honor you. Endeavor to keep always cool and calm, never suffer your passions to rule you. Govern your passions, so that your students will never be able to see any changes in your looks, talk or actions.

Be ever kind to your students, and endeavor to gain the strongest affections of each one of them. At the same time let them know that your requirements must and shall be complied with. I hope you will be successful in advancing the students at the same time, recollect that you never have and perhaps never will occupy a better place for your own advancement. Let not an hour pass unimproved- particularly improve your mode of spelling and hand write. I hope to see a perceptible change in each letter you write me. <u>Let me not be deceived.</u>

I rec'd. letters from A.J. & A.N. which I would answer if I knew they would get them but as I do not I shall decline writing them at present. I am truly sorry A.J. would not take my advice & get off the muster roll & remain at home. I know he could have done so- and I well know he is not able for military service. I hope he will consider the importance of so doing and get off before it is too late even if he has neglected the proper time for doing so.

Write me soon after the reception of this and give me full particulars of your school. Where you are boarding, what you are making, who is sending, &c. &c. &c.

Give my love to Father, Mother and Sis with the connection & friends who may enquire for me.

Your affectionate Brother
W.H. Proffit

P.S. You wished to know if that diamond-shaped purse sent with A. Walsh's things was a money purse, I will inform you it is.

W.H.P.

N.B. Adopt the best system in your school and faithfully carry it out.

Camp Hill, N.C.
August 24th 1862
Wm. Proffit

Dear Father,

I seat my self this sabbath morning for the purpose of informing you that we are all well and doing as well as we can. We have plenty to eat and good water as I want and as good as a tent as you cold wish for. We have been drilling a little of mornings and evenings, but vary little. The buoys are coming in evry day from evry county a round.

News is as scarse here as hens teeth concerning the ware [war]. I hardly have herd it maned [mentioned?] since I came in to camp. The news came here this morning that we wold start from this place in a short time. I can't tell when but you needen't to write till I write again. I must close by subscribing my self, your affection son,

A.N.P.

P.S. A.J., T.C., W.C., A.V. are all well and vary well satisfied.

C.L.P.

Dear Father,

These lines lave me well and I hope they may find you in joying good health and prosperity. I haven't any good news to write you but if you ware here, I and the rest of the buoys could tell you some rich jokes. I have formed sevrel aquaints sence I came here. I can't write this morning, thare are so many passing, you must excuse sutch a letter as this and I will try to do better. Give my respects to all my friends and except [accept] for your self. I must close. You needen't to write till I write again.

P.S. We haft to charge the battry twist pr day- we flank him and throw the [bunbs?] hevily we had torn him almost to mutch. You and Whig and Th. aut [ought] to come and se it. It is worthy of attention tell [illegible] that Kib is well and doing well W.C. is well- in form his folks of this, if you can.

No more,
A.N.P.

Camp Lea, two miles west of Richmond, Va.
August the 29th 1862
Wm. Proffit

Dear Father,

Theese lines are to inform you where we are and what we are doing, &c. On last Sunday we received orders to prepare 4 days rations in order to start to Gordonsville and on Monday the 25 of this inst. we took the cars and traveled all day and all night and arrived at Raleigh about 10 A.M. We, there, changed cars and continued our travel and arrived at Weldon about 12 o'clock that night and slept in the streets on our blankets. Next morning we took the train for Petersburg and got there about 12 o'clock. We rested a few hours- had a fine shower of rain- we, then, started for Richmond and got there at 10 A.M.

We then started on foot 2 miles for Camp Lea and lay on our blankets in a grove. Next morning we drew tent and pitched them and drew rations of first rate beef, rise and loaf bread. We are doing nothing but cooking and eating. There came about 300 with us from Camp Hill. We were all glad to leave that point and left without a tear, for we had no liberty there, but we have as much as we want here. Our station will be in the 18th N.C. Regiment. I forget the Col's. name- it is Branche's Brigade and Jackson's Division. We have not seen any of the boys from the 1st Reg. nor the 53rd and do not know where they are. We heard the 1st was away up this side of Washington city but cannot say. Wm. Walsh is with us waiting to hear from them.

We had right smart of fun on our hard travel to this place. The ladies, gentlemen and little children greated us with many harty cheers and the darkise found it not agains their conscience to cheer us, too, and give us peaches, &c. I do not know how long we will stay here but I think we will leave in a few days- as soon as we can get transportation. The cars are now taking provisions up to Gordonsville. There are a great many men here- none of them are doing anything, except the artillery- they are drilling beautifully. Sum few of the boys from Wilkes are not well satisfied but the Stony and Lewis Fork boys are dong finely waiting for the wagon and anxious for the ride.

I want Calvin to continue teaching school until I find out some things and if he has to go to the ware, I will try to get him with me. Tell him to hold on and teach school until I tell him what to do. I am anxious to here from you and to hear what trades and arrangements you have made. I do not know whether you need write to me or not but if you do, direct to Richmond, Va.

I must now close. I will write soon and give you information where to direct your letters. Trade and do the best you can, &c. Theese lines leave us all well, hoping they may find you all in good health. Give my love and compliments to the connection and neighbors. Tell them to write to me. I will close by subscribing myself, your mos[t] affectionate son, &c.

Andrew J. Proffit

>State of Maryland
>45 miles from Washington City
>Sept. the 8th 1862
>Mr. Wm. Proffit

Dear Father,

This note will in form you that we waded the Potomac yesterday and are now in Maryland. We are all well and doing very well. We have had a hard time marching to this place- we have marched 8 days and are much worn out. Gen. Jackson's division is all in Maryland.

We crossed the river with two brigades- the river was about as wide as from your house to T.C. Walsh's. We do not know anything about the movements of the army.

One thing is the yankees are whiped out of Virginia and our forces are in Maryland in abundance, &c. Tell T.C. Walsh's folks that he is well- also A. Vannoy's folkes that he is well and all the boys that came with us are well. Wm. Walsh has got to his Co. this morning. I have not time to write anything about our trip but will in a few days. We are in the 18th Reg. and they are now dividing us out. Now the 1st Reg. is in this place. Harrisson was not able for the march and was sent back to Gordonsville I suppose he has written to you when you write, write how he is and where he is. Tell C.L. to be shure to stay at home and teach school.

When you write to us direct your letters thus

A.J. Proffit

18th Reg. N.C. Troops

Gordon'sville Va.

Tell T.C.'s wife and his father's folks to write to him and direct in the same manner. He has not time to write today- also, A. Vannoy's. Please inform all our friends how to write to us and tell them to write. No more at present, but remain yours, &c.

>A.J. Proffit

State of Maryland, Camp Thunder
September 9, 1862
C.L. Proffit

Dear Brother,

Thes lines are to inform you that we are all well, greatly hopeing these few lines may reach you and find you, withe all the rest of my friends, injoying the same blessings.

I haven't any news to write you of mutch importance more than we have had quite a frisky time sines we left Richmond. We left thare Monday, the 1st of September, and hav marched 8 days in succession and cooked our rashions evry night. We waided the Rhappadan and Potomack Riv[ers]. We have past many scines, bouth plesant and unplesant. We passed many battell grounds. Though not exactly through any, we have passed many beautifull townes and villedgs.

When we left Richmond, we expected to go to Gordonsville and stay thare some time, but we diden't tarry thare and from thare, we started to Manasses and we turned before we got quite thare on the account of a hard fought battal which had ben fought a few days before we got thar and the [illegible] was vary bad in which the Southern buoys ware sucsessfull it was some [illegible] to see the armes that was taken from the yankess. We all have yankee guns of the best quality.

The men in this stait [state] are volunteering fast. We will soon have a larg army of Marylanders- then we may recross the Potomack, but I don't know what the intentioun of Jackson is- he is unwell at this time. When he gits well, he will do some thing. We are encamped on a steepe hillside without tents- so is all the army on this side of the P. [Potomac] We have plenty to eat to leave here in a few days. I wrote you while I was at Richmond, which I suppose you have recieved. The chance for sending letters here is bad on the account of the railroad being tourn up. We haft to have our provisions from the Rhappadand on wagons. I must soon close- I will in form you how to direct you letters on a little scrap of paper and then I want you to write me as soon as you can. Give my respecks to F.M. and Elizabet and family. No mor but remains, yours,

A.N.P.

Miss R.L. Proffit

Estemed Sister,

    These lines will inform you that we are all rite on the goos. I am now in Maryland and in joying my self finely. We have plenty to eat and not mutch to do since we taken the sourt martch [short march?] of 8 days. Thare was not mutch fun in that, for the dust was so thick that you could not see- onon [on and on for?] 10 miles. Sis, I have not taken off my clothes since I left home and it will take some rubing to git them clean. I wish you had the chance to wash them for me. A.J. and some of the buoys are goan [going] to the creek to wash now. I must close for want of space. You must write me soon,

                                                      A.N.P.

Solid shot (foreground, above) was used, primarily, for destruction of material, fortifications or ships. Canister shot consisted of balls in a cylindrical steel tube (lower-right, above) & grape shot consisted of balls held together between steel plates (top, above), Both broke apart into shrapnel, when fired, and were used against personnel.

RICHMOND, VA. PILES OF SOLID SHOT, CANISTER, ETC., IN THE ARSENAL GROUNDS; RICHMOND & PETERSBURG RAILROAD BRIDGE AT RIGHT.

Photo by Alexander Gardner, United States Library of Congress

Near Martisburg, Va.
Sept. the 22nd 1862

Dear Father and Mother,

It is with great pleasure that I write you a few lines which will in form you that we are all in the land of the living and en joying a reasonable portion of health, &c. I have in deed stood the trip well- have had no sickness. I have stood it better than the other boys. We have been gone one month & 2 days- have been in three battles- the 1st at Harpers Fary where we took about 1,000 prisoners. 2- in Maryland which was indeed a bloody battle. We did not get to fire ther but was exposed to the fire of the enemy in an open field for a bout one half mile.

Severil of our Reg. were killed and wounded we lay all day, next, behind a fense exposed to their sharp shooters & A.W. Dunkin[1] was shot through the thigh. That night we crossed back in to Va. Al thow [Although] we ran the enemy from the field when we left, they persued us and crossed day before yesterday. We turned on them and had a bloody engagement. We formed in line of battle a bout one mile from them and made a generil charge, exposed the hole way to the heavist bombing, said to be by old soldiers, that they ever saw. But we routed them and drove them back across the river about 9 or 10 o'clock. I suppose we lost a great many, but the yankees lay on the field in heaps and piles. We got all their arms, knap-sacks and all they had, with many prisoners. As they crossed the river we give them fits. A.N. and I shot as long as we could see a blue coat. Exposed to the fire of 3 batteries, the bombs burst round our heads with terrific fury and showers of grape and canister fell, mingled with limbs of trees thick around us, but the God of heaven protected us from their power- which I hope he will ever do. We wer so much exhosted from the fatiques of the charge that we threw away all our clothes & blankets, only [keeping] what we have on, but that is all right- we will get more. A.N. was slightly struck on the arm with a piec of shell or something. He droped his gun. I asked him if he was hurt, he said not. He grabed his and fought like a heroe while the sweat droped fast from his brow.

T.C. Walsh, A. Vannoy,[2] John Ferguson,[3] R.M. Blankinship,[4] Vincent Hendrix & others wer all engaged & fought like veterans. Wm. C. Proffit was struck on the knee with a piec of a bomb and knocked down, so he did not go through, but was not hurt much. He is not very well now but is able to march. A.N. & W.C., T.C.W. have not stood it as well as I have, but have kept up and done good service and for bravery cannot be excelled. We have not been drilled exceeding 4 hours but our officers give us much praise for fighting.

---

1 *Andrew W. Duncan, Co. D, 18th N.C. Infantry*
2 *James A. Vannoy, Co. K, 53rd N.C. Infantry*
3 *John F. Ferguson, Co. D, 18th N.C. Infantry*
4 *R.M. Blackenship, Co. D, 18th N.C. Infantry*

Well Pa, as it is all right on the goose a bout the war, I will now ask you a few questions. I want you to write me all the news about our domestic conserns. Have you bought you any land? If so, where & what price? Are you done fodering? Have you sold my mare or jack and what price? Have you made any trades of importance & what are they? If we have any free school and who is teaching- where H.M. Stokes is & what he is doing, if you have heard from Jesse Miller & how he is, how Bethe's family is doing and how the church is getting a long. Please answer theese interrogatives and give me the news a bout all the connection and neighbors, if cousin Fanny got well. Write if you have heard from Harrisson, lately. He was broken down and not able to travel when his Reg. left the Rhapadan and he was sent back to Gordon's ville or Orange Ct. to rest. I saw some of his Reg., yesterday. [I] thought that Wm. Walsh was gone home when I wrote before but he did not start then, but I suppose he has or will go soon, for he will not be retained in service, &c. Tell H. Bingham's connection that I see him almost every day. He is in our brigade & is doing well, &c. Pa, I want you to keep Calvin at home, if posible, in an honorable way & I know he can stay if he will continue teaching school for he is not able for such service as is required, &c.

I believe I have written about all I know. I am anxious to hear from you & to know what you are going to do about a home. I know not what plan to suggest. If you could get that set of mills I would be much pleased- if not, I think you could do well on Gap Creek, if you could get a good chance. You must do the best you can. Sell any of my propperty and apply it to the most needful purpose. Write whether Capt. Ball took my wagon or not, &c. and take it all in all. Get some man to write a day for you and write every think that will be of interest to me. Tell all my friends to write often to me & I will write to them but my chance is bad. I have to send them by chance to Gordon's ville to be mailed which is about 150 or 200 miles. Therefore, if you do not get many letters from us, you need not be uneasy. When you write, direct thusly. Writing thus they will follow me where I am:

A.J. Proffit
18th Reg. N.C. Troops
Branches brigade
A.P. Hill's division
Gordon's ville Va.
Co (D)

I will now close by subscribing my self, your most obedient son till death, &c.

A.J. Proffit

P.S. Please in form my friends how to direct their letters, &c.   A.J.P.

Near Winchester, Va.
Oct the 13th 1862
Wm. Proffit

Dear Father

I now write you a short note which will inform you that we are well at present, hoping that when theese lines come to hand that they may find you all well. I have no news to write you at present, more than Calvin, Thos. Walsh, Wm. West, H.M. Hamby, S. Cox [and] L. Lewther came to our camp last night they were all well and galy. They belong 13th N.C. Reg. which is in D.H. Hill's Division about 4 miles from here [illegible] all night with us and went on this morning. I am going to try to swap for C.L. and Thos. Walsh if I can- they are in the same division with Harrisson, but not the same brigade I do not think.

I have not seen Harrisson and do not know [illegible] he is but I guess he is with his Reg., now. I am quite sorry that C.L. and Thos. had to come. I do not know how you will do without us all, but there is no other chance now. I want to know where you expect to live next year. I am uneasy about that and what you will do with Betty and her children as I know you cannot maintain them all by yourself without help and I know not what to say for the best. I suppose you have made sum arrangement before this time. I want you to do what you think would be the best. I would be glad for you to stay where you are next year if you could make the arrangements- if not, I think you might do well on Gap Creek if you could get a good chance.

I hope that peace will be made and we will all be home before this time next year. I have written every week for a long time to you but have got no answers so send our letters with out paying the postage for that is all the chance we have taking money- and pay the postage. C.L. told me you had been trading. That is all right on the goose.

When you write, direct your letters A.J. Proffit, Co. D, 18th Reg. N.C. Troops. Branches Brigad, A.P. Hills Division. I have been in three fights since I left home but none of us got hurt. The battles were Harpers Fary, Va., Sharpsburg, and Shepardstown, Va., of which I have written before and I hope you have got my letters and they will tell you all about it. C.L. told me that you had sold my Jack for a wagon- Well hold on to that for wagons are good trade. I suppose you have bought A.B. [West's?] wagon well I want [illegible] to come home [illegible] when you write, give me all the news you have a bout all our concern. Take good care of all the money you can get, for we spend lots here. We have not drawn one cent, yet- what you save for me will be all I shall have if I ever come home- but take what you stand in need of that belongs to me. You will have to sell my mare. Do something with her, for I know you cannot keep her. C.L. and his squad got their $50 bounty and one soot of clothes but they had spent a good deal before they got here.

    I will cease writing for this time hoping to hear from you soon I will close by subscribing myself, yours, most affectionately, &c.

A.J. Proffit

VIEW ON THE POTOMAC — NEAR HARPER'S FERRY.

Currier & Ives Lithograph drawn by Frances Flora Bond (Fanny) Palmer, United States Library of Congress

10 miles North of Winchester, Va.
Monday, Oct. the 27th 1862
Wm. & Mary Proffit

Dear Father & Mother,

In answer to your interesting letter of Oct. the 12 which came to hand in due time & grattified me greatly by informing me that you were all well, &c. I have no news to write at present to interest you more than A.N. & I are stout & harty. I feel just as well as I ever did in my life, but it rained so much last night & was so cold I could not sleep.

There are severil of the boys gone to the hospitle from our Reg. Wm. C. Proffit has been gone about ten days- he had the measels- & I have not heard from him since he left. The Measels & Mumps are common in camp. With that exception, the health is good. T.C. & Phillip Walsh are both well, &c.

You wanted to know if we wanted any clothing. We will draw as much as we need in a few days. I think they are making out the pay rolls to draw our money and have sent sometime ago for our clothes. Calvin drew his bounty and 1 soot of clothes at Raleigh and he came by to see us & gave us some of his clothes. We are so far from home that you could not send us any, but you may make us some socks & gloves as we are needing them & I think that we will come nigher home in a few weeks & I will write again & perhaps you can send them to us. Blame the yankees- they caused me to loose all- but we thrashed them out of this part of Va. & I have not seen them since & do not want to any more.

You wanted to know if I had seen C.L. & Thos. I have [seen] C.L. 3 times he is in Gen. Penders Brigade, 13 Reg. N.C.T., Co. H, A.P. Hill's Division- in the same division that I am. He says he has a first rate Capt. & likes him well, &c. I have not seen W.H. & do not know where his Reg. is. I was glad to hear that his health was improving. I think I will see him this winter. When you write to him, inform him how to direct letters to me & you direct yours the same as you have till further orders, &c. I was much pleased to learn that you were going to live another year wher you are. Do the best you can with all our stock. You done well with the Jack, I am well pleased. Tell the girls that as soon as I get my new short coat & my face clean and move to some city, that I will send them the best likeness that they have seen for I am mending very fast & looks pretty well, considering. Tell cousins, Wm. & Nancy Ball that I have rec'd. their letters and will write to the in a few days, as I have not time, now

Being that I have no news, I will close for the present. Theese lines leave us well, hoping that they may find you all enjoying the same blessings, &c.

I remain your affectionate son until death, &c.

A.J. Proffit

State of Va., Clark Co.
Nov the 2nd 1862
Miss R.L. Proffit

Dear Sister,

I now write you a few lines which will in form you that I am quite well at this time, hoping that theese lines may find you all in good health. I have no news to write you at this time of an in teresting character. I rec'd your kind letter of Oct. the 19th, which was rec'd with many thanks. It came to hand in due time & I hope you will not fail to write to me often as it appears that no one else will.

I was quite sorry to hear that Wm. Walsh & Minervy were sick I hope they are well now. We are falling back toward Richmond eating & mooring all before us. I do not know whether we will have any fighting to do before we get back or not. It will take a bully to whip us.

I saw C.L. a few days, since. He & Thos. was well then. He has written to you but has rec'd no answer, W.C.P. is at Winchester in the Hospitle with the measels. He has been gone about 3 weeks- I think he will be back soon. Wm. Cotrell was sent to the Hospitle. I heave heared he was dead & I suppose it is so.

You stated that you had not determined to stay where you are. If you do not, I want to know where you expect to go and what chance you have at another place. I want L. Land to be shure to come and see us this winter, but he had better wait a few weeks & I think we will be nearer the railroad station. I want him to bring me some socks & gloves & a box of chestnuts, sweet potatoes, butter, molasses and any little thing he coveniently can. I will write to him on the subject, &c.

I remain your brother with great respect &c.

A.J. Proffit

Camp Near Buryvile, Va.
Nov. 5, 1862
Miss R.L. Proffit

Dear Sister,

I write you a few lines which will inform you that I am moderatly well at this time, hoping that this may find you all well. I have no vary good news to write you.

I hav had a vary easy time since I left home- especialy for a soldier. I hav never stood gard, yet- I hav not yet receved arms. I am vary glad that our machine has done so well. I saw A.J. & A.N a few days a go. They informed me that they rec'ed. a letter from you a day or two before. I want you to write me how many bushels they hav thrashed, on what conditions pa rented that farm, what he is doing, how much wheat you hav sown, if the mules hav mended much, &c. &c. And I want you to be certain to write where W.H. is, if you are going to school, &c. &c.

Inform unkle McAlpin's folks that Thomas is well & doing first rate. Wm. West[1] & Smith Cox[2] went to the hospitle at Winchester a few day[s] ago. I think Wm. will get a dis charge- Smith had the Measles. I will close. If you hav any respect for a brother, write one just as soon as you receive this, I remain, &c.

C.L. Proffit

Direct to C.L. Proffit

A.P. Hill's Division

Penders Brigade Care Col Ruffin 13st Reg. N.C. Troops Co. H.

---

1 *William West, Surry County, Co. H, 13th N.C. Infantry, d. May 21, 1863, at Hospital, Richmond, Virginia..*
2 *Smith Cox, Co. H, 13th N.C. Infantry d. May 27, 1864, at Hospital, Gordonsville, Virginia.*

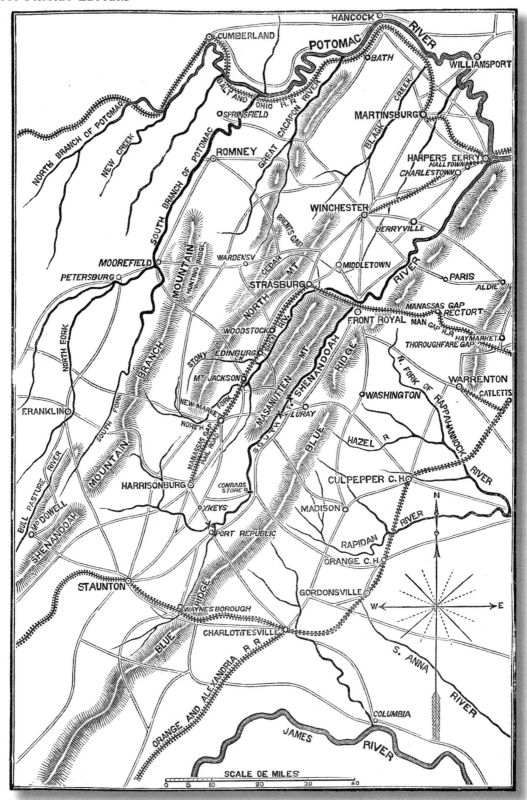

Map of the Shenandoah Valley.

Near bary vill, Va.
November 10, 1862
R.L. Proffit

Dear Sister,

I again take pleasure in writing you a few lines which will in form you that we are all well, hopeing these lines will find you all injoyin the same great blessing.

I havent any news to write you of im portance, more than our side still keps whipping the yankees. They have whiped then twice not far from hear, lately, and will whip then a gain when ever they fight for they don't expect anything ells. For when we hollow at them, they brake like thunder.

Sis, I think will come back to N.C. or S.C. to stay this winter. Give my love to F.M.E. and family and except [accept] for yourself. Write soon and ofton.

A.N.P.

Near Fredericksburg, Va.
Dec. 19, 1862
R.D. Proffit

Dear Sister

These lines are to inform you that we are all well at this time, greatly hopeing these lines may find you injoying the same bessings.

I have seen W.H., C.L. and Thomas since the battal (an account of which you will see in Whigs letter.) They are all well and come through the fight safe. We whiped the yankees out slick. Now it is said they lost 15 thousand. Thare was nobody killed on our side that I was acquainted with but Wm. Robins. He was shot dead.

John B. Miller came and staid all night with us and per haps discouraged you about how we ware gitting along havin a bad time we war scearce of provisions at that time, but we now have plenty we draw pork, bacon and beef and flower and crackers.

I will close. Write soon. So no more,

A.N. Proffit

Camp 8 miles East of Fredericksburg, Va.
December 18, 1862

Dear Father and Mother:

I embrace this opportunity of writing you a short letter for the purpose of letting you know that I am enjoying good health at this time. I am sorry I could not write your more frequently than I have done of late, but as we have been almost all the time on the march, we could not write as we would love to have done.

I will here say to you not to make yourselves uneasy if you do not get letters from me often, however I will write every good opportunity that is offered, but they will no doubt be few.

I will here inform you that I have been in the battle of Fredericksburg but our division was not actively engaged. We were held in reserve and were only exposed to the fire of artillery. There were very few of our Reg.'s killed, but several wounded. Lieut. W.W. Vannoy[1] of our Co. B was wounded. His eyeball is said to be bursted.

The battle was a very hard one particularly on the 10th day of the month. We gained one of the brightest victories of the war. The next day after the battle we were sent forward and occupied the front lines. We were near the enemy we could plainly see three of their lines of battle, and were near enough to have reached them with our small army.

We expected every minute to hear the next battle begin, but in the evening the enemy sent in a flag of truce asking permission to bury their dead. They carried off about one half of their dead, when the time expired that night, they all moved off or the most of them crossed the river and when day appeared the <u>blue lines</u> were not to be seen.

The retreat was so conducted that we did not take many prisoners nor much booty. We are now waiting to see when they will make another demonstration. Then, I guess we will meet them with the intenion of using them as we have been in the habit of doing. I understand that the Yankees seem very much cowed and some of them say they can never whip us. I think it is getting time for them all

---

1 *William W. Vannoy, Second Lieutenant, 1st N.C. Infantry*

to acknowledge it. After the battle was over I went to the 18th N.C. Regt. and saw Andrew and Alfred.

They were tolerably well and in good spirits. They were were in the battle but were not hurt. Alfred had seen Calvin and Thomas Walsh[1] a day or two before I saw them- they were well and in good spirits. I had not heard of the death of T.C. Walsh and Wm. C. Proffit[2] until I saw A.J. and Alfred. I was indeed sorry to hear such sad news.

I have not received a letter from you since I left the hospital. I hope to receive a letter from you soon.

Give my love to the family and neighbors. When you write me again, give me a long letter and let me know how you are getting along. If you want money, I guess I, or A.J., can send you as much as you are needing- if you are needing any. I expect to draw $116 today or tomorrow. I am oweing Andrew $87 to finish paying for (Joe) which I shall either take or send to him first chance.

Write me soon and direct to W.H. Proffit
Co "B"
1st Reg. N.C. Troops
Richmond, Va.

I shall be compelled to put you to the trouble and expense of paying postage, because we neither have nor can get stamps at present.

Your affectionate son,   W.H. Proffit

P.S. Tell Uncle Samuel that I advise him to learn what is necessary for him to do in order to draw Alfred's[3] bounty money and wages and to come or send after it. I learned, also yesterday, that Alfred's overcoat was give to Lieut. Saml. Ginnings[4] who is responsible for it and will pay for it whenever required to do so.

W.H.P.

Tell Wm. Walsh I am looking for a letter from him.   H.

---

1 *Harrison's Brother, Calvin, and cousin, Thomas Walsh enlisted and served together in 13th Infantry*
2 *William Chapman Proffit, Co. I, 58th N.C. Infantry, d. Nov. 19, 1862, Son of Thornton Proffit and cousin of W. H.Proffit.*
3 *Alfred Walsh, Co. B, 1st N.C. Infantry, killed at Malvern Hill, July 1, 1862, Son of Samuel Walsh and cousin of W.H. Proffit.*
4 *Samuel Jefferson Ginnings, Co. B, 1st N.C. Infantry, Promoted to Full Sutler on Dec. 1, 1862.*

Camp in the woods Near Goldsboro
January the 6th/63

Der Companion,[1]

    I with please drop you a few lines in anser to you kind letter wich came to hand on last satterday baring date the 7 of December, wich gave me grate sadisfaction to hear that you was all well, to the exseption of bad colds & you statid that you had bout [bought] some corn & whet at of Wm. Dyer, wich I was glad to here for I dont think corn can be bout next sumer. You said that J.B. Miller had not bout you any hogs, yet I fe[a]r that hogs can't be bout for any price for the spulatons [speculators] will [gethe] all the hogs & wheat & corn thar is in the cuntry and pore wiming [women] and childern must suffer for if tha [they] had the money, it is worth nothing, &c.

    We ar expecting a fite her evry day. The news is that the yankees ar advancin up the Nuse [Neuse] river again to give us annothe trial & if we whip them again I dont think thay will fite any more this winter. We have a large forse her[e], &c.

    I want to see you all verry bad but than is no chance of giting furlows, now. I think the hardst fiting is over and a terms of peace will made in a short time, &c.

    Got a letter from me A.J.P. he said he & A.N. came out safe. He sed he had saw Wm. H. & D.M. Carlton & C.L.P. a[nd] tha[y] all was well.

    These lines leavs me about, but not well. I grately hope when these lines reachis you tha will find you and family wel. So I must close. I remain yours, as ever. Write soon- direct your letters to Goldsboro.

                                                  Jesse Miller

---

1 Elizabeth Proffit, oldest sister of the Proffit family.

Camp near Fredericksburg, Va.
January 9, 1862 [1863]

I agan drop you a note for the pupose of informing you that I am enjoying fine health, at present. Indeed I am stouter than I have been, perhaps, at any period of my life and I think I am much heavier than I ever was. C.L. Proffit came to see me yesterday. He is [in] elegant health; he looks the best I ever saw him. He says he weighs 140 lbs. He said he saw Andrew and Alfred day before yesterday, they were in tolerably [good] health and improving. He said Thomas Walsh was also in tolerably good health. I am unable to interest you with news from the army. We have been very quietly encamped since the termination of the battle. Our forces occupying the South and the enemy the North side of the Rappahannock river. Our forces are fortifying very strongly near the river, more, I suppose as a matter of precaution than of necessity. It is not generally believed that they will ever make another demonstration in the vicinity of Fredericksburg, but if they should do so, all seem to entertain the gratest confidence that they will meet with a much grater defeat than they did on the 13th Dec'r.

I have become quite impatient in looking for a letter from you. I have not yet received a line from you since I left the Hospital. I hope you are not so unlucky in getting my letters as I am in getting yours. I am axious to know what you have done in regard to buying land &c. &c.

I have written you my opinion upon the subject before, therefore I shall decline offering any suggestions at the present, and rationly await an answer to the letters, heretofore sent.

I learned yesterday from Calvin that cousin John Wesley Proffit[1] was dead. Calvin has also become acquainted with cousin Ora Proffit. He is a Lieut. in a company from Madison Co. Calvin said cousin Ora wanted you to buy land and move to Yancey county. I believe it would be a good idea to do so, when the war is ended but for the present I could not recommend it.
Direct as follows
W.H. Proffit, Co "B" 1st N.C. Troops, Richmond, Va.

My love to all the family and enquiring friends, Yours as ever,
W.H. Proffit

---

1 *John Wesley Proffit, Yancey County, North Carolina, Copporal, Co. C, 16th N.C. Infantry, d. Nov. 5, 1861, at Bath Alum Springs, Virginia.*

Camp near Ginea Station, Va.
Jan 11, 1863
Miss R.L. Proffit

Dear Sister

I again seet myself for the purpose of dropping you a short note which leaves me well, hoping this may reach and find you all well.

I hav no news to interest you with. I visited W.H. Proffit last Thursday. He is vary stout, waying at least 180 (or at least he looks like he might.) I saw A.J. & A.N. last Tuesday. They are doing finly. Furloughs are being given out now- I do not know wither I will get a furloug soon or not, though I hope to get one about March.

You spoke of my sending you my [tin] type in a letter some time ago. There is no chance for me to hav one taken at this tim, though if an oppertunity presents its self I will be apt to hav one taken. I suppose your school is out by this time. If so, you take a considerable portion of time in reading which will improve both your reading facultys and memory. Suppose you take your N.C. Reader[1] and read it through. Point out every place you read about, then the history of North and South America, then the Indian captive, and by that time you can read with the best of them. I want you to write me a long letter. Write what H.M. Stokes is doing; who is going to live where Calp and Luther did, if Pap talks like buying land, etc. Send me some thread and a kneedle. Give my respects to all of my friends. Tell them to write me for I have looked in vain for a letter a long time and, &c., &c.

C.L. Proffit

---

1 *The North-Carolina Reader: Containing a History and Description of North-Carolina, Selections in Prose and Verse, Many of Them by Eminent Citizens of the State, Historical and Chronological Tables, and a Variety of Miscellaneous Information and Statistics* was written by Calvin Henderson Wiley, the first superintendent of North Carolina Common Schools, in 1851.

Camp near Goldsboro, N.C.
January the 12th 1863
Wm. Proffit & Mary Proffit

Dear Father and Mother,

With pleasure I drop you a few lines wich will in form you we ar stationed one & half miles from Goldsboro, in the woods. We have suffered considerably from cold since we have bin here, for we had but one blanket a pease for some three weeks & the wether was sever and cold.

We got our things about one week ago, but tha wount [won't] let us have but two tents and flies to a company and ordered us to box up all of our things- only what we cold carry on our backs and box and some boxt up thir things and sent them to Goldsboro but our mess, we thout, we would keep what we had as long as we staid her for what we have won't do much good if tha was sent home, &c.

Times is hard her with all of us for we don't git but half rashins of meat and meal and don't git anything else, at all and that is close living. We bie [buy] some sweet potatoes when we can git them, but tha ar giting scearce, &c.

I no you have a hard time to git along, for thar is no chance for to hire any help and times will git worse for the men up to forty is ordered out now- for if tha don't come willing, tha will be forst, &c.

I want you too to do the best with mi family that you can til I come home, if ever. I want to see you all just as I ever wanded but thar is no chances. These lines leaves me well, hoping tha will reach you and family in good helth, so no more but remains, yours, as ever,

Jesse Miller

Write soon.

Ten miles below Fredericksburg, Va.
Jan. the 18th 1863
Mr. & Mrs. Wm. & Mary Proffit

Dear Father & Mother,

I take this opportunity of writing you a few lines in answer to your very kind letter of the 4th of this inst., which gave me great satisfaction by informing me that you were all well, &c. I can inform you that I have nothing of interest to write you at this time, more than we are well & doing very well, more than the weather is cold & the smoke is bad. I can say to you that my health is better than it has been since I left home & A.N. is much stouter than he has been for sometime. I have not heared from the other boys in a few days- they were well the last time I heared from them.

I can also inform you that we received orders last night to be in readiness to march at any time & I guess we will leave here in a short time.

I do not know where we are going but our Col. says that we are going back to N.C.- which we are all willing to do- but, I guess there will be hard times in N.C. this winter, but as we are acquainted with hard times we will not think hard of seeing them in our own state.

Well, Mother, you seem to be uneasy about our clothing which you need not be, for we have plenty of clothing except socks & gloves and we are not suffering much for them but would be glad of them if you could have a chance to send them.

Well, Mother, I want you to see as little uneasiness about us as you possibly can as it will be no advantage to us, but an injury to you. You kneed not think that the government will allow us to starve or go necked, although we get scarce sometimes. Well, Father, I sent you $75.00 and a short letter the other day by David Hufman[1] which I hope you have receivd.

I have written to you concerning buying land- W.H. and I have written two letter each on that subject- but I fear you have not rec'd.

---

1 *David Huffman, Co. E, 18th North Carolina Infantry, died of disease on December 10, 1862, at Winchester, Virginia.*

them for we have been looking for an answer on to them. If you have got them, I think you would do well to do as they direct. If you have not, I think you would do well to spend all my money & stock & buy you a home- as far as it will go & we will try to make money enough to pay for such a place as you can make a good support on. I desire to hear from you soon on this subject as I feel much interested concerning the same, &c.

Mother, I guess that you can send us our things by David Hufman as he is coming to our Reg. again in a short time to draw his son's money (who is dead.) He will be shure to come, I think, no differance where we are but I hope we will be in N.C.

W.H. & C.L. say that they write to you frequently. I do not see why they do not reach you. I can tell you how to direct to W.H. if you have not had a letter from him yet. Direct thus:

W.H. Proffit
Co. B.
1st Reg. N.C.T.
Doll's brigade
D.H. Hill's division
Richmond, Va.

Well, as the weather is cold and news scarce, I will now close. Please write soon as this comes to hand, and fail not, but you need not write me until I write again, as you will not know were I will be. Tell Wm. Walsh to write to me soon. Give my respects to all my friends and relatives & tell them to write soon, &c. No more but remain yours, &c.

A.J. Proffit

Camp Gregg, Va.
Jan. 22/63
Mr. William Proffit

Dear Father,

 I, again, drop you a short note which leaves me well, hoping this may find you well. I am void of news at this time. Times are calm in this part of Va., so far as I know. I want to have a letter from home as I have not recived a single line in two months. I want you to give me a long letter just as soon as this comes to hand and let me know what you are doing- if you hav bought any land or if you expect to by any, how the mules look, &c.

 W.H. visited me the other day- he is well. There is some talk of our going to North Carolina. In fact, we are now under marching orders. If we got to N.C., I would like for you to come and see ous or if you cannot come I would like for you to send me a few things I know L. Land would like to come and see ous. Though if we do not move, I shall not look for any person to come from home. Be certain to write me vary soon and let me know what trades you hav made. I hope you will keep the mules.

 Tell Ma and Sis to send me some thread and a kneedle. I will close. Write soon. Direct as before.

C.L. Proffit

Camp Gregg, Va.
Jan. 26, 1863
Miss R.L. Proffit

Dear Sister,

    I, again, write you a short not which leavs me well, hoping this may find you all well. I am anxiously wating for a letter from hom, though I have almost dispeared [despaired] of getting one. I know you could write me a short letter and inform me how the family are getting a long, &c. News is scarce at present. Though that is generally the case, especially relyable news. We are still looking for orders to march to North Carolina, which I hope soon to do. All your friends are well in camp, so far as I know. I have understood that you could not or had not received any letters from me. I am truly sorry you cannot get letters from me and am more so becaus I cannot get som news hom you. If you take the notion to write me a letter, please put in a good knedle and as much thread as you can and I would like to hav my fin[e] comb.

    I believe you can send it in a letter, any how, and if ever I can see any stamps I will risk sending a few hom. Write if there is any talk of peace in Wilkes. Write what Pa is going to do, &c. and what he is doing at present. Giv my respects to Pa & Ma, and in a purticular manner to Elizabeth. Tell Betty, if she is a little dark, I would powerfully to see her and the childern. I will close for I am in no fix for writing today. Direct your letter to:

        Richmond, Va.
        AP Hill's Division
        Pender's Brigade
        13 Reg. N.C. Troops
        Care Col. Scales[1]
        Co (H)

I remain yours truly, &c.

        C.L. Proffit

---

1 *Alfred Moore Scales, Rockingham County, Co. D, 13th N.C. Infantry*

Camp Gregg below Fredericksburg, Va.
Jan. the 27nd/63
Miss R.L. Proffit

Dear Sister.

It is with great pleasure that I now write you a few lines to let you know that we are tolerably well at this time, hoping that when these few lines come to hand, that they may find you all well, &c.

I can say to you that I have no news of interest to you to write at this time. We have been at this camp ever since the battle of Fredericksburg and doing but little. There is some talk that the yankees are going to cross the river and try us again, but I do not know how it will be. There has been some talk that we would come back to N.C. but I fear we will not get to come. I had seen W.H. & C.L. also Thos. of late. They were all stout. W.H. and his Reg. have been exchanged and are not under their same Gen., therefore I do not know how for you to direct a letter to him, but I guess he will write you soon.

I have written home frequently, of late, but get very few answers. The last time I wrote, I said not to write to me again until I wrote home as I thaught we were going to move but you may continue to direct as you have been doing until I give you further directions. I have written severil times of late to Father about buying land- which I hope he has done. I want you to write and let me know if he has & where, the price & all about it. Give my love to Elizabeth and family and all my [illegible]. Tell them I would love to write to them all, today, for I think of them all every day but I have nothing to write, therefore I cannot tell them all to write to me. I will now close, hoping to hear from you soon. I close by subscribing myself yours, very respectfully, &c.

A.J. Proffit

Camp Gregg, Va.
Feb. the 7th: 63
Wm. and Mary Proffit

Dear Father and Mother,

After my love and best wishes to you, I can in form you that your sons are all well. I saw W.H. and C.L. too or three days ago. They look the best you ever saw them.

I haven't any news to write we are still stationed whare we hav been evry since the fite. We recieved your vary kind and interesting letter in dew time and it give us great sattisfaction to hear how you was gitting along with your bissness. I think you have done as well as you could- and perhaps the best- for you nead just sutch a place. I want you to do the best you can till we come home and then we will help you to do make all you can and be surtain to keepe thee mules if you can, for that is W.H.'s request. You spoke of selling one yoke of oxen. Do so if you want to. I want you to let me know what you have don with my pig. If you have killed him, I want to know his wait. I would like to bee thare to help you move as I am youst to it. Fath[er], be shure to set you out an orchid for I see the nead of them.

I am paing $3 for apples (green) and fifty cents a quart for dride ones. If you send any boxes, send some butter and mulasses and brandy, if you can, and evry thing you please. Send some soap, it is one dollar a pound. I must close. Writ soon.

A.N.P.

Camp 1st N.C. Troops
15 miles below Fredericksburg, Va.
February 7th 1863

Dear Father and Mother:

I drop you a note for the purpose of letting you know that I, at last, have had the pleasure of reading a letter from you, which was full of such information as I delighted in receving.

First, in regard to your late purchase of land, allow me to say that you have my full concurrance and approval. In my opinion you could not have made a better selection at the same price in the county. I think you got the land at a reasonable price. I am glad to know that you have near enough mony in hand to pay down for the land, my advise is to pay what you have in hand and then to sell enough property of some kind to pay the last cent, and do it immediately. Then have the right made in a proper manner and in such a way that it will be perfectly secure. By no means allow the right to remain unsafe one day after you shall have finished paying for the land.

You said you had both of my mules, yet, and would keep them on condition you could finish paying for your land, &c. I would be glad if you could do so but I would not have you to go to any unneccessary expence and trouble on account of anything in your possession that belongs to me, I have told you several times to dispose of anything of mine as suits your own convenience best.

I suppose the other boys will draw $50 bounty each which I guess they can send home. I could have sent some also, but it took all I had to spare to finish paying A.J. for Joe ($80). I saw A.J. and A.N. last Sunday. Alfred had seen C.L the same day- he and Tho's. Walsh were well.

In your answer to this letter, inform me who owns the land lying just below yours, on the Summerlin Road, formerly owned by Triplett Ferguson (I think Geo. Minton lives on the land) How many acres there are, and if it could be bought at all, what it would cost.

Let me know what is your chance for a corn crop this year, if you will have plenty of pastures, &c. If you have any wheat sowed at al-

Sunday morning, February 8th

I will now finish my letter. I suppose you would like to hear some war news, but I have comparatively none to communicate. We are still encamped near the Rappahannock River, and the enemy encamped on the opposite side, everything is unusally quiet. Nothing is being transacted except picketing. The pickets line the bank of the River on each side, in plain view of each other and sufficiently close to admit of talking to each other, however, very little conversation is allowed. Some think the enemy will cross the River again and attack us, but none seem to doubt our ability to hold our position, and repulse them as often as they choose to advance. The papers give repeated accounts of dissatisfaction and confusion in the North Western States, which are said to be ripe for secession. The Lincoln administration is denounced throughout the whole United States to a grater or less extent. They have commenced suppressing public newspapers and imprisoning the editors. It is said by one of the yankee congress members that the term of service of of 300,000 of their troops will expire in May, and they will not be able to raise 50,000 more, therefore a bill has been passed in Congress to raise a large force of negros. (I believe 150 Regiments.) In view of all these circumstances and hundreds of other convincing ones, I think a speedy termination of the war may be expected.

Let me hear from you as often as you conveniently can. We have lately been transfered to Taliaferro's Brigade, Trimble's Division, you will now direct as follows,

W.H. Proffit,
Co. "B" 1st N.C. Troops,
Taliaferro's Brigade,
Trimble's Divisions,
Richmond, Va.

My health of late has been remarkably good. I am well at present except a cold, &c.

D.M. Carlton sends his respects to the family.

Yours, as ever,
W.H. Proffit

Camp Gregg, Va.
Feb. 15, 1863
Mr. Samuel Walsh

Dear Cousin,

With pleasure I seet myself for the purpose of writing you a few words which leavs me well- though void of such news as would interest you. 'T is thought by some that there will be a fight at this point. Though I think quite differant from the fact that <u>we</u> hav such good fortifications at this place, that I hardly think the yankees will make the riffle at [paper torn, missing] me I would take a [missing] n living at home so [missing] night go a sproocing [missing] ly enjoy my self with [missing] ls and I hope

C.L. Proffit Co. H

13th Reg. N.C.T.

Wm. Proffit
Lewis Fork
Wilkes County N.C.

Camp of the 1st N.C. Troops,
Near Port Royal, Va.,
Monday Morning, February 23d. 1863

Dear Father:

I write you another short letter to let you know that I am enjoying good health and getting along very well. Our Regiment has just performed another hard task of picket duty. We started from camp on Saturday evening and returned yesterday evening. On Saturday night and Sunday morning, we encountered the worst snow storm that has fallen this winter. Our Co. was stationed at a house near the bank of the River, therefore we fared tolerably well. The snow was about 12 inches deep.

We have comfortable quarters and are well supplied with clothing, blankets, &c. Our rations have been considerably reduced- we draw only half as much bacon as we did in the first part of the winter, but our wages have been raised $5.00 more per month, which make privates pay $16.00 per month. I have very little war news to write you at present. All operations on land are necessarily suspended on account of the inclemency of the weather.

I believe no attack is now expected in the vicinity of Fredericksburg; some think that most of the Yankees are leaving here. I should not be surprised if it were true. I suppose that Charleston, Savannah and Mobile, will be attacked bery soon. It is also very probable that another attack will be made on Vicksburg. I think if ithey are unsuccessful in these attempts, that active operations will cease, and our independence soon after acknowledged, but if the enemy should be successful, I have no doubt that it would tend grately to the prolongation of the war. Grate disaffection exists in the North Western States, and a North Western Confederacy is strongly spoken of. It is said that Gen'l Longstreet's Corps of this army is going South. I think part of it has already gone. We belong to Jackson's corps, therefore it is probable we will remain in Virginia.

I have not seen the other boys since I wrote you before, but heard from Andrew and Alfred a few days ago, they were well. I hope you received the letter I wrote you some time ago. I directed it to Lewis Fork P.O. Would it be more convenient for you to get letters from Lewis Fork? Write me as often as you conveniently can. Fearing that your letter are not backed correctly, I will send you an envelope properly directed.

My love to Mother and Sis, with all who may enquire for one.

Yours, as ever,
Wlm. H. Proffit

Camp of the 1st N.C Troops,
near Port Royal, Va.
February 25, 1863
Miss R.L. Proffit

Dear Sister:

Having an opportunity of sending you a note by Esq. James Eller,[1] I take pleasure in doing so. I wrote Pa a day or two ago, and gave him all the news in circulation, consequently a repetition of it would be unnecessary. I heard from the other boys a day or two since, Mr. Eller saw A.J. as he came down. They were well. I am looking for A.J. down to-day to see me. I heard he was coming. I inclose you a few needles, stamps, &c. Not knowing that you are needing them, but thinking they might be of service to you. I also send you a small book, containing a few, brief sketches that I have taken since I have been in the service; please do me the kindness to take special care of it. Let no person have it under any circumstance, unless I direct you to do so. I have lately directed you two a letter to Lewis Fork P.O. however they went backed to Pa.

Your Brother,

W.H. Proffit

P.S. You will find inclosed in the book some envelopes, properly addressed to me and the other boys which you will use when ever it suits you. I send them backed because there are very few who are not in the army that know how to address a letter to a person in the army.

W.H.P.

N.B. I am very well at present.

---

1 James Eller, born in Wilkes County in 1827 enlisted in Co. K, 53rd N.C. Infantry at the age of 33 in 1862 and was rejected in camp due to an unlisted disability. Mr. Eller eventually moved to Ashe County and lived there until he passed away in 1926 at the age of 98.

Camp Gregg, Va.
Feb. 26, 63
Wm. & Mary Proffit

Dear Father & Mo[ther]

I take pleasure in droping you a short note which leaves me enjoying the vary best of health, hoping this may reach and find you well. I cannot interest you with any good news- every thing in this part is calm so far as I know. Ther is some talk of peace in camp, now, though I do not pretend to say that it is relyable. I can say that on last Monday I saw a man shot for crimes which I suppose deserved death. He was shot by eight or ten men all at the same time which would appear to you I suppose rather a horable sight, though it did not appear so terable as I had anticipated. He belonged to the 38 Reg. N.C.T. I do not recolect his name at this time, though if he is as mean as has been represented, I do not know that is vary much matter.

I guess by this time that you hav done moving and is fixing for a crop and though I was never vary industrous, I would take a delight in assisting you in fixing for a crop. I hope I will git home time enough to prepare for a large crop of wheat &c.

I want you to write me soon and give me all the news- how times are going on at home, if there is any talk of peace, also, the prices of diferent articles &c., if you hav commen[ced] an orchard &c. A.N. came over yesterday and stayed with me a good while. He was well. Also, A.J. & W.H.

A.N. said he heared from W.H. the other day. I will soon close. Write soon and direct as before. I remain obedient son till death,

Calvin Luther Proffit

PS. Giv my respects to Sis. Tell her I will take a pair of socks if she will be so kind as to prepare a pair for me.

C.L. Proffit

Camp Gregg, Va.
March the 1st, 1863
Mr. & Mrs. Wm. & Mary Proffit

Dear Father & Mother

Yours of Feb. the 16th is at hand, to which I hasten to reply. Your letter gave me great pleasure by informing me that you were all well, &c. I am much pleased to learn that you have bought you a home.

Well, the plan is to stick closet to it. I would love to know if you have a deed to it and how you have got it fixed. I was sorry that you heared that I was sick & caused you to be uneasy. I will say to you that there has been but little the matter with me. I had the diarhea a few days and did no deauty, but that is so common here that we hardly call it sickness. I believe my health is better than it was when I left home.

I do not know that I will have an opportunity of coming home this Spring as there are severil who will get furloughs before I can.

Well Mother, when you write a gain please send me a little skain of thread & a large needle, if you have one. By so doing you will oblige yours, &c. I will close hoping to hear from you soon. These lines leave us well, &c. I remain yours, &c.

A.J.P.

Camp Gregg, Va.
March 1: 63
Mr. Wm. Proffit and Mary Proffit

Dear Father and Mother,

I again write you a few lines in ansur to your vary kind and interesting letter baring date of Feb 16th, which came to hand last night, which was a sourse of the greatist pleasure to me for it had been some time since I had recieved a letter from home. I have now [no] interesting news to write any more than I with A.J., W.H. and C.L. are all well. I saw C.L. this morning and heard from W.H. yesterday

I hope these lines may reach you soon and find you all well. You wrote that you was going to moove soon. I think the sooner the better, as Spring is near at hand. So mutch trouble to moove and get things regulated again.

I have written you concerning your trade, so it is unnecessary to say any thing a bout it at this time. I only recommend your course.

Well, it has been the hardist winter I all most ever saw, the most fawling [falling] weather. It is rain and snow all the time. The last snow was next to the largist I ever saw. We wrote you some time ago concerning a box of provision we wanted. I think you had better not under take it as spring is so near at hand and so mutch to do and we don't nead it. We have plenty to eat now. Pap press forward and doo the best you can and I think we will all return and help you before long, I want to see you all the worst in the world and I want you to write us. Oftimes, if I can't see you I want to hear from you. I will close. No more, but ever remanes yours, &c.

A.N. Proffit

>Camp of the 1st N.C. Troops
>Near Port Royal, Va.
>March 10th 1863

Dear Father,

As I have leisure time to denote to something, I'll drop you another short note of which I'll inform you that I am in common health and getting along very well. I saw all the boys a few days ago, they were all well. Calvin had been a little unwell a few days before I saw him but was very gaily when I saw him. Thomas Walsh was also as well as he generally is. I saw a man today who is a member of the same company to which A.J. and A.N. belong. He brought me a note from A.J. They are well.

All continues quiet along the Rappahannock and it is believed almost all of the yankees are gone from about Fredericksburg. It is now thought the gratest efforts of the enemy will be to take Vicksburg.

They fear that if they do not open the Mississippi River and do something to give satifaction to the Northwestern States, that they will secede and start a Northern Confederacy[1].

If they fail to take Vicksburg and make an unsuccessful attack at Charleston and Savannah there is no doubt it will have an effect to bring the war to a succesful termination.

I would be glad to know if you received the last two letters I wrote you. I am anxious to have an answer from one of them in particular. I would be glad if it were so that I could assist you in moving and making a crop, &c. Be shure to keep enough corn, wheat and bacon for your own use for I fear that those who get without will be compelled to remain so, and I hope there is enough in the country to supply the people. I advise you to plant a large crop of potatoes and vegatables as you have just bought land destitute of an [illegible] and I hope you will adopt the quickest and shurest means for improving your land in this important particular.

I hope you will not consider that I am taking improper priviledges in offering these suggestions. Let me hear from you as often as you can conveniently. Give me all the news you can, how you are getting along, &c. My love to Ma and Sis,

>Yours, as ever,
>W.H. Proffit.

---

1 *This wasn't just empty rhetoric. "Northwestern states" at that time were what we would consider midwestern states, today. They stretched from Ohio to Minnesota, and depended on the Mississippi River for commerce. Indiana governor Thomas Hendricks said in 1862, "The first and highest interest of the Northwest is in the restoration and preservation of the Union but if the failure and folly and wickedness of the party in power render a Union impossible then the mighty Northwest must take care of herself and her own interests."*

State of Va., Caroline Co.
March the 12th 1863
Mr. & Mrs. Wm. & Mary Proffit

Dear Father & Mother,

I take this opportunity of writing you a few lines which will inform you that I am well at this time. A.N. is also in good health. I have nothing of interest to write at present. Times are about as usual in camp. We are still hear where we have been all winter. There is said to be a large force of yankees on the other side of the Rappahannoc & we have a strong force on this side ready to meet them. We have good breastworks thrown up for miles up and down the river with any amount of rifle pits. There is no doubt that it will take a large froce to rout us from our position, though we may never have it to try. We have had a hard winter and the weather is very changeable now, We are not doing much at present more than drilling twice a day in good weather.

Sis said in her letter sometime since that you was going to commence mooving the next day. I hope you are all through that hard & unpleasant job. I hope you are now settled for life & I earnestly think that you had better be for you can make a good support & that is sufficient.

I hardly know how you can make out about house room. I wish I was at home to help you put up a good framed house to live in. When you write again, please inform me where you are going to plant your crop of corn. Also, I wish to know if you sowed any wheat last fall & another thing I will suggest: I think that when you get your land broken up, you had better turn Ginny in a good pasture & give her rest & make your crop with Jo. I do not want you to let any person work either of them or have anything to do with them but I am not uneasy about that.

Well, Father, I am well pleased at the way you have been doing since I left home. It appears that you can do better without us than with us. I hope you will make a good crop this year & I have no doubt that you will. You must try to hire Major Polly & Sis to help you. Then your force will be strong & I have no doubt that all will move on smoothly. I would know what became of A.N.'s pig- if he is still alive.

As I have no news I will close, hoping to hear from you soon, I remain yours, with great respect, &c.

A.J.P.

N.B., W.H., C.L. & Thos. were all right the other day, &c.

A.J.P.

Camp Gregg, Va.
March 18/63
Miss R.L. Proffit

Dear Sister,

    I take pleasure in responding to your kind letter which came to hand in due time and found me well; hoping this may reach and find you all well. I believe news is as scarc[e] an article as you will generally find in this part at present, however day before yesterday, I heard vary heavy canonading a cross the River (Rappahannock) but the cause or effect I am unable to recite. Our Col. said that it was the yankee a fighting within themselves; mose suppose that it was the yankees a practicing there Negro Regts. to the fire of canon and musketry. I suppose we will hear from them in a few days.

    You spoke of my getting a furlough- I can say to you that furloughs are stopped, though nothing on earth would please me better than to have an opportunity of comming home though there is no use in talking of a furlough this summer and I beleive I would not take one as A.F. Ball did.

    I was truly glad to hear that you had set out a nurcery for that was a part which I feared would be neglected. I hope I will get to come home to stay and assist in setting an orchard but if I do not, I will gladly accept these things which you spoke of Sunday by P. Walsh. Well, Sis, how do you think Unkle McAlpen's folks means by moving so much? Who was the cause of there breaking up from Ash? Well, I have written over a considerably space without interesting you. I will soon close. I hope you will take the notion to write more frequently, for I tell you I am glad to have a letter from home at any time. Give my love to Pap & Ma and all who may inquire for me.

                                                  C.L. Proffit

P.S. The first N.C. Troops have moved near Ginea Station some five or six miles from this camp.

                                                  C.L. Proffit

Camp Gregg, Va.
March 25th [1863?]

Dear Sir,

It becomes my duty to convey the melancholy intelligence of the death of your son, Calvin Proffit, who died very sudenly this morning of Congestion of the brain. He was in good health on yesterday, retired as usual last night, but never lived to see daylight. His effects have all been delivered to his brother of the 18th Reg. who is here with the corpse.

Accept my sympathy in this, your time of affliction and also my evidence of the noble, virtous and patriotic disposition of your deceased son.

He had been in my Company but for a short time but enough has been learned to know he posessed every qualification to make a son dear to a parent.

Hoping that He who feeds the young ravens will comfort you in your affliction and that your son's spirit may now be residing in the climes of a better, [fairer?] world where no war is, and where eternal rest remains, I am
y'r obt. Svt.

J. Macklin Smith[1]

1st Lieutenant Comdg Co. H

13th Reg. N.C. Troops

---

1 *James Macklin Smith, of Rockingham County, North Carolina was a medical student who enlisted in March of 1861 as a Private in Co. H, 13th N.C. Infantry. He was promoted to 2nd Lieutenant in 1862 & to Full 1st Lieutenant in 1863. He was transferred out on April 30, 1864, and survived the war.*

Camp of the 1st N.C.T.
March 28th, 1863

Dear Father, Mother and Sister:

I drop you a few lines to give you the sad news that brother Calvin is dead. He died about daybreak on the morning of the 25th Inst.

I suppose that the brain was affected which was the principal cause of his death. It is, indeed, an appalling thought to think of the death of one so dear, but sad as it is, we have some consolation to know that he remained unusually pious while surrounded with the vice and immorality of the camp, and instead of participating in them, devoted much time in reading the scriptures. Some of his companions expressed the thought that he was prepared to meet his God in peace. We have another consolation that he had won the confidence and esteem of his officers and fellow soldiers, and that every possible means was applied in burying him decently. A good coffin, clean clothes, &c. were procured. Sad as the thought is, it is no worse than thousands have endured since the commencement of this unholy war. I hope you will all try to refrain as much as possible from unecessary grief, as it is a thing of no avail.

I have sent the <u>Biblical Recorder</u> to Sis. It will come to Lewis Fork, P.O. You will see in it an account of Brother Calvin's death. You will find it under the head of <u>Obituary</u>.

Be sure to find it and preserve the paper. A.J. and Alfred were down to see me yesterday. They were well as common. They will write you the full particulars of Calvin's death and burial as they were there soon after he died. They sent for me also, but I did not go, as I was unwell, myself.

Let me hear from you as often as you conveniently can.

Yours,

W.H. Proffit

P.S. My health is very good at present.

W.H.P.

Camp Gregg, Va.
March 28, 1863
R.L. Proffit

Dear Sister,

After my love and best respecks to you I am thank full to have the good news & to write you that I am yet numbered a mong the live ing, while hundards & thousands are dailey deprived of the sweatness of life, This is all the good news I have but I have the sad and hart braking news to write you of the death of our beloved brother C.L.P.

He departed this life March the 25. The doctor who attended him in his last hours said it was an inflamatioun of the brain. He had not been sick but 3 or 4 days and had not been bad of[f] untill a few hours before he died. He had been able to walk about and do his cooking untill the night before he died. He complained of his head and brest.

I have been informed by Wm. West[1] and Thomas Walsh that he died quite easy. Without a word or a groan, he closed his eyes and seemed as if he had just drooped into a sweat [sweet] sleep.

His doctor was sent for, and he came immediatly, but could not doo any good. He staid with him untill a few minutes before his departure. Allso, his sargeon sat by him untill he was dead. He has a high repitatioun in his companey- mutch loved by his officers and, in fact, by the hold Reg. who was acquainted with him. They sent for A.J. and I fourth with and we went and saw him deseantly [decently] put a way. We had him washed and dressed in white, nicely.

His officers had a good coffin made for him and put him a way with thare own hands. They said he was a good soldier. They never heard of his grumbling at any duty he had to do since he had been with the Reg.

It is hard to give up one so dear, but these are things that we haft to do when the Creator of all things sees fit to call his people from time to eternity. We might just give the up without a groan, but the human nature can't be satisfied so easy. Look on the next sheat.

A.N.P.

---

1 *William West, Surry County, Co. H, 13th N.C. Infantry, d. on May 21, 1863, "at Hospital," Richmond, Virginia.*

But I hope you will all consider the matter and not grieve, for he left evidence that he is better of[f] in the arms of his Redeemer, than to bee hear on this dull Earth whar trouble is no strainger nor rest is never found, as I have give you a bout all the news a bout him, I will soon close.

Give my love to F. and M. Tell them not to grieve for thare departed son for he was the naturelist looking corps and the prettiest one I ever saw. He looked just like he was asleepe.

A.N.P.

[March 28, 1863]

R.L.,

A.J. and I went to see W.H. yesterday, He is injoying reasneble health. He sent you the Biblical Recorder and it is a bout time for it to come. R.A. Spainhower[1] is going to write out a piece a bout C.L. and have it printed in that paper. It will come in a few weeks, The paper will come to Lewis Fork P.O. Write soon and let me nou [know] how you are gitting a long.

These lines leaves me well, hoping they may find you all injoying the same blessing. I will send you a lock of C.L.['s] har.

A.N.P.

---

1 *Rufus Adkins Spainhour, born in Burke County, Co. B, 1st N.C. Mr. Spainhour survived the war and lived in Wilkes County. He passed away on March 23, 1928. A personal account of the war from his diary begins on page 298.*

The Biblical Recorder was founded in 1833 by Thomas Meredith, a Baptist pastor from New Bern, North Carolina, and is still published today by the Baptist State Convention of North Carolina.

Rufus Spainhour's tent-mate[1], W.R. Gaultney, turns up in the book, *Christ in Camp, or Religion in Lee's Army* published in 1887 by John William Jones, former Chaplain of the Army Northern Virginia:

Rev. W.R. Gaultney writes to the Biblical Recorder, that, during the battle at Fredericksburg, he saw a large number of soldiers reading their Testaments with the deepest interest, while lying in the entrenchments awaiting orders. He witnesses the same every day in camp.

Rufus Spainhower's letter, printed in the April 22, 1863, edition of the Biblical Recorder relating the death of Calvin Luther Proffit.

"We were present not long since," says the Soldier's Visitor, "when a chaplain, at the close of a public service, announced that he had a prospect of being able to get a supply of Testaments for the portion of the men still destitute, and that those who wished a copy could give him their names after the benediction was pronounced. Scarcely had the 'Amen' died on the minister's lips before the war-worn heroes charged on the chaplain almost as furiously as if storming the enemy's breastworks."

---

1 See Rufus Spainhour's diary, page 298

Images of The Biblical Recorder are used courtesy of the Z. Smith Reynolds Library, Special Collections and Archives, Wake Forest University

Camp Gregg, Va.
March the 28th 1863
Wm. & Mary Proffit

Dear Father & Mother,

I take this opprotunity of writing you a few lines to let you know how we are doing. A.N. and I are in tolerably good health, able to do anything that we have to do, but I must tell you the painful story that Calvin is dead.

He departed this life March the 25th, 1863, a bout day light. They sent for A.N. & I to go & see him, which we did. His mess informed me that he had been unwel for 3 or 4 days & the doctor had excused him from deauty, but he was up a bout & thaught there was but little the matter.

The morning before he died the next, he told the boys that he would get the doctor to excuse him that morning & he thaught that he would be able for deauty by the next. He was up attending to his things all day before he died & done his own cooking or a part of it. He was taken very bad a bout two o'clock that night. Wm. West found out that he was very bad by feeling of his pulse & he got up & sent for the doctor & he came and staid with him until he died but could do nothing. The doctor said it was inflamation of the brain & I suppose he acted like he had sever colic, but he never spoke nor opened his eyes from the time they found out he was so bad until he died. They told me that he died very easy & never moved or made any fuss at all. Theese are the particulars of his death, so far as I could ascertain. I suppose you would love to know how he was put away.

Well, he was washed and clean clothes put on him & his officers had a very good pine plank coffin made for him & buried him in a very nice place in an orchard. I would have sent him home but I had no chance at the time.

Well, Father & Mother, all the comfort I can give you a bout his death is that he was universally beloved in his Reg. and Co. He had gained the respect of all his officers by being a brave & obedient soldier. They said they had never heard of him murmuring at any deauty which he had to do & I know that they did love him for his officers buried him with their own hands- a thing that I never have seen done before, since I have been in the service, &c.

And as to his future welfare, I cannot say. All that I could find out about that was that he appeared to be very diligent in studying the scriptures and that a man in his Reg. in another Co. told me that he had often talked to him on the subject of religion & he talked freely on the subject & appeared to be very much disgusted at the wickedness of the soldiers. He also told me that he thaught that if ever a man died happy, that Calvin did. I do not know whether he was a man to be relied on or not, but I could not think he would have told me a falsehood a bout so important a thing.

Father, I hope that you and Mother and all the family and friends will take it as light as possible, knowing, as we do, it was the justice of God that called him away from us & I feel to hope that he is praising God for his countless mercies while the rest of us are so journing on this dull Earth with nothing to cheer us but a glimmering hope that we will, one day, meet around the throne of God to join with the happyfied millions who have gone before in anthemes of prais to God for redeeming grace & dying love.

I feel & know the stroke to be a sever one, but I do admonish you all to consider it well and bear it as light as possible & ask God to give you fortitude to bear up under it.

We did not know that anything was the matter with him until we heard that he was dead, for we had mooved some little distance from him & had not seen him for some time. I sent for W.H. to go & see him, but as he was unwell & the distance a little two far for him to walk, he did not go. Calvin had, when he died, $8.00 in his posession & he owed $5.00 of that to one of his Lieutenants which I paid & we have the rest.

There is but little coming to him- perhaps not more than will settle his clothing account. His lieut. wrote you the same day that he died a bout that.

Well, Father, as yesterday was proclaimed as a day of thanksgiving, A.N. & I went down to see W.H. His health is improving. He is able for deauty. We heard a fine sermon from Rev. Mr. Gaultney & returned to camp. I must now close, hoping to hear from you soon. These lines leave us well, hoping that they may find you all in good health, &c.

Yours, most affectionately, &c.

A.J. Proffit

>   Camp Gregg, Va.
>   Apr. the 5th 1863
>   Wm. & Mary Proffit

Dear Father & Mother,

I am again blessed with another opportunity of writing you a few lies, though as news is scarce, I shall fail to interest you. There has been no movements made by the enemy of late. All appears to be quiet, &c. as this is Easter Sunday. We have a fine snow on the ground & more falling. I would love to know how the weather is at home today.

Well, Father & Mother, I have the painful news to write you that C.L. Proffit is dead. He died on the 25th of March with inflamation of the brain. I wrote you a full account of his death & buriel immediately. I had him decently intered in a good coffin. You will see an account of his death in the Recorder which W.H. sent to Sis. It was written by R.A. Spainhower & will be published in a short time. If you do not get the account I sent you & wish further information a bout it, let me know & I will give you all the information I can. I am well a ware that it is hard to give up one so well be loved, but as we know not the design of God, in taking him from us, we should try to reconcile ourselves to his will in all things & ask him to give us grace to support us in our trials.

I can say to you that I hardly think that it was by any exposure that C.L. had that killed him for his health had been better in camp than it ever was before. I am of the opinion that it was one of those spells of fever & pain in the head that he was given to at home.

Well, Father, I do not see any particular prospects of peace. I am like Calvin was- I think that sin is the sole cause of the war & I do not look for peace until the people humble themselves & puts their hole trust in God. I would love to be at home & take a long talk with you a bout such things for I have but little chance of a delightful conversation, here.

I will now close. These lines leaves me well, hoping that they may find you all well, &c. I remain yours, with great respect, &c. Please write soon

A.J. Proffit

>   Camp Gregg, Va.
>   Apr. the 5th, 1863
>   R.L.P.

Dear Sister,

Yours of March the 22 is at hand to which I hasten to reply. I gladly rec'd. your kind letter which gave me great satisfaction by informing me that you were all well, &c. I would love to give you a full letter, but have not room but as I write once a week, I will do so soon. I get letters a bout once a month. I do not not know why they do not come oftener, &c. We gladly rec'd. the thread & needles you sent us. I will close by subscribing myself, yours with great respect,

A.J.P.

>Camp Gregg, Va.
>April 5::1863
>Miss R.L. Proffit

Esteemed Sister,

These lines are to inform you that A.J., W.H. and I are all well, hoping these lines may reach and find you all injoying the same blessing. I received yours of March 22nd last night which was a sourse of the greatest pleashure to hear from you all for your letters comes sildomm [seldom]. We allso found in the inclosed 2 kneedles and some thread which was gladly received by us for thread is hard to get here.

I have no good news to write. We are waiting for the yankees to make a moove and then we will give them a cawl. We are strongly fortified from Fredericksburg to Fourt Royal and it is the jeneral opinion of all, if they do cross here, they will git the worst whipping they ever have got. R.L., as I gave you a full account of the death of C.L. in a letter, I will say nuthing about him in this. Sis, tell Father and Mother we have plenty to eat and but little to do. Tell them I want to see them the worst of all things and will write them soon.

I understood by James Howlmon[1] that F. [Father?] had taken R. Jones in as a [share] cropper. All write, I think, they will come it like a beauty. Write soon.

I remain, as ever, yours, &c.

>A.N. Proffit

---

1 *James Holman, Co.F, 37th N.C. Infantry*

Camp Gregg, Va.
April 11th 1863
Wm. and Mary Proffit

Dear Father and Mother,

I, again, seat myself to address you tho I have no news to communicate to you that would be of interesting caracter. Times are mutch like common- we are still waiting the movement of the yankees. I understood they had a small fight at Charlestown a few dayes a go and the confederits thashed them out and sunk one ship.

Pap, I saw a man taken and one side of his head shaived and he hast to toat [tote] a stick of wood waying 50 lbs. round a ring 30 feet in diameter evry other hower in the day and then ware a barrell shirt throu the streets with two drums after him beating Yankee Doodle. Allso a man after him with a bayonet for desearting. On his barrell shirt[1] thare are big letters, "Deserter."

They are running a way like thunder. Thare has gone 15 from my Co. for the last few days. Pap, I would like to be at home to help you work as the weather is fine and I suppose you are making good youse of it. I was vary sorry to learn by P. Walsh that you had not paid up for the land and got a deead [deed] for those are vary quare [queer] folkes and will take any turn they can to keepe from making a rite. If it in your power, pay for the land and git a wright to it and if I am so fortunitate as ever to git home, I will stay at home and help you farm.

I want to see you all the worst in the world and tell you some of my past seanes. I must close for want of news. These lines leaves us well, hoping they may find you well. Write soon.

A.N. Proffit

R.L.,

I must write you a few lines in ansur to your vary kind and interesting letter which came safe to hand by P. Walsh and found me well. I was mutch pleased to reseave the things you sent me and to hear from home and how you are all doing.

All so, to see a spessimon of your hand right. I want you to do your own writing from know on. I can read it as fast as I can talk. You said you was vary lonesome and wanted me to come and stay all night. I hope I can come and stay all the time before long. I want to bee thare to help you fix the gardon and walk but you must do that.

I must close. Write soon and give my respects to all my friends except for R.L.

A.N.P.

---

1 From Miles O. Sherrill's "A Soldier's Story: Prison Life and Other Incidents in the War of 1861-'65": "The mode of wearing the barrel shirts was to take an ordinary flour barrel, cut a hole through the bottom large enough for the head to go through, with arm-holes on the right and left, through which the arms were to be placed. This was put on the poor fellow, resting on his shoulders, his head and arms coming through as indicated above; thus they were made to march around for so many hours and so many days."

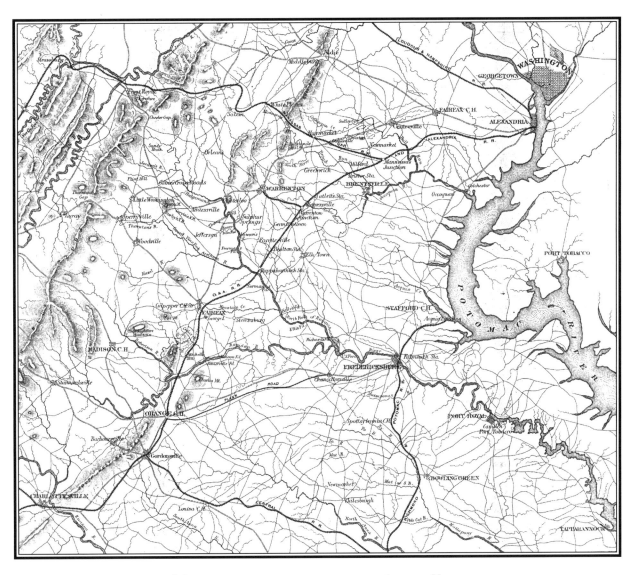

MAP OF THE FIELD OF OPERATIONS OF THE ARMY OF VIRGINIA.

Camp Gregg, Va.
April 15th 1863
R.L. Proffit

Dear Sister,

I, again, write you a few lines to let you know how we are gitting along. We are well and harty as you ever saw us and trewly hope these few lines may reach and find you all well.

Sis, I have no news to write, for I wrote you the other day and I have nothing to write at present. I want you to inform me in your next, how you are gitting along with all your work- farm, gardon, &c. how you are of for fead and how the mules look and how many cows you have and if you git plenty of milk and how many hogs you have and how they look and many other things to tedious to mensioun [mention].

A.N. Proffit

Camp of the 1st N.C. Troops
April 22nd 1863
Miss R.L. Proffit

Dear Sister,

I suppose my time is spent in vain writing you as I learned, yesterday, that none of the family and scarcely any person in the neighborhood could read my letters. I am, indeed, sorry that such is the case, but know not how to remedy the defect. I would, however, say that in my opinion, you are all under as much obligations to improve in reading as I am to improve in writing.

I will here inform you that I went to see A.J. and A.N. yesterday and spent most of the day with them. They are enjoying the best health and looking much the best they have since I saw first, last winter, in fact, A.J. looks better than he has in ten years. Alfred had lately seen our friends in the 13 and 37th. Regts. Thomas Walsh, Wm. West, James Holman and most all acquaintences are well. P. Walsh is not very stout, but is performing camp duty.

Your acquaintences here are all well. I have not been very well for some time, but am improving.

There is no very interesting war news that I cooould write you at this time. Instead of writing about the war, I will advise you to read your paper carefully which will contain all the important news relative to the war.

I received a letter from you all dated March 28th which was quite interesting to me. It contained an inquiry of the fate of Smith German,[1] Co. D, 18th N.C. Regt. I enquired of A.J.P. concerning him, who informed me he was dead. I do not know the circumstances of his death.

Well, R.L., I guess I saw a letter you wrote the boys some time ago. I was well pleased to see that you had improved so fast as to be able to write so good a letter. If you have learned to write that well, you can learn to write better. I advise you to depend on no other person to do your writing, but do it all yourself. Write me a letter as soon as you get this. I can read your letters if you can't read mine.

---

1 *Smith German, b. 1833, Wilkes County, Co. D, 18th N.C. Infantry, d. Nov. 2, 1862, at Winchester, Virginia, and was buried at Stonewall Cemetery, there.*

Friday 24th-

I expected to have started to have started my letter before today and have been disappointed. Yesterday was one of [the] wettest days I ever saw. Almost 10 o'clock in the morning, we were ordered to get ready for marching immediately; we did so and marched about five miles forward, Port Royal- wading creeks, marshes, &c., some of which were very deep, meantime, the rain poured down in perfect torrents. In the evening we returned to camp wet, hungry and weary. The excitement proved to be nothing of grave importance.

I hope to hear from you very soon.

Your brother,
W.H. Proffit

Cliffburn barracks
City of Washington
[Mount Pleasant, Washington]
May the 7th 1863

Mr. Wm. Proffit,

This is to inform you that I am a prisoner of war at this place. Was captured at U.S. Ford above Fredericksburg on Sunday the 3rd inst. I am well and doing well. I now have a paroal and expects to be exchanged before a great while.

I do not know whether I will get to come home or not- it is probable that I will. W.H. and A.N. were not hurt the last I heared of them. A.N. had given out & was sent to the rear. He was not a long when I was captured.

Father I know that you will all be very uneasy when you hear that I am missing, but you need not be for I am well treated and no doubt will get back before a great while. I hope that these few lines will reach you soon and find you all enjoying good health.

I will close for the present & write you again the first opportunity. I will close by subscribing myself your mos affectionate son until death, etc.

A.J. Proffit

Scene on the U.S. ford road, (battle of Chancellorsville) on the night of Apr. 30, 1863.

Drawing by Edwin Forbes, United States Library of Congress

May 8th 1863

Dear Father and Mother:

I avail myself of this opportunity of informing you that I am still alive and in good health, although, I have just passed through another of the bloodiest battles of the war. [Chancellorsville]

We have had another desperate battle on the Rappahannock, but I am glad to inform you that victory is ours.

Our Regiment was in the hardest part of the battle and suffered severly.

I received a wound in the jaw on Sunday evening and have since then been at the hospital, but am not seriously injured and will rejoin my company in a few days (the hospital to which I refer is near the battlefield where the wounded were carried during the fight.) I have not received any correct news from our connection and friends in other Regts.

About 30 of our company are killed and wounded. Thomas Eller, William Pilkenton, John Pennel, Samuel Pennel and I.N. Martin have all died on the field.

John Estes[1] had his right arm broken near his shoulder. Sergt. D.M. Carlton was slightly wound[ed], but is now at the company. Anderson Vannoy and perhaps, others, of our co. who were your acquaintances are wounded.

I will write you again soon and give you fuller accounts. I will also very soon write Saml. Walsh, Jr.

Yours,
W.H. Proffit

---

1 *John L.J. Estes, Caldwell County, Co. B, 1st N.C. Infantry, wounded at Malvern Hill and Chancellorsville and also lost an arm.*

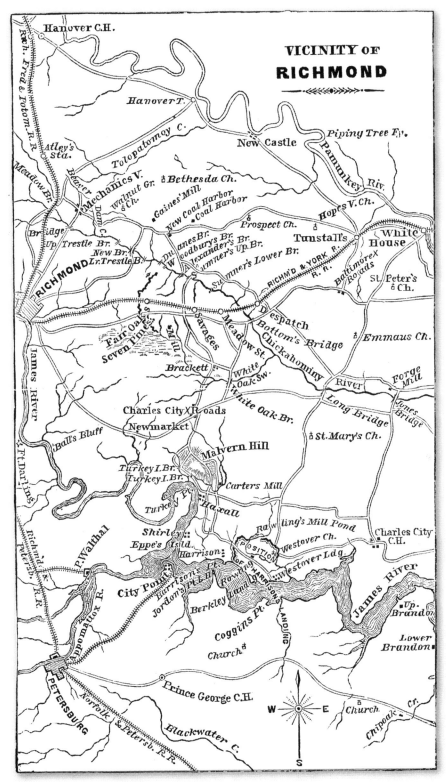

Map of the Vicinity of Richmond, Virginia.

Harpers Pictorial History of the Civil War

Camp Lee, Richmond, Va.
May the 15th 1863
Mr. Wm. Proffit

Dear Father,

I take this kind opportunity of writing you a few lines which will inform you that I am again on the Southern soil well and doing finely.

I am sorry to inform you that I unfortunately fell into the hands of the enemy on Sunday the 3 inst. I will now try to tell you how it happened as we were on the march to the battlefield I with another Corporal were appointed to guard the flag- one of the most dangerous positions in battle. On Saturday night there fell a bomb in my company & exploded in 4 or 5 feet of me and wounded the flag bearer and five or six of my Co. taking off one man's leg & wounded my lieutenant.

When the flag of my country fell to the earth I grabed it with my own hands. My Colonel told me to throw down my gun and hold on to my flag which I did.

That night, the yankees charged on us but we soon repulsed them. Next morning we made a charge on them, routed them from their first breastworks & proceeded to the second- was ordered to charge them which part of us did. I carried the flag to the breastworks. We routed a long line of them and held our position but the 28th N.C. Reg. on our right failed to charge them.

The enemy commenced firing up our lines & give them a chance to retake their works again, which give us no chance to escape. I lay there with two lines of cross fireing at me a short distance & three batteries throwing grape at me not more than 3 or 4 hundred yards distant.

The first I knew the yanks were in five steps [of me] when two jumped over the breastworks & grabed the flag out of my hand & said to me, "Fall in John." Ha ha ha.

John fell in but did not like to do it.

They took us to Washington and kept us about 13 days. They treated us with great respect- give us plenty to eat.

When they brought us from Washington we came down the Potomac through Chesipeak bay by fortress _____ then up the James river to Citty Point near Petersburg where we landed. We came here to Camp Lee, Richmond last night.

I do not know when we will be carried to our regiments but I suppose shortly. I am unable to say what became of A.N. & W.H.

A.N. give out the night before I was taken and had had nothing to eat for a day or so & marched hard which made him sick & he was sent back to the rear. I think that nothing but fatigue & hunger was the matter. W.H. was in the fight. Some of his Co. is here as prisoners. They say that he was not hurt the last they saw of him & I hope he was not, &c. My Col.[1] was killed & my Lieut. Col. wounded & the great Gen. Jackson was mortally wounded by his own men & is now dead.

Father, I am getting use to all kinds of hardships in warfare & though I say it myself, I know nothing of cowardice & God forbid that I ever should. The Lord has been very merciful to me & I fear as I have not a heart to praise him as I ought. I want you and all my friends to remember me at a throne of grace.

I will now close. Give my warmest love to Mother &c. and all my friends. Write soon & direct to Co. D, 13th Reg., NC T. Richmond Va.

I remain yours with great respect,
A.J. Proffit

---

1 Thomas J. Purdie, Colonel 18th N.C. Infantry, killed May 3, 1863, at Chancellorsville

Camp of the 1st N.C. Troops
May 19th 1863
Miss R.L. Proffit

Dear Sister:

    I take pleasure in acknowledging the receipt of yours of May 4th which would have been replied to immediately, had I not written only a day or two before I received yours. In my last I could not give you any satisfaction regarding the probable fate of A.J.- I had very little hope of his safety. All the reports I heard regarding him led me to believe that he had fallen in battle, but I am happy in announcing to you that he is safe and unhurt.

    I was told by Lieut. Vannoy[1] of our company who arrived here last night that he saw him in Richmond- he had been taken prisoner, and had been either paroled or exchanged and sent back to Ricmond. Lieut. Vannoy said he was looking well. The last time I heard from A.N. he was well and had not been hurt in the battle.

    Our Brigade remains on the Rappahannock about 10 miles above Fredericksburg, doing picket duty. We expect to leave here in a day or two and go down about Fredericksburg. All has been quiet since the battle. The enemy have been carrying off their wounded who fell in our hands in time of the battle- so grate was the number of their wounded, that a part of the time from 100 to 200 ambulances have been employed in hauling them off. Those of the enemy who carried who carried away their wounded, were admitted into our lines under flag of truce.

    My health is good and my wound is very nearly well, at least, I am doing duty in the Company!

    As I have no special news to communicate I will close. Write me soon after the reception of this and give me all the news you can. Please let yourself next appear in your own handwriting. My love, as ever, to Father, Mother & the connection and neighbors who may enquire for me. I send you an envelope properly backed in which to inclose your return letter.

Your brother till death,
W.H. Proffit

---

1 William W. Vannoy, 2nd Lieutenant, Co. B, 1st N.C. Infantry

Camp Gregg, Va.
May 21st 1863
Wm. Mary & R.L. Proffit

Dear Father, Mother & Sister,

I now write you a short note which will inform you that I have just returned to my regiment. I was taken prisoner on the 3rd day of this month a bove Fredericksburg & the yankees kept me 13 days. They treated me very well. I am now with my Reg. I do not know whether I am exchanged or not. If I am not I guess I will be in a short time &c. I can say to you that I had the pleasure of staying all day and part of the night, night before last, with the 53rd N.C. Reg.

Harvy & Wm. Walsh were well & gaily. Thos. Walsh is at Camp Winder slightly wounded in the knee with a buckshot. Wm. W. & I went to see him.

A.N.P. is here stout and well. W.H.P. got struck on the mout with a piece of shell & which cut through his lip & knocked some of his teeth loose. P. Walsh is sick and gone to the hospitle. I find that I am reported killed in the news papers.

I would not have had you to have heared such news for nothing in the world but I have written you a full account of my trip & imprisonment which I hope you have rec'd. I am well except cold hopin to hear from you all soon & to hear that you are all well I am with respect &c.

A.J. Proffit

Camp of the 1st N.C. Troops,
near Fredericksburg, Va.
May 30th 1863
Miss R.L. Proffit

Dear Sister:

I have neglected writing you a few days longer than usual because I was expecting a letter from you, but as it has not been received I will continue to look for it & write you a short letter also. When I wrote you last, we were on the Rappahannock about 10 miles above Fredericksburg. Since then, we have come down near the town and encamped near the rail road leading from Fredericksburg to Richmond. We are now faring the best we have for twelve months. Our rations have been increased- the quantity furnished is very plenty & the variety, tolerably good.

Capt. Miller's Company is encamped with the Reg. (53) near here- I have visited them once and found many old friends and acquaintances among them. Capt. Miller, Lieut. Eller & Land, William Walsh and Jesse Miller have been to see us. They are all in fine health Harvy Walsh also looks finely. Jesse had good luck on his return- brought his boxes through safely &c.

I have not seen A.J. and A.N. since the battle- Lieut. Land and William Walsh and others who saw A.J. at Richmond say he is looking finely. I expect to go and see them in a few days. I have no news from the army that has reference to future operations that would be likely to interest you. Most of our troops are stationed along the River, pretty much like they were before the fight.

The yanks, what few we did not kill in the late fight are occupying the other side. We are ready to whip them again whenever they choose to come on our side of the River.

The weather is remarkably dry here. There has been very little rain here during the last month and a half. My health is tolerably good at present. My love to father, mother with all enquiring friends,

Your till death,

W.H. Proffit

Monday morning June 1st 1863, Since the above was written I have received letters from A.J. & Alfred. They were well. Nothing of special interest has transpired since Saturday. All remains quiet. I hope to hear from you soon.

W.H. Proffit

P.S. Tell S. Walsh that I consider his letters as becoming few & far between.

W.H.P.

Camp Gregg, Va.
June the 4th 1863
Wm. & Mary Proffit

Dear Father and Mother,

I, again, am blessed with another opportunity of writing you a few lines which will inform you that I am in good health at present hoping that these lines may find you all well etc.

I have no news of interest to write at present. Times are very good in camp. We have plenty to eat and but little to do. I can not say when there will be an other movement made, but I would not be surprised if there is shortly.

I suppose that you have seen an account of my being killed (before this time) in the late battle, but I hope that you have heared it disputed as I have written you three letters since in which I give you a dull account of being taken prisoner. I would take great delight in being at home now so that I could tell you all about my travels, etc. We had a letter from W.H. written the 15th of May. He was doing very well. His wound was not very severe.

Well Father, as this is the 4th of June, I suppose that you are 60 years old to day. I feel to hope that you are stout and harty. You and mother has lived & been highly blessed for a number of years although the days of trouble are now on us.

I feel to hope that you will not let the troubles and turmoiles of this life molest your peace but little. Try to live as cheerful and as much contented as possible. The Lord will bring all things right in due time.

I am anxiously waiting for a letter from you. Your last letter was written the 4th of May. Please write soon and often. Let me know how you are getting a long with your crop- how it looks- how your rye is doing & give the news in full a bout the little domestic concerns & if the dry weather is likely to injure you &c. Tell Sis to write me without fail & be certain not to marry until I come home. I will now close, hoping to hear from you soon I remain your old yellow boy &c.

A.J. Proffit

Camp Gregg, Va.
June 4th 1863
Wm. and Mary Proffit

Dear Father and Mother,

I again write you a few lines not in ansser to a letter for the last one I got was dated May 4. I all most decline the ida [idea] of writeing you any more untill I git some- all tho, they may git misslaid. I want you to write us oftines for nothing on earth givs us more satisfaction than to hear from home.

I have no news to write times are still in camp. A man was brandied [branded] on the left hip with a letter D for deserting. He belongs to our Co. And one was druned [drummed] through our Regt. from the 87th Regt. with a board to his back with letters on it, "deserter" on it for the same &c.

We got a letter from W.H. this evening. He is not far from hear. He is well. I saw Harson Brown[1] day before yeterday from Capt. Miller's Co. Jesse Miller is well and all the beuoys [boys] of that Co. I suppose you have heard before this time it was a mistake a bout A.J. being killed. He is hear and well and doing well. He was a prisoner and taken to Washington and was vary well yoused [used] by them &c.

Pap, we want to know how you are gitting along with your work- how your corn looks and how wheat looks in that cuntry. We want to know how what sort of a wagon you have- whare you got it and what it cost &c. What you are doing with the mules? Whether you have got them boath at hom or not- how they look &c.

I must close for want of news. Write soon and fail not. We have a division of N.C.T. now and General Pender for our Gen. A.P. Hill has taken command of a corps. I suppose you have received letters before this time in forming you a bout A.J. & W.H. so I will say no more about it. It is reported our men has whiped the yankees at Vixburg vary bad with the loss of vary few &c.

I will seace writing by saying these lines leaves us in good health and truly hope they may reach and find you all well, &c.

Yours as ever, A.N. Proffit

---

1 William Harrison Brown, Sergeant, Co. K, 53rd N.C. Infantry

Camp of the 1st N.C. Troops
near Culpepper Court House, Va.
June 10, 1863
William Proffit

Dear Father:

As I have a leisure moment this morning, I devote it in dropping you a short note, to let you know that my health is good and that I am getting along well. We left our camp near Fredericksburg about 9 o'clock on the morning of the 5th Inst. and have been marched to Culpepper C.H. a distance of about 50 miles. We arrived at the C.H. day before yesterday.

Yesterday there was a hard battle[1] fought about 5 miles below Culpepper. The Yankees landed a heavy force of cavalry & some infantry and artillery. They were met by our cavalry & artillery and as usual, were whipped & driven back. We started to meet them again but our services were not needed. It is said we took about 400 prisoners. It is said the Col.[2] of the 2nd N.C. Cavalry was killed also another Cavalry Col. & two of our Generals wounded (Jones & Lee[3]). The 1st N.C. Cavalry was also in the fight. Our Co. is in fine health. I have not heard from the other boys since I wrote last. I think they are yet about Fredericksburg.

I am very anxious to hear from you. I think the last letter I received from any of you was dated May 4th.

Direct to Richmond Va.
Co. "B" 1st N.C. Troops
Stuarts Brigade
Jacksons Old Division

My love to the family & neighbors,

Your affectionate Son,

W.H. Proffit

---

1 *The Battle of Brandy Station, June 9, 1863, the largest cavalry engagement of the war.*
2 *Solomon Williams, Colonel, 2nd N.C. Cavalry.*
3 *William Henry Fitzhugh Lee, Brigadier General, son of Robert E. Lee, wounded at Brandy Station.*

Near Fredericksburg, Va.
June the 13th 1863
R.L. Proffit

Dear Sister,

These lines are to inform you whare I am and what I am doing. We have been in line of battle 8 days expecting a fight but have failed to git it. The yanks have all disappeared from before our lines and we have moved out in the woods and camped. We have been faring vary well. We have had plenty to eat and lay on our backs and read and sing. We taken some prisoners that was on picket to the amount of 20. They have been afraid to raise their baloon[1] in frount of us evry since we have been hear.

Times are quite still at presant Longstreete and Ewell are making movements some whare. Sis, I have had the pleasure of seeing many of my friends in the 26th and 52nd. I saw Bennet Walsh, Pinkney Walsh, T. D. Hawl [and] John A. Foster of the 52. They are all well. John A. Foster sends you all his best respeckes. I have seen all our friends in the 87th. They are all well &c.

I recieved your vary kind and interesting letter a few minuts ago baring date of June the 8, which grattified me much to hear from you and that you ware all well. If I am not mistaken, by reading your letter you have paid for the land all to $80.00. If I am, inform me in your next.

Sis, as the Troops have so many left N.C., I think thare will be a vary good chance for our brigade to come to N.C. this fawl and then I can git a furlow and come home and see you and have some good times.

Tell Rebcca she can sing for me. Tell the girles, all, I have not forgotten them and I want to see them the worst in the wourled. Sis, as I can't interest you, I will close these lines- leaves us well hoping you are all well. Tell Pap and Mother we are all rite on the goose.

Yours as ever A.N.P.

P.S. Write soon and fail not- direct as ever.

When this you see, write to me, tho in the ware [war] I be, &c.
A.N.P.

---

1 *The yanks' "baloon" is described on page 16.*

Near Fredericksburg, Va.
June the 14th 1863
Wm., Mary & R.L. Proffit

Dear Father, Mother, and Sister,

I again write you a few lines to let you know where I am & what I am doing. We have been laying in line of battle for the last nine days but we have just now left the line & moved back a short distance as last night was a dark rainy night.

The yankees thought it a fit time to leave this side of the Rappahannock and they done so leaving a wagon load of spades shovels and picks on this side, which we got. They have taken up their Pontoon bridges and are gone I know not where. I am not of the opinion that there will be much fighting at this point if any as this is the same place where we whiped them on the 13th of Dec. last. There are movements going on for a fight some where, but I have no idea where it will be. I am not very uneasy that I will be in it- provided we stay here.

I do not know where W.H. is. I have not heard from him since the 31st of May. He was well then. I guess he is a long the river sumplace. As news is so scarce, I will soon close. We have just reed letters from T. and R. Land, R.C. Proffit and Elizabeth Miller which was a great pleasure to us.

Father, I rec'd, your kind letter a few days since, which was read with much delight. I was very sorry that you had had so much trouble a bout my being killed.

I want you to live as cheerful as possible even if I do get killed. I am yet alive and well and enjoying myself very well- no doubt much better than you who are at home. I will now close. Please write soon & give me all the news. Tel Whig that I have his letter & will answer it soon. Give him and all his folks my respects. No more, but remain yours with great respect &c.

A.J. Proffit

Near Shepardstown, Va.
June 18, 1863
Miss R.L. Proffit

Dear Sister:

Yours of June 3d came to hand in due time and I use this as the first opportunity of writing in reply. We have been marching 13 days. We went from Fredericksburg to Winchester & whipped Gen'l Gilroy's[1] [Milroy's] forces & captured from 3 to 5000 prisoners- all his comissary and quarter master stores- artillery- wagons, horses &c. &c. Our Reg. fought bravely. We came in contact with the retreating yanks just at the break of day after marching all night. They charged us furiously, three times and were as often repulsed, when they raised a white flag & surrendered. None of our company was killed.

The Reg. lost very few- Capt Miller[2] of Caldwell was killed. We are now in a bout 2 miles of the Potomac River. I do not know whether or not we will go into Maryland. I am now in the best health I have been for several months, except that I am very much wearied & have sore feet.

I have not heard from the other boys since I wrote you last. I think they are yet about Fredericksburg. Gene. Ewell's Corps only has been on this march.

You need not expect to get letters from me but seldom. I shall not have the chance to write but seldom. Write me every chance.

I will send you some stamps as soon as I can get them. My love to father & mother & all who enquire for me.

Yours,

W.H. Proffit

P.S. I recvd. those socks you sent me by William Brown (of Color)

W.H.P.

---

1 Robert H. Milroy, Major General Union.
2 John S.R. Miller, Captain, Co. G, 1st N.C. Infantry, d. June 15, 1863, at Winchester, Virginia.

Camp 1st N.C. Troops
near Sharpsburg, Maryland
June 22, 1863

Dear Father:

I use this leisure time in writing you a short letter to let you know where I am and how I am getting along, &c. I will inform you that Lieut. General Ewell's Corps, which is comprised of the divisions of Major General Johnston, Rodes and Early, left the vicinity of Fredericksburg on the morning of the 5th Inst. and started in the direction of Winchester, Va. We arrived there on the morning of the 13th. The federal general, Milroy, was in possession of the town with a force of from 5000 to 8000. The yankees were strongly fortified- Gen'l. Ewell lost no time in attacking him; a regular bombardment and skirmish was kept up on the 13th & 14th.

On the evening of the 14th, it was ascertained that the enemy were going to evacuate the town and, if possible, escape during the night.

Between Sunset and dark our brigade was put in motion and marched the entire night- just at the break of day we met the yanks retreating in haste.

Their advance guard fired upon us and retreated. Our brigade was quickly formed in line of battle, stretching across the road on which the yankees were retreating. The yanks then saw that their only hope of escape depended on breaking our line & forcing their way through, and I tell you they went to work in good earnest. They raised a most hideous yell and came at us like as though they expected to accomplish all their designs. Our boys <u>lay low</u> and <u>kept cool</u> until the yanks came within about 30 or 40 steps, when a most deadly volley was poured into them which caused them to change directions quickly. They made two other charges with like results, when they found there was no chance of escape & raised the white flag and surrendered.

I suppose we took from 3 to 4000 prisoners. Large quantities of Quarter master and Comissary stores- horses- Wagons- artillery, &c, &c.

Genl. Milroy, himself, narrowly escaped being taken prisoner. Our Regiment lost but few although it performed a noble part in the fight. None of our company was killed. After the battle was over & the captured horses collected, our Regiment was mounted and went in full chase after the Yankees who escaped. We rode all day and overtook several straggling yanks which we carried back with us. Our boys enjoyed the sport very much.

All having been satisfactorily arranged at Winchester, at least on our part, we resumed the march in the direction of Shepardstown, at which place we waded the Potomac and entered Maryland on the 18th. We are now encamped on a part of the battlefield of Sharpsburg about one mile from town. (Sharpsburg) I was in town, yesterday, and did some trading. Confederate money was taken and goods much cheeper than I expected to find.

I know nothing of the movements of our army. It is said one division of our Corps (Gen. Rodes) is at Hagerstown near Pennsylvania and that our Cavalry is in Penn. I suppose it is so, as about 700 fine cattle passed here yesterday from that direction going to the rear of our army.

We are faring finely and if no bad luck I think we will continue to do so. Our Brig. Gen. is a Marylander and I am shure he will look out for his men. You need not expect letters from me regularly. We may not have an opportunity of sending any letters for weeks. You need not expect to hear from me but seldom. Let me hear from you as often as you conveniently can. My health is good. I hope you may all be blessed with health and prosperity. My love to the family and neighbors.

I have had no late news of A.J. & A.N.

Your affectionate son,
W.H. Proffit

William and Mary Proffit

State of Va.
Warren County
June 24, 1863
Wm. Proffit

Dear Father,

I write you a short note to let you know where I am and what I am doing. I am at an old gentle man's house by the name of James Sealock. We have had another hard march from Fredericksbur to ward Winchester. The march was so hard, and the weather so hot, that hundreds give out. I marched three days til I could go no more. They halled me one day, but the ambulances were so crowded that they broke part of them down, so the doctors give me a pass to shift for myself.

I am at a first rate place- I can stay as long as I choose. I do not know when I will be able to go on but I suppose I will in a week or so.

There is nothing the matter more than I am broken down, my feet worn out and my head pains me right smartly.

All of which make me quite weak. I can say to you that A.N. give out and was sent back to Culpepper. He was right sick but I hope not dangerous.

It was said that many marched until they fell dead on this march. You need not be uneasy that I will do that. I guess that I have been somewhere since I left home.

Do not be uneasy a bout me- I am treated as kindly as I would be at home. I would love to hear from you all again. I do not know where to tell you to write unless you write as you did before. I will write you again the first chance & let you knowhow I am.

There is a young calf in Fredericksburg with 2 heads 3 years [ears] 4 eyes, 4 nose holes & 2 mouths. (There is a sick Georgia soldier here who has seen it & examined it.) It sucks with either mouth & it 3d year [ear] is between its heads.

I will close yours with great respect,
A.J. Proffit

>Gordonsville, Va.
>June 24, 1863
>Wm., Mary and R.L. Proffit

Dear Father, Mother and Sister,

    I again seat myself to drop you a few lines to let you now where and how I am. I am hear at Gordonsville hospittle. My health is tolerable good. We started on a march some time ago from Fredericksburg to wards the valley of Va. I, with many others, give out and could not go- the weather was so hot and we marched through the heat of the day and, that, more than we could stand. I was only broken down, as for being sick, I am not.

    I have quite a fine time plenty to eat I have eaten mower [more] cheries since I came hear than I ever did in the same length of time. A.J. went on with the Reg., but he was very tired. He was well as for health but broken down with the march. But they ware going to do the marching in the evening and morning after I left it, so will not be so hard on them. General Ewell has given the yankees a glorious whipping at Winchester. They came a train by hear this morning loaded with prisners and I hear thare are lotts behind coming on. Our fources are all mooving to wards Mariland and I hear some are thare now.

    As I have no news to interest you with I will soon close.

    P.S. You nead not to write till I write again. They are leaving hear evry day- I dont know but what I shal leave hear to day.

    I don't want you to make yourselves uneasy a bout me. I am in tolerable health- I goo [go] whare [where] I please. I dont keepe [to] my bed any at all- only of a night.

    I will close hopeing you are all well,

>I remain as ever yours, &c.
>A.N. Proffit

Richmond, Va.
June 26, 1863
R.L. Proffit

Dear Sister,

These lines are to in form you that I am now at Richmond faring tolerable well. Thare is but little the matter with me- I only broke down on the march. I wrote you a short note the other day while at Gordonsville. I left thare in a few hours after and came hear to Chamborazso[1] Ward "I". We have enough to eat and good bunkes to ly upon.

Thare are many of my acquaints hear- P. Walsh is hear, Eli Robbards Henry Hamby- Thomas Walsh is at Camp Winder not far from hear. He is well, he had the shot taken from his knee the other day. For fear you diden't git the letter I started from Gordonsville, I will tell you some thing about A.J. He was well, as far as health, but he broke down the two last days that I was with the Reg., but he stil went on. It is said our fources are in Pensylvania at this time. I dont know what thare idea is. It is expected that the yankes are landing below Rich.

Thare is a call for volunteers out of the hospittles to meat them. It is said old Jeff has orderd out the malatia [militia] to defend the Citty. I must soon close by asking you to write soon and fail not,

Direct thus
A.N. Proffit
Chamborazo Hospittle
3 Division
Ward I
Richmond V.A.

Write as soon as you get this for I dont know how long I shall stay hear. These lines leaves me tolearble well, hoping they may find you all enjoying the same blessing. Give my love to F. M. allso to unkle Samual's Walshes family, &c. Excuse bad writing and spelling.

No more but remanes yours, &c. A.N.P.

---

1 *Chimborazo Hospital.*

Chamborazo Hospital
July 8th 1863
Wm. and Mary Proffit

Dear Father and Mother,

These lines are to inform you that my health is good. Greatly hoping these few lines may reach you and find you all well.

We have it in today's paper that General Lee has had another great battal in Pensylvania. It is said he captured forty thousand prisoners and they are on thare way to Richmond and have refused to be paroled. But on the other hand it is near as bad as it was reported this morning that the yankees have taken Vixburg- which I hope is not so and I rather think it is. So I will not write much now as I shall leave hear in the morning. I recken I shall go out to Camp Lee and stay a while. I can't tell when I shall git to my Regt.

I have written home twice since I came hear and got no anseer and I expect to leave hear in the morning. You need not to write hear if you haint [haven't] and if you have, don't direct any more to hear- I cant tell you where to direct. So you nedent [needn't] to write no more til you hear from me again.

I wll now close. These Lines leaves me well. I remain yours as ever,

A.N. Proffit

Eli Robbards is hear- he is not well. I may not write any more soon if I start on a long march, &c.

Chimborazo Hospital on the Eastern edge of Richmond - the "hospital on the hill."

Camp 1st N.C. Troops
Near Hagerstown, Md.
July 9th 1863
Miss R. L. Proffit

Dear Sister:

I have received two letters from you since I had an opportunity of writing you. Yours of June 20th was received last evening and was read with much pleasure. I believe the last time I wrote any of you was when we were at Sharpsburg, Md. Since then I have passed through a variety of scenes, which I think could not fail of being interesting to you if I could have the pleasure of relating them to you, but time & space will not admit of writing full accounts. I will, however, inform you that our army has been through a grate part of Maryland and Pennsylvania. The Corps to which we belong (Lieut. General Ewell's) went within a few miles of Harrisburg which is the Capital of Penn., and I have very little doubt that we could have taken the city had we not been ordered to rejoin the main army which penetrated far into the State in other directions.

The Yankee army was compelled to retire from Virginia and Maryland and fight us in Penn. if they chose to fight us at all. The two main armies met at a town called Gettysburg in Penn.

The fight commenced on the 7th day of July and continued three days, when it closed without either army being routed or driven back. The enemy secured an elevated position and fortified it well which saved them from their usual fate.

Since the fight both armies have fallen back- most of our army is now encamped near Hagerstown, Md. The yankees are said to have fallen back to Baltimore City. It is said the Yankee papers admit a loss of forty two thousand and say it is the gratest defeat they ever sustained. I suppose we took 19,000 prisoners.

Two of our company were killed- Sergt. N.G. Martin and Corporal Ja. E. Purvis- 7 men wounded, I suppose you are not acquainted with any of the except Rufus Eller- he was slightly wounded in the arm- I was not hurt. 18th N.C. Regt was in the fight but I learned that A.J. and Alfred both gave out on the way and were left in Md. or Penn.

I suppose there was nothing the matter with them more than being exhausted by hard marching. Capt. Miller's Company was in the fight and sustained a heavy loss. I am sorry to announce that Capt. Miller, J.W. Triplett and Franklin Hamby were killed. One or two others with whom I was not acquainted with were killed. Lieut. Miller was badly wounded. William Walsh was very slightly wounded, but is with the Co.

Harry Walsh is unwell. He was not in the fight and was not with the Co. when I saw it, I suppose he is at the hospital. Jesse Miller and Lieut. Land are tolerably well. William Walsh is also in good health. I have no idea of future movements of the army. I hope it will not be long till the war will be prosperously terminated. My health is good at present.

Please inform Mrs. Elizabeth Miller that I received a letter from her some time ago and would have answered it immediately, but we were then in Penn. I had no chance to send letters to Richmond or any place where they could be mailed.

Tell S. Walsh Jr. that I received a letter from him yesterday which I will answer as soon as circumstances will admit.

You need not expect letters from me often as we very seldom have a chance of sending one off after it is written.

My love to Father, Mother and all enquiring friends, if any. Let me hear from you frequently.

Your brother as ever,

W.H. Proffit

P.S. I will send you some envelopes and stamps as soon as I have an opportunity.

H.

Stanton, Va.
July 16th 1863
R.L. Proffit

I again seat myself to drop you a few lines to let you know whare I am. I am now in the hospital at Stanton- I left Rich. At the time I wrote you, I was going to come on hear and not thinking I was quite stout enough to stand the long march from hear to Maryland I went in to the hospital but I think I will go on in a few days.

This is a vary good hospital. We have plenty to eat. We have beeaf, bacon, molases and milk- for supper, coffee & soup

I would like to hear from home and know how you are all gitting along and to know when you have heard from A.J. and W.H. I have no chance to hear from them.

Our wounded are coming in every day from the battle in Pensylvania. All that can walk, has walked all the way from Pensylvania hear. They are tyered fellows. They are going to Rich. every day.

As I am destitute of news, I will close. These lines leaves me tolerable well, hopeing these few lines may reach and find you all well.

It is not wort while to write me until I git to my Regt., but I will still write you onse and a while.

No more but remains, your brother until death, &c.

A.N. Proffit

Danville, Va.
July the 23th 1863

Dare Cousin,

I take my pen in hande to lete you no that I am well as comin [common] at this time, bute not well like I youste to bee bute am beter then I have bin fore six month. I hope when this letter come to you hande hit will finde you well an unkl an ante allso. I have no nuse to rite to you of eny intereste. I am heare at Danville. I wente oute to hunte bares [bears?] yesterday with some young men. I no note [know not] when I will goe to my campine bute I will hafte to goe before longe I woulde like to come home an see you all worse time mos bute I no note [but I know not] when I will.

I saw Alfored in Richmond but he hase gone to hise company. I woulde rote [would have wrote] to you all before now bute I have been moving aboute, so I have no chanse [missing]

I hope you will excuse [missing] and rite to me soon [missing]

gite this letter. [missing]

I wante you to give my love to Unkl Saml an Ante Poly an all the galse an [sumay?] an tell them to rite to me an lete me no how thay are doin. I will rite to you all as soone as I gite settle.

I hope you will all remember me, all tho I may never see none of you no more, bute I hope I will gite to come home againe. Give my love to Mr. Mcgee family.

I muste soone close my bade rote letter. You no that I can'te rite much, nohow.

I cane to say to you that I have note hade bute wone letter sens the fite at Chanservill. I doe hope the ware will soone close an lete all the men come home that is left alive, bute ther is meney of our relason lefte on the rede hill of VA., so I muste close my letter.

[missing] you can direct you letter to Danville
the generl hospitl the 3 ward D
[missing] R.L. Proffite, from P. Walsh

Stanton, Va.
August 1st 1863
Wm. and Mary Proffit

Dear Father & Mother,

I, again, write you a few lines to let you know how I am. I am still at the hospital and am well, as for health. I am the stoutist I have been since I left the Reg. I expect to go back be fore long.

I have heard from A.J. and W.H. since the great battal in Pa. They ware not heart- also, Jesse Miller was not heart. Capt. Miller, John Triplett[1] [and] H. Hamby ware killed. Tad John. Lipps [and] A.B. West- wounded. Thare was but one killed in my Co.

Several wounded, allso Jesse Triplett[2] of the 26 was killed, &&

I want hear from you all the worst I ever did but had mutch rather see you. It is not worth while to write me til I get to my Regt. I am doing vary well now. I have pleanty to eat but if I was at home I could do better. I want to hear from crops gardeans and fruit &c in Wilkes.

As I have no news to write you, I will close, hopeing these lines may reach and find you all well. Give my love to Sis. Till her I an [am] "all rite on the goose."

I ever remain your sun burnt buoy til death, &c.

A.N. Proffit

---

1 *John W. Triplett, Wilkes County, Sergeant, Co. K, 53rd N.C. Infantry, d. on July 3, 1863, at Gettysburg, Pennsylvania. (Brother to Jesse F. Triplett)*
2 *Jesse F. Triplett, Wilkes County, Sergeant, Co. C, 26th N.C. Infantry, d. on July 3, 1863, at Gettysburg, Pennsylvania. (Brother to John W. Triplett)*

Bivouac 1st N.C. Troops
near Orange C.H., Va.
August 2d 1863
Miss R.L. Proffit

Dear Sister:

I have been expecting a letter from you for several days, but as I have received none, I write you again; although I wrote last.

We have not been marching so hard for ten days, as we had previously been doing. You may be shure the rest we have lately been enjoying was duly appreciated. We are now encamped near Orange Court House. We came here yesterday and are resting today.

As this is Sunday morning, I suppose you are all preparing to go to meeting at Lewis Fork, I would be happy to be with you, but duty demands that I should be elsewhere, therefore I am [as] content as circumstances will permit.

I know nothing of the future plans of our army. All is quiet here now.

Some think we will fall back to Fredericksburg- some think to Richmond.

Although we have sustained several reverses of late, I have not dispaired of our final triumph, I am as far from being willing to submit to Northern despotism as I ever have been, but I am sorry to say all are not so.

The latest news is that our army in the West has gained a grate victory. Also, in N.C., the yankees have been repulsed at two points. I hope the independence of the Confederacy will be gained and that, soon.

I have not yet heard from A.J. and A.N. I have written to the commander of their Company for information of them and am looking for an answer. Wm. Walsh and Jesse Miller were well a few days ago. Harvy Walsh was inproving in health.

Write me often and give me all the news you can. Do you receive your Recorder regularly? How are crops of corn, weat &c? Is there much fruit in your neighborhood?

Have you a school in your dist.? Who teaches & are you going? Does Pa keep his machine & is he going to thresh this year? My love to all the family & neighbors. Is Pa's & Ma's general health as good or better than when I saw them?

My health is good
Your brother,
W.H. Proffit

Camp near Madison Courthouse, Va.
August the 3rd 1863
Miss R.L. Proffit

Dear Cousin,

I take my pen in hand in order to drop you a few lines which will inform you that I am well, greatly hoping these lines may reach & find you enjoying the same blessing. I can inform you that we are now encamped near Orange Courthouse. We have been here two days. I dont know when we will leave here. I dont know as ther is mutch prospect of a fight here. It is reported that they had a fight at Culpepper, day before yesterday. They say our men whiped them. It is also reported that the yankees are advancing in this way, but I don't know the truth of it for we seldom here the truth.

I guess you have seen a few accounts of our grand raids through Penn. and Md., so that is [un]necessary for me to attempt to give you and account of it now- from the fear that I would not be able to give you anything like as satisfactory an account of it. I will only say that if I can live, I hope I will never see such another time. You have, no doubt, seen an account of the men that wer killed & wounded in our Co. and Reg.

I can inform you that we are left almost without a Co. an entirely without officers. Lt Eller & Land are both sick. Our men have nearly all deserted- two left us last night. I dont know who will go tonight- I expect some of them will, though. If they don't it will be a wonder.

I wish one thing, and that is for them all to say [stay?] or go on & not be sliping off one or two at a time.

Jesse Miller & two others left us- yesterday was a week ago.

I guess they have got nearly home if they had good luck I can inform you that Harvy Walsh is left behind. He was in verry bad health. I saw W.H. after the fight- he was well. A.J. & A.N. wer both left sick in Va., so I have been informed, & did not cross over the Potomac, so I recon none of our connections wer killed. I can tell you what I have come to conclude: that we are whiped if some change does not speedily take place. I dont think anybody regrets it more deeply than I wanted but I can't see any other chance.

The soldiers are all discouraged. They dread the thought of meeting the yankees again & loosing thier lives in a cause they consider to be nearly hopeless. It is reported Gen. Lee has resigned- this I don't believe. I must close soon. I want you to write me a long letter as soon as you receive this. Give me the news. Tell all about what is going on in Wilkes, if you all have any fun now when you all get together.

Yesterday was meeting time at Lewis Fork. I thought of you all & how I would like to be their to hear some good man preach. We don't get to hear any preaching since we left Penn., as our preacher was left their with our wounded.

Give my respects to uncle Samuel's girls. Tell them to write to me & not wait till they receive letters from me, fore I have not had the chance to write a letter till yesterday, in two months. Tell Lilly I would like to here from her & to know if she begs mutch these times.

If evrybody don't know, I think they ought to. I shudder when I think what I have passed through- the balls fell thick as hail & men fell all around me.

Must close- direct to: Richmond, Va. Co. K, 53 Reg, NCT, Daniels brigade, Rhodes division.

Give my respect to uncle Wm. & Aunt Ninny.

No more at present, but remain yours, &c.

Wm. Walsh

Camp of the 1st N.C. Troops
near Orange Court House, Va.
Monday morning, August 10th 1863

My dear sister Louisa,

Another week has gone bye, and I have not received a letter from you or any of my friends in Wilkes, neither have I heard a word concerning Andrew and Alfred, consequently I am becoming quite impatient, as well as uneasy, although I have no thought that it is any fault of yours.

All has been quiet since I wrote you last. We are enjoying most all the comforts of a quiet camp, but how long we will be permitted to remain in camp is not known.

The two grate armies of the Potomac, I believe, are both quiet and, at least, tempoarily stationary- the Yankees in the vicinity of Culpepper C.H. and the Confederate at Orange C.H.

The weather has been excessively hot for the past ten days, but as we have very little to do, we lie in the shade and pass the time as agreeably as possible. I have three or four books including my bible with which I spend a grate part of my time.

We have had three or four fine rains within the past week. Crops look remarkably well in this neighborhood, indeed, I do not see how they can be better. I understand the people of Wilkes are badly whipped and willing for our patriotic old state to return to the pretended Union, and, claim Abraham Lincoln as their chief magistrate, I have also been told that the country was full of deserters and no efforts being made to arrest them, but that they are more highly respected than a soldier who is toiling and fighting to redeem their country from chains and slavery.

I would be glad to hope that such were not the case, but no grounds for believing the reports are untrue.

I am not in favor of a termination of the war, until it terminates in the independence of the Confederate States. Our late reverses are not cause for submitting to our enemies, but should cause us to make the more determined and vigorous efforts to accomplish what we first began.

And as regards desertion, I would as soon hear of a Christian friend of mine being shot through the brain or heart as to hear of him deserting the army and resorting to the rock houses of his native mountains.

My health is good. Tell Pa & Ma that I would be happy in seeing them and will get a furlough as soon as possible and visit them.

When you write me, give me all the information you can of A.J. & A.N. Your acquaintances in this company are well- those who are present.

It is feared that John Estes is dead, although we have no certain account of it.

Affectionately your brother,

W.H. Proffit

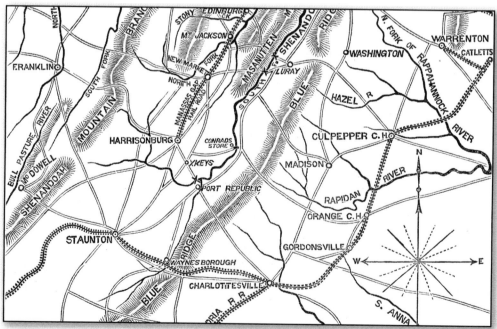

DETAIL OF A MAP OF THE SHENANDOAH VALLEY.

>
> Warren Co. Va.
> Near Front Royal
> August the 19th 1863

Dear Father,

 I, this day, seate my self to drop you a few lines to inform you that I am yet a [live?] & I think I am a gitting well. I have bin very low & I am very weeke, yet, but I think that I am improving slowly. I am still at Mrs. Celocks, yet. [They?] have bin good to me & has treated me like a mother. I want you to rite to me & let me know how you all air & whether you have heard eny thing of brother W.H. & A.N. or not.

 A.N. was sent to the hospital befour I was taken sick. I think if I was at Richmond Hospital I cold git a furlow, but I can't git thair untell I git able to walk. It is a bout 80 miles to the railroade & the yanks is all a round us. Their is but won way to git out from hear.

 You kneede knot bee uneasy a bout me for I think I will be well in a few weeks & will com hom as soon as I can. I have not mutch to rite at this time.

 I will rite soon again & tell you more a bout it, so nothing more at this time- only I remain your until death, so do write soon. Direct your Letter to:

> Front Royal Va
> Warren County

>> To Mr. W. M. Proffit
>> From A.J. Proffit

Stanton Hospital, Va.
Aug. 20, 1863
R.L. Proffit

Dear Sister,

These lines are to inform you that I am yet in the hospital. I should have been gon to my Regt, before now, but since I last wrote you I have had a vary savear [severe] attact of disintary- which weakened me vary mutch- but I am now over it and tolerable stout. My stomach is vary good and I have lots to eat and that is good.

I have milck 3 times a day and butter & molases once and all sorts of vegitables, &c. Sis I am the loansomest chicken you ever saw- no person to stay with, nor talk with of my acquainte. I walk the streets of those long eavenings by myself- no person to communicate my thoughts to. I have to take it out in studding [studying]. I oftimes think of my native home and the many pleashures I have enjoyed with my friends and long to see the time rowl [roll] round when I can, again, meat my friends again, in peace, at home.

This day, 12 months ago, I taken my leaf of home. The time has passed of fast, but I have sean hard times since I saw you.

I would like to see you all, the best of all things and I think I will git a furlough this fawl and come home. I am quite anxious to hear from you all but thare is no chance now. I have been gon from the Regt. 2 months and I have not heard from home since.

I should like to know how times are in Wilkes, &c.

As I have no news to write, I will close. Give my love to P. & M. and all my friends and except [accept] the same your self, &c. Theses lines leaves me tolerable well and I truley hope they may find you all well, &c&c

I remain, as ever, yours, &c.
A.N. Proffit

Camp near Orange C.H.
Aug. the 21th 63

Dear Cousin,

It is with great pleasure that I avail myself of the present opportunity to drop you a few lines which will inform you that I am well greatly hoping these lines may reach & find you all enjoying the same blessing. I have no vary interesting news to write you at this time. This is the day the President set apart as a day of fasting and prair, but from what I see going on in camp, I think vary little regard is paid to it. I see some of the men engaged in playing cards and others engaged in cooking eating cursing & swearing, &c. We have no interesting war news. I believe it is the opinion here, that the yankees are pulling back from Culpepper. I think a fight is not expected here soon.

The last news we had from Charlestown, the were fighting tar & it is the general opinion here that they will take Charlestown. If they do this will be a vary heavy loss & will cause men to desert in greater numbers but I think they will all go unless something is done to stop it. They are going more or less very day. 8 left yesterday out of this reg. I don't know whether any have gone today or not. If they hant yet, I expect they will before night. It takes one half the brigade to guard the other now and if many more deserts, I reckon they will keep us all on guarde all the time. They have released all the prisoners they had on guarde. Jesse Miller is with the Company.

Now I understand Wilkes is _____ full of deserters and almost running over & I have also heard that they are received by people thar with joy. I have believed only a part of what I have bin hearing & am waiting patiently for the truth.

I can't hardly think any of you have got so that you would like to see me desert the army & come home in disgrace. I don't beleive that we ar whiped & I woulde like to git out of this war soon, myself, but I don't hardly think that I will desert, yet a while, unless we start back accross the Potomac River again & if we do that, I don't know what I might do. I can't deside I wouldn't go thar any more but I reckon if the rest wer to go I guess I would go with them. I have heard by some letters from Wilkes that it looks like olde times in Wilkes again- so many young men ar stepping about thar. I think times would be a little more encouraging here if we could see them all return us. They ought to do without delay as this is a time of need.

I have heard nothing from A.J. nor A.N. since we left Va.- only they wer both left behind sick. You will please inform me when you write if you know whar they ar. I heard from W.H. a few days ago- he was well. Harvy Walsh has gone to the Hospittle. I hear they ar holding Union meeting in Wilkes- have raised the Union flag, &c. I want to know if all this is so.

I must close. Write soon & give me the news. Give my respects to all my connections & friends &c. So no more at present but remains Yours, &c.

Wm. Walsh

Danville, Va.
August the 23, 1863

Dare Cousin,

Hite [It] is with much plasor, [pleasure] I take my pen in hande to write you a few lines to lete you no I am giting alonge toleber well. I all so recive you letter a few days agoe an you made shore I was glade to hare from you an to hare you wase all well. I have gote no nuse to rite to you about the ware. I can'te hare mush nuse.

I have binne goine to meetin, day an nite, fore some time. Ther hase binn [illegible] every sens I came heere. I am glade to tell you of the nuse- their hase binn some Eighty soles [illegible] sense this meating coments [commenced] an a large amounte are sick an wound solgars [soldiers] hite [it] is in this church.

I miss you all vary mush. Hite [It] wase so mush like old times. Thare is some thirty or forty [mornes?] yete I no note whene hite will close. I wante you to give my love to all my frends an naber [neighbors]. I wante to see you all vary bade. You rote to me somethinge about thay wase holdin pase [peace] meating I hope the ware [war] will sone [soon] close an we will all gite to come home to stay. I woude rote to you all before now, bute I dide note no when I wase starte to my Compine. I wante you to rite to me whene you harde frome the boys. I wante to see them. I may starte to my Compine soone- I no note when. I muste soone bringe my letter to a close, by saying, rite soone an fail note, an direct you letter to the Generl hospitl no. 2, the 3 Divison, Ward D, Danville, Va. I wille sende you apase [a piece] of [illegible] an you cane see whate [illegible] is [illegible] from.

Farewell,

Philip Walsh

to R.L. Proffit an Nancy Walsh

Near Orange C.H., Va.
August 28th 1863

My dear Sister Louisa:

Yours of August 18th was received on the 24th, and I am sorry that circumstances rendered it impossible to respond immediately. We have been on picket near two and a half days. We returned to camp this morning.

I received news of Andrew and Alfred a few days ago that I suppose is correct. I told Alexander Faw of our Co. who was going to their Reg. to enquire for them. They told him that Alfred was at Staunton and A.J. was at Hugenaught Springs Hospital,[1] which is on the James River a short distance above Richmond.

It is very strange you get no letters from them. I would write them but don't know how to direct my letters properly.

There is very little news afloat in the camps. All the soldiers are enjoying rest and quietude, except those who are either deserting or contemplating how to escape. I suppose that I could be as glad to see my parents and relatives & friends as almot any man, but if there is never an opportunity offered for me to visit them honorably, I have no idea of ever seeing them again. Thank God there are many who have not and will not desert. I hope there are yet enough who are willing to continue the war until it ends in the independence of the Confederate States. If it ends otherwise than in our favor, the end of the war will be the beginning of trouble. I hope I shall never hear of any of my relatives shamefully deserting their posts & leaving their comrades to fight alone for their freedom, of which they had made themselves unworthy.

Cousin Bennett Walsh (Co. "C" 26 N.C.T.) came up to see us a few days ago, he is well. He said Jesse Triplett, Samuel and David Hall were taken prisoner and are at New York.

I am going to see Cousin William Walsh and the rest of my acquaintances in that Co. in a few days, but I can't tell whether or not any of the rest of our relations are with him.

---

1 *Huguenot Springs, Confederate Hospital.*

You wanted to know if I wanted any clothing. I will inform you that I am not needing any at present, but if I should live to see Winter I would be much obliged to you for a pair of yarn gloves and about two pairs of good socks.

If you have a chance to send these by a safe hand I would be glad for you to do so.

My love to Father and Mother with all my relatives & friends who may enquire for me.

Affectionately your brother

W.H. Proffit

P.S. My health is good, except that I have pains in my limbs a good deal like Rheumatism.

H.

N.B. Let me hear from you again soon, Why did you not answer those questions I asked a short time ago?

H.

You wanted to know how we are faring. We are faring well. We draw 1lb. & 2 oz. of flour, 1/2 lb. of bacon or 1 1/4 lb. of beef a day besides which we frequently get peas, rice, green corn, shugar, &c.

H.

> Staunton, Va.
> September 1st 1863
> Wm. & Mary Proffit

Mutch beloved Father and Mother,

After some delay I again seaze the presant opportunity of droping you a few lines to let you know how I am doing. I am tolerable well at presant. I am now helping to nurs until I get entirely stout.

I am faring vary well- pleanty to eat and the weather is vary cool for this season of the year. We haft to ware our coats of mornings.

The sick had been cawled [called] on to defend the Town of Stanton some three or four times. The last cawl, I shourled [shouldered] my musket and went out but saw no yankees. The[y] turned out- all that could walk. If the[y] had come we would have give them [Jesse?]

I begin to want to want to go to the regiment vary bad to see A.J. and hear from home, as I suppose you write him and git ansurs from him and W.H. I want to hear from you all the worst in the wourld and I think when I git to the Regt I can hear. I am out hear whare I dont hear anything but lyes.

Crops ar fine in this cuntry also fruit and vegitables and I hope they are in N.C.

As today is inspectionn of the Hospital and things flousterated I can't write and I will seace to write.

You may think, as I have been writeing you so long a bout going to my Regt. and am not as yet, I have been vary sick, but I have never been confined to my bed a day- yet I have been so I could go any whare I wanted to, &c. These lines leaves me well, hopeing to see you soon. I will close. I remain your beautiful buoy till death, &c.

Give Sis my love and respeckes,

A.N. Proffit

Camp near Orange Court House, Va.
September 8th 1863
R.L. Proffit

I spend these few moments in writing you a few lines to inform you that I am with the regiment and am well at this time and hope these few lines may soon reach and find you all in like health. I left Stanton last Sunday & got hear the same day. Times are mutch like common in camp- enough to eat and not mutch to do. I miss A.J. vary mutch. He is not hear. I have not heard from him since he left the Regt. The (Dr) told him whar thar was a privat house and to go to it an he would [be] attended to & I suppose he is thare yet.

I heard from W.H. since I come hear. He is well- all so the buoys of Capt. Millers (Co)- they are all well and P. Walsh is now by my side- stout as a buck

I want to go to see W.H. in a day or two I left J.E. Lewther at Staunton. He was nocking about but had the hooping cough. Sis I want you to write me just as soon as you git this. It is near three months since I heard from you or since I have gotten a letter- just one from you some time ago and I heard by that, you was all well. Give me a long letter and let it contain all the news about our home affars and a bout the union and about the deserters in Wilkes. Let it contain all the news you can hear.

Write soon and fail not and direct as heretofor, &c. Give my love to Pa & Ma and all my friends and allso, to [too]. Sis, tell him I would like to be at home vary mutch & I remain, &c. &c.

A.N. Proffit

Camp 1st N. C. T.
Sept. 22nd 1863

My dear Sister Louisa:

I received a letter from Pa on the 15th, dated the 6th, by which I was informed you were not well but the rest of the family were. I hope that before this reaches you your health will have been restored and you will be going to school, &c.

There has been nothing but excitement and marching here since the 14th Inst. There has not been a general battle yet and it is doubtful when there will be. We are fortifying our position along the RapidAnn River and waiting for the enemy to advance.

We are now on the East side of the Rapidann 20 miles below Orange C.H. Since I wrote you last I saw Alfred, he was with his Company and in fine health. He looks the best I have seen him since he has been in the army. He knows nothing at all of A.J.

I wrote to the citizen at Front Royal with whom he was staying when last heard from. I had received no answer and think it doubtful whether or not I do. I do not know whether or not our mail runs there at this time. I also saw P. Walsh. He was well. I wrote a letter to H.M. Stokes today and directed it to Wilkesboro- if he is in your neighborhood inform him of the same. I will write more when I have more time & better opportunities. My love to Pa & Ma.

Affectionately your brother,

W.H. Proffit

My health is good. H.

Seven Miles west of Gordonsville, Va.
At the Rappadan river on Picket
Sept 25, 1863
R.L. Proffit Est. &c.

These lines, &c. will inform you that my health with A.J.'s is vary good. He returned to the Redg. last Monday just a month from the time he left until he returned. He has been at a privat house all the time and was attended to, vary well by the people of the house and neighborhood.

The doctor who attends him was an army sergeon. He has had quite a sevear spell of fever and fluckes [flux], all of which he has conquered, and came out all right on the goose. He can eat as mutch as A.J. Hudson and my stomach is the same as Unkle Jas.

As I have told you all about us, I will now say to you that we left our camp near Orange and marched up hear expecting a brush with the Yankes but we did not git into them. Old Steward's Cavalry whiped them like a beauty with little or no [laws?] and we are now on picket watching to see if any of them attempt to come on again.

We don't expect them hear any moor and we have gone into camp. We an our brigade have a vary nice camp. As I have give you all the news I know I will soon close.

I have written you two or three times cince I came to camp and I have not received any from you yet.

Please give me an ansur, if you please. When this you see remember me. These lines leaves me well, &c.

Return our love to Father and Mother and except [accept] for yourself, &c.

I remain yours, &c.

A.N. Proffit

Camp of the 1st N.C. Troops
20 miles N.E. of Orange C.H. Va.
Sept. 29th 1863

Dear Father, Mother and Sister:

I received your very kind letters of 18th and 22 inst. today. I was happy in learning that you were all in the enjoyment of good health and also to receive a short history of your domestic affairs with the general news from the county.

I suppose you have learned ere this that the Army of Northern Virginia has again been in motion and another bloody contest expected, but no general engagement has yet taken place.

We have just returned from the banks of the Rapidan were we have been performing our part of the picket duty. The yankees picket the West side of the river with cavalry who never forget to keep a sensible distance from us- as the cavalry of this Army seem to posess a genuine hatred for infantry. I think we now have all the fords and most of the hights from below Fredericksburg to Orange C.H. tolerably well fortified and I have no doubt that it is the intention of our Genl's to hold this present position; neither do I have any fears of our ability to do so. It is true that the yankees may, as usual, out number us and make another desperate effort, but it is to be remembered that the Army of Northern Virginia led by the gray haired Veteran Lee has never been whipped, while on the other hand, "The greatest Army on the Planet," as the Army of the Potomac claims to be, knows nothing but defeat, retreat and panic, save on two occasions and in these they have no grounds to claim anything more than holding their positions with greatly the advantage in both positions and in numbers. Lest I weary you on this subject and add nothing to your information, I will dispense with it by saying all is now quiet along the lines and I know of no demonstrations denoting an early advance.

I will here inform you that I received a letter from Andrew a few days ago under the date of September 16th. He said he was quite weak but his health, he said, was improving fast. He said he was still at Mr. Sealocks, but expected to start to his Regiment that day, (16th) As it is getting dark I will wait til morning to close.

Sept. 30th- Since writing the above, nothing of interest has occurred, I hope we may have another season of quiet, and enjoy the advantage of a perminent camp.

I have not seen or heard from A.N. since I wrote you last. Cousin William Walsh, Jesse Miller and Lieut. Land have all visited us within the past few days- they were all enjoying good health. I expect to go and see them tomorrow.

You wished to know in a letter of previous date whether or not I wanted any clothing. In reply I informed you that I would be much obliged to you, if you would send me two pairs of socks and a pair of gloves. If you have an opportunity of sending them by a reliable person, do so. If not, I will get some of the boys who come home on furlough to bring them to me. They are giving a few furloughs now. Those who have been from home longer, get the first furloughs in our Co. I think if I live till the latter part of Winter, it will be my time.

Cheering news from Genl Bragg's Army has been received. There is no doubt of our gaining a great victory in the West. I wrote a letter to Mr. Stokes a short time ago, and directed it to Wilkesboro. I hope he will get it, I enclose you a few stamps.

My love to the connection and neighbors.

Affectionately yours,
Harrison

> Camp near Moten Ford, Va.
> Sept the 29th 1863
> Miss R.L. Proffit

Dear Cousin,

I take my pen in hand in order to drop you a gew lines which will inform you that I am well, greatly hoping these lines may reach & find you all well.

I can inform you that I received your kind letter which you sent by Lieut. Land. I was vary glad to hear that you wer all doing well I have nothing strang to write you at present. We are encamped about 20 miles from Orang CH on the Rapadan river. The yankees are on the other side in plain view of us. We have been expecting a fight here for some time but it has been delayed for some cause or another till the present time.

Ther may be a fight here soon or ther may not- I can't tell & should not be surprised for a fight to commence here at any time. We have orders to keep our rations cooked and be ready to move at a moments warning. If the yankees should make an attack on us here, I think they will be vary apt to get a whiping. I think that is agreed on by all our men. No one seems to have any doubt but what we will whip them this time. I hear that the gard is playing a rough game with the deseres & conscips [deserters & conscripts] in Wilkes. Poor old fellows, they were not over half as smat [smart] as they thought they were.

Guess it would have been the best for the men not to have runaway & for the conscips to have come out and us kept peace in the country as mutch as posable.

I hope they will not leave a cowardly deserter in the county & I want them to bring all the conscrips who are able to come but such men as J._____, I am in favour of litting alone but I hear they had him & will no doubt bring him into the servis. I hear they have taken old B._____, two [too] because they could not catch T._____ & G._____- that looks rather hard. I reckon G._____ an't quite as popular as he thought he was. He wrote back here that "no one stood so fair in Wilkes as the deserters."

I can inform you that I saw W.H. the other day- he is well. His Reg. is in camp about one mile from here A.N. I suppose is with his Reg.- I have not seen him. I have not heard from Thos. nor Phillip since we left Orang. I have not heard from Harvy Walsh since he left us. I must soon bring my letter to a close. I want to come home about Christmas if I live. I want you to tell Davy that she must have a fine quilt as I would expect her to have a fine quilting, a play and a heap of fun, &c. Tell Lilly to keep on begging Uncl.

Maby peace will be made sometime. Tell Davy & Lillly, Mary & Martha I would like for them to write me as I have written to all of them. I heard the gard had taken up J._____ . I wunder what they will do with him? What has gone with H._____ has the gard got him to?

I reckon N._____ has taken to the brush again. Is General B._____ in Wilkes? Tell Lilly she had better mind or the General will be taken old A._____ & J._____. What has gone with them?

I would bring my letter to a clos. Give my respects [to] Uncle Billy [and] Aunt Ninny & all my connections & friends. No more at present, but ever remain yours, with greate respect,

Wm. Walsh

Near Gordonsville, Va
Oct. the 8th 1863
Mr. Wm. Proffit

Dear Father,

This note is to inform you that I am with my regiment enjoying a reasonable portion of health. I have been absent three months, sick with the fever. I was at a private house & treated very kindly. The fever fell in my feet and legs so that I could not walk nor get off of my bed for some time. I was not out of the house for seven weeks, and no one who saw me thought there was any chance for me to live, but the God who rules and governs all things saw fit in his tender mercies to raise me up again for which I shall ever feel greateful.

I have no news of interest to write at this time. We have been cooking three days rations, today, in order for a march, but to what place I am unable to say. As news is scarce & my hand is quite nervous, I will soon close.

A.N. is quite stout and look finely. You will please write me as soon as this comes to hand and give me all the news- how you are getting a long & how your crop is about to turn out. Give my love to Mother, Sis, & all my friends. I will close by subscribing my self, yours with great respect, &c.

A.J. Proffit

Co. 'D' 1st reg NCT

Lain's brigade

Wilcoxe's division

Richmond, Va.

Head Qa. Co F 37th N.C. Troops
In Camp Near Liberty Mills, Va.
Oct. 8th '63

Dear Father and Mother,

I wonce more seat my self to drope you a few lines with will enform you that I am well an not forgting to hope this will fine you all well an doing well. I hant [haven't] got any good nuse to rite at this time. I will say to you that we have orders to cook three days rations an be ready to march. We are cooking them today. I dont know whar we will go, but it is thought that we will advance on the yankee an I think we will by all apperence. I wood much rather not go, but it is not as I say. It is sead thar troops ar moving now, and I recond it is so for I see the artilery going to wards the River. It is [no] telling what this move will [attain?]

It may be for our good an it may be for our worse- I can't say, but I hope it will be for our good. A.J. and A.N. Poffit is here an ar both well an sends you all thar love an best respects. I rec. a letter from W.L. Welch an Elisebeth an I answer it the next day but I dont know wether thay have got it or not. W. Church an family, I send you all my love an best respects an would love to see you all but I can't say when I will. but I hope it won't be long until this war will come to a end so I can come home.

I want you all to rite to me an give me all the nuse you can. So I will close [from?]

Phillip Walsh

Thomas Walsh

Brandy Station
8 M. North of Culpepper, Va.
Oct. the 27, 1863
Wm. & Mary Proffit

Dear Father and Mother,

I drop you a short note to let you know that A.N. and I are in good health at present, hoping that these lines may find you all enjoying the same blessing.

I have no news of interest to writ. I saw D. M. Carlton the other day. He informed me that W.H. was gone to the hospitle.

He had been unwell for some time & give out on our late march to ward Manasses. I held out to get there & it was a sevre fight, though my brigade was not engaged- neither was W.H.'s. I saw Henry Hamby[1] & Smith Cox[2] the other day. They were well & harty. I have no news further to write, there fore you will please excuse me for not writing a long letter.

I can inform you that Thos. Walsh is at the Hospitle.

P. Walsh is here- he looks fine

I want you, if you can, to have A.N. & I a light wool hat made a pice & try to send them to us this winter, for I do not know whether we will get to come home or not. When this comes to hand I desire you to write me a long plain letter stating the particulars of your business- what you are doing, what you expect to do and how you are getting alog in general for I am anxious to know. I will now close, hoping to hear from you soon.

Give my respects to Uncle McAlpin & family, to Uncle Samuel & family & all enquiring friends. I close by subscribing myself, yours truly, &c.

A.J. Proffit

Co. D, 18th Reg. N.C.T.
Lane's brigade
Wilcoxe's division
Richmond Va.

---

1 *Henry M. Hamby, Co. H, 13th N.C. Infantry*
2 *Smith Cox, Enlisted Co. H, 13th N.C. Infantry, d. May 27, 1864, at Hospital, Gordonsville, Virginia.*

Campe nare Liberts Mills, Va.
Nov. the 15, 1863

Dare Cousin,

I seate my self to rite you afue lines to let you no that I am well at this tim an I hope, when this letter come to you hande, it will finde you an all the rest well. I recive you letter some time agoe an hav failde to anser it, but I think when you hare the reson you will fore give me.

We have binn marchin an fitin some. We had a fite Sunday, laste, but not mush harme done. We have got back to hour olde campe. I don'te no how longe we will git to stay hare. I think we will stay hare some time. I am sorrey to informe you of the deth of J._____. He wase shot yesterday at 11 o'clock. I cod not bare to see it all thoy [although] I hope he is beter off. He said that he wase prefurd to die he though[t]. I rote his wife a letter an started it to day. I am sory fore his wife an childern- I done all I cod to save his life but it was all in vane.

I can say to you that I saw your brother to day an he wase well an said A.J. wase well. I wante to see you very bad, an all the rest, I think if I cade [could?] git to come home, some of you woud have aqaints in, an we would have some fun. I no not when I will git to come. You have hard of the deth of Cousin Thomas Walsh[1], no dout, before now.

It dose seeme like all of hour lines will die an git kill before this ware will close. I doe wante it to seese some time.

I must soone close. Giv Unkill an Ant my love an all my frends. I Reciev a letter from Cousin S. Walsh[2] an he sed he had volintard so I have not rote to him. I rite this letter to you and Nancy Walsh an I wante you to rite to me as soone as you git this letter. Give my love to Elisbeth, Marthe, Mary an all the rest. Tell Unkle an Ante to rite to me. So I will close my bad rote letter at this time, by subsin [subscribing] myself you[r] frend tell deth, you[rs] truly,

                                                        Philip Walsh

---

1 *Thomas Walsh, Co. H, 13th N.C. Infantry, d. October 14, 1863, at Hospital, Charlottesville, Virginia.*
2 *Samuel Walsh, Enlisted Co. K, 53rd N.C. Infantry on December 10, 1863, d. February 28, 1865, at Point Lookout, Maryland.*

Orange Co., Va.
Nov. the 16th 1863

Dear Father, Mother & Sister,

    After my love to you, I drop you a few lines which will inform you that my health is quite good at present hoping that this short note may find you all well.

    I have no news worth your attention to write. Times are tolerably good in camp- the boys are well.

    I can say to you that I had the mortification of seeing J._____ shot to death on the 14th of this inst. which was quite a trying scene. I have seen 10 men shot for desertion, which is a shocking scene, but I have seen do many horrible things that nothing has much affect on me.

    We have not heared from W.H. since he went to the hospitle. I am quite uneasy about him- if you hear where he is let me know soon.

    Father, I am quite sorry that you will have to sell one of your mules I have nothing to say about that as they are not mine. All I can say is, do the best you can & try to keep plenty to eat. I will now clos by asking you all to write me soon.

    Yours very respectfully, &c.

    A.J. Proffit

to R.L. Proffit an Nancy Walsh

Near Gordonville, Va.
Nov. 17
R.L. Proffit

Dear Sister,

After some delay of time I again write to you to let you know that I, with A.J., are well, hoping these lines may reach and find you, with all the rest of my relatives and friends, enjoying the blessing.

I have no good news to write. Times are good in camp. Cince I last wrote you we have moved- we run the yankees to Manasses, then fel back near Culpeper and we camped thare some 2 weekes. We then started to fall back a cross the Rappadan River. We went but a vary short distance before we formed a line of battle and had a heavy skirmish with the yankee cavalry. We drove them back killed a few and wounded some.

We then fell back to our old camp whare we first started from. We have put up some fine houses and a fixen to live at home. We have a fine Company and it is increasing all most dailey. They have stoped deseartioun in the army by shooteing a few. I have witnesed the death of 12 by musketry for desearting- the last one was J._____. He was shot last Saturday. I have sean as many men shot as I wish to. Some haft to be shot the second time and that is quite a sight to see.

I saw cousin James Proffit some time ago- he was well- and all his friends in his Co. P. Walsh [and] J.E. Lewther[1] are well.

I recieved your kind letter baring date Nove. 10 last night and was vary glad to hear from you all and to hear that I have another neace on Stony Fork. I should like to see it. Tell Rhoda I am entitled to the name an will come home to see it as soon as I can.

As I am out of news, I will come to a close by asking you to write soon.

Give my love to Pap and Mother, &c.
A.N. Proffit

---

1 *Jesse Elihu Luther, Co. F, 37th N.C. Infantry*

Four Brothers In Gray

Jesse Elihu Luther and Amelia Marieh James Luther. Mr. Luther was born September 10, 1843, in Randolph County, N.C., and his family moved to Wilkesboro when he was twelve. He enlisted, Co. F, 37th N.C. Infantry, at Wilkesboro, May 10, 1862. He served at the Battle of the Wilderness, Spotsylvania Court House, Chancellorsville and in the Second Battle of Manassas and was wounded three times.

Mr. Luther was captured near Chafin's Farm and held at Point Lookout Prison for about eight months before being paroled and sent home. He was, again, detained and brought before General Stoneman who allowed him to go after hearing that he had been paroled.

Mr. Luther was one of the longest living Confederate soldiers in Wilkes and attended the 75th anniversary event in Gettysburg. He was reported to have been "the only man to carry the southern flag across the rock breast-works occupied by the federal soldiers in the famous Battle of Gettysburg."

Jesse Elihu Luther died in 1946 at Stony Fork, North Carolina, at the age of 102 years. He and Amelia were buried at Gap Creek Community Cemetery.

—Publishers.

Photo Courtesy of Mike Read

Camp 1st N.C. Regt.
Near Raccoon Ford, Va.
Nov 21st '63
Mr. William Proffit,

Much esteemed friend,

The occasion upon which I address you, I am sorry to say, is one of deep mortification to the writer as well as the person addressed.

I am sorry to say that it has become my lot to be the communicator of the sad fate of my ever affectionate and most highly esteemed friend as well as your blood son, Sargt. W.H. Proffit who died in the hospital at Gordonsville, Va. on the 25 of last month, the disease not known.

He left the Company on the 18th while on the march near Manassas and we never heard anything from him until this morning and, alas, by Surgeons Certificate to L.A. Curtis he was reported dead.

I am sorry that I cannot state the full particulars of his death. He had some money when he went away and if you will try you can be enabled to get it and all that is due him which is probably one hundred or more dollars. I will close.

I would be glad to hear from you at any time.

Your ever true friend,

Wm. H. Witherspoon[1]

---

1 *William Harrison Witherspoon, Corporal, Co. B, 1st N.C. Infantry*

FROM THE LAND OF WILKES
BY JOHNSON J. HAYES.

Among the original Proffit papers is the diary of W.H. Proffit covering his daily activities. Here is his entry on election day, November 6, 1860:

"Taught school until 1 o'clock; A. Walsh taught the rest of the day. I went to the election and voted for Stephen A. Douglas of Illinois, and no other person voted for him."

This teacher enlisted in Company B, of Col. Montfort Sidney Stokes' First Regiment, later becoming a major, and was wounded at Chancellorsville. His assistant teacher, who finished teaching on election day, Alfred Walsh, enlisted with him in the first company of volunteers, but he was killed at Malvern Hill, July 1, 1862. Thomas Land, who enlisted with Proffit and Walsh, was likewise wounded at Malvern Hill. Prof. J. Henry Spainhour was another volunteer. He was a chaplain and died in the service.

US SENATOR FROM ILLINOIS STEPHEN ARNOLD DOUGLAS

Here is a copy of an original report... to William Proffit on the progress of his son, A.J. Proffit, a student at New Hope Academy:

We have similar reports on A.J. Proffit dated August 12 and November 11, 1859. This file of Proffit's original papers includes a letter[1] from Thos. C. Land of Teleco, Tenn., dated February 4, 1860, to A.J. Proffit.

Land was teaching school in Tennessee and was encouraging A.J. and C.L. Proffit to continue in school and to take advantage of their chances. He rejoiced to hear of the progress at New Hope Academy:

---

1 See page 98

"It appears that the spirit of education has been considerably aroused in North Carolina recently and I hope that this excitement will continue until there are none to advocate the cause of ignorance."

Land taught school in Wilkes before going to Tennessee. He attended Beaver Creek Academy while Hugh Stokes was principal. He returned from Tennessee and joined Col. Sidney Stokes' company and became lieutenant colonel of the 53rd Regiment...

Andrew J. Proffit taught school before attending New Hope Academy. An original contract employing him to teach school in district number 55 August 25, 1856, is as follows:

> We the undersigned School Committee for Dist. No. 55 has employed Andy Prophet to teach School in said district, at the rates of Twelve Dollars per month and him boarded, he is to teach Reading, Riting, and Arithmetic, agreeable to his skill, he is bound to keep good order in time of school.
>
> If there should be any that is too large to correct and is not willing to come under the rules of the School, they shall be dismissed from sd. school.
>
> We obligate our selves as committeemen to give an order to the Chairman for the money agreeable for the time taught by sd. Prophet. August 25th, 1856.
>
> Wm. S. Witherspoon
Thos. Kindall
Harvey Dula
Committeemen

William H. Proffit taught the school in District 55 from September 1857 to March 4, 1858, at $12.00 per month.

> Camp of the 53 Reg.
> 8 miles Northeast of Orange C.H., Va.
> January 3, 1864
> Mr. Wm. and Mary Proffit

Der Father and Mother,

I with grate plesure drop you a short note wich will inform you that I am in tolerable helth owing to hardships and privations of camp life. I do grately hope when thse lines comes to hand, you and famely may be injoying good helth. I have no news for to communicate wish would interest you. I have no war news at present times- a peas still in this vicinity at present & we have just got up some of our huts. I got mine done the first of this instant all to the door shelter. I had not laid in a house nor under a tent for eight months- we have just taken the wether as it come and you can give a guess how we have fared & the wether is powerful cold her[e] at this time and we ar scearce blankets but if we can get to stay her[e] in our huts, I think we can doe verry well. We have a grate menny that is sick in our brigade and some ar dieing. John P. Wodey[1] died at Orange the 15th of December. Harrison Brown[2] was sent to the [hospittle?] yesterday. Barnet Owens[3] was sent this morning. Both was vary sick men. I have no thout [thought] that Owens will live. We have been so exposed, I fe[a]r that we shod have a grate deal of sickness.

Orders come round last nite to furlow one man for every twenty men in camp. That [illegible] some of them will be coming home constant, &c.

We have a close time her[e] at this time. Tha [They] have cut our rashins down to a qarter of a pound of bacon and one pound of flower and evry third day we don't git that. We drew, today, one spoonful of shooger and not so much coffee and no bacon. We have close living. A.N. was in fine helth. I received a letter from home baring date 22 of December. I [learned?] from that you was all well, &c. I have bin looking for a letter from you for some time. I wrote you a letter just as soon as I herd W.H. was ded, but has far[e]d for to see ur ansur, yet & when these lines you reecve, please respond to me. So I will close by acknowledging myself, as ever,

Jesse Miller

P.S. Write soon and often.

---

1 *Jonathan P. Woody, Co. K, 53rd N.C. Infantry, died of disease December 15, 1863, at Orange County Court House, Virginia.*
2 *William Harrison Brown, Co. K, 53rd N.C. Infantry*
3 *Barnett Owens, Co. K, 53rd N.C. Infantry, d. January 4, 1864*

Camp Near Orang C.H., Va.
January the 23rd, 64
Miss R.L. Proffit

Dear Cousin,

I take my pen in hand in order to drop you a few lines which will inform you that I am tolerable well at this time, greatly hoping these lines may find you all enjoying the same blessing.

I have no news of any importance to write you we are doing the best we can. We have pretty hard times, though. I can inform you that A.J. & A.N. came down & stayed with us night before last & Whig & I went up and stade with them last night & have just returned, so ther has been a good deel of visiting here lately.

A.J. & A.N. were both stout and hearty. We went to the 67th Reg & Phillip went over & staid till bed time so ther was a right respectable crowd of us together once more & we enjoyed the time finely. Phillip looks the best I ever saw him. He is going to come home before long- then you can see for yourself.

A.J. & A.N. are going to come home, to[o], before long. I hope you will have a heap of fun when they all get thar. I don't know whether I will get to come home or not. If I do, I will not get to come before the last of March. I want to come vary badly to see you all. They are now giving furloughs, one man for evry 8. We send 5 men out at a time.

We have left the brigade- our Reg has- & are attending on two steam saw mills. We have to work nearly evry day & night, to[o]. They don't let the mills stop at all.

We have put up 3 sets of wintr quarters this winter and have been, two-thirds of the time without any selter [shelter] all, at that. As soon as we got sorter fixed up down at the brigade so we could keep dry & warm, the[y] took us out- moved us off up here & sat us down in the woods again- the ground covered with snow. We set right in & put us up another cabin & are fixed vary well again, if they will let us stay here.

If they turn us out again, I shall try to live the rest of the winter without any house, for it won't pay to bild so many houses unless we could get to stay in them.

It's a vary still time with the yankees, now. We here nithing from them, hardly. I don't know whar they can be. I am in hopes they have all gone home & will stay thar. It is reported here that old Lincoln has called for one million more men & is going to make a shure trip this time & most of our fellows that has always been whiped has given it up, that we can't stand such a force. I don't think that it is necessary to be scared before we are hurt. As for my part, I care but vary little how many men he calls for, for if he is going to crush us, I about care how soon, but I don't hardly think he will accomplish any greate things. If he does it will be more than he ever has done.

I must soon bring my letter to a close. I want you to write soon & give me all the news. Write if ther is any prospects of any weddings & who is going to marry &c. What is our old friend there doing? Is he likely to get him a wife or not? Tell Davy she may begin to fix up pretty soon & have her quilt ready for she may know who is coming. Tell Lilly to beg on maby peace will be made sometime.

I fer she has not done her duty or peace would have been made before now.

I must close. Give my regards to Uncle Wm. & Aunt Ninny & all my connection & friends. Write soon, no more at present but remain, your cousin till death.

William Walsh

P.S. Whig, Harvy & Jesse Miller are well. Whig sends you his respects.

W. Walsh

Camp of the 18th N.C.T.
March 9/ '64
Wm., Mary & R.L. Proffit

These lines will inform you that myself with A.J. returned to camp yesterday. We lay over 1 day at Richmond. We had vary good luck on the way. We never lost anything on the way. We drank all our brandy before we went to camp. We drank thee last in cite of camp.

We found evry thing straight. The yankees has made a raid or two and caused some moveing to be dun, but we are in our same camp. I found my house in Bad order. It looked to me like it had not been swept cince I left it, alltho they said it had.

I guess I gave it a brush this morning &c.

We are drawing tolerable good rations as they are giving us shugar, coffee, rice and molasses, beeaf and corn meal. I wish we could draw flower. We are tired of meal. I have not seen Philip nor J.E. Lewther. I heard from them, they are well. I expect to go to the 37 Regt. to day and I look for P. over hear to day.

It is raining hear to day and A.J. is on gard, &c.

Cis, if you recollect, I brought Enoch Spivey's[1] letters and a little blank book- just a few leaves, no lids to it- containing the number of peaces of clothing he had washed for the men. Please send the book and one letter as soon as you can put them in an envelope and direct them to me.

The letter he wants is from Tincy Jane Starlin. You can burn the rest of the letters if you please. I left them in a map in the bookcase, &c.

As I have no vary good news to write, I will soon close. Write soon and fail not.

Yours, as ever,

A.N. Proffit

---

1 Enoch Spivey, Co.D, 18th N.C. Infantry

When this you see, [illegible] me
knowing miles apart we be.

Mr. A.J. Proffit, Co. D, 18th Reg. N.C. Troops
Lanes Reg. Wilcoxes Divition
Miss Mary Walsh
Lewis Fork, PO

A.N. Proffit, Co. D, 18th Regt. N.C.
Laines Brig. Wilcox
Division Richmond
Va.

Liberty Mills, Va.
March 10/64
Wm. Proffit

Dear Father,

I can inform you that we are now in camp. We arrived in camp on the 5th day after we started. Our health is quite good. There has been but little done since we left camp. The yankee cavalry made a raid on Richmond and sum other points- tore up sum railroad between Richmond and Gordonsville and burned sum buildings, got whipped and left.

There is nothing of interest going on at this time. The health of the Regt. is good, &c. Pa, I hope that you will not think hard of us for taking J.A. Hudson all the way to Statesville with us, for we could not get a long well without him.

I will send back the duplicate I have of Harrison's money, which was sent to the second auditors office at Richmond and you can get some person to attend to it for you. As it was Sunday when I came through that place, I could not do any thing with it.

There is sum talk that we are going to be swapt for a regiment in N.C. & go to Wilmington, though I have but little faith in the report.

As I have no news to write, I will close. Please write soon and let me know how you are all doing. I feel much better satisfied since I have seen you all, &c.

No more at present, but remain yours, &c.

A.J. Proffit

April 2nd 1864
Camp of 18th N.C.T.
R.L. Proffit

Beloved Cister,

I, again, attempt to write you, not in ansur to a letter from you, for I have not had any inteligence from home cince I left- only what I heard through other letters. I have wrote hom- allso A.J. has done the same. If you have not got them, you should have written us, anyhow. I expected to git some letters when J.E. Lewther[1] came back but I failed to do so and I have almost sworn off even writing any more.

If I knew you had not started me a letter yet, I would find my oath, but as I have a better opinion of you, I will try you a little longer and see if you think any thing of me. I don't know that you have much right now to think any thing of me, but still if you don't, I think you could write me onse and a while, anyhow. I think this will do on this subject so I will stop these remarks & Cis, I will now give you a sketch of the times. I can inform you that we have the most rain and snow I ever saw. It is raining and snowing now- the wind blowing, &c.

As for rations, it is like Pap says- what we draw and what we by, we make it do. I guess we make the wild onions git up and git. We fish a good part of our time- that is a vary good traid- mutch like whare you live, we generally have fisherman's luck- a wet ass and a hungry gut, &c. &c.

Governer Vance is in our Brigaid. He was to speak yesterday [but] the weather would not admit of it. Then today. Today is worse than yesterday and I don't know when he will speak.

I have news of 53rd as late as 27th March. The buoys are all quite stout and harry. I saw P.W. [Phillip Walsh] [and] J.E.L. with others of your acquaintances, yesterday- they are in good health. Myself with A.J. are vary stout and harty.

I trust you, Father and Mother and the rest of my friends are all in good health, &c. Write me as soon as you get this. Give me a long and interesting letter. Let it contain the important news from home and Wilkes. Give me the account of our private affairs, &c.

As I have no news to write, I will soon close. I remain your affectionate brother, until death,

A.N. Proffit

Josef Jones

---

1 Jesse Elihu Luther, Co. F, 37th N.C. Infantry

LETTERS FROM
NORTH CAROLINA GOVERNOR ZEBULON BAIRD VANCE

STATE OF NORTH CAROLINA, EXECUTIVE DEPARTMENT,
RALEIGH, DECEMBER 30TH, 1863.

His Excellency President Davis:

MY DEAR SIR: After a careful consideration of all the sources of discontent in North Carolina, I have concluded that it will be perhaps impossible to remove it except by making some effort at negotiation with the enemy. The recent action of the Federal House of Representatives, though meaning very little, has greatly excited the public hope that the Northern mind is looking towards peace. I am promised by all men who advocate this course that if fair terms are rejected it will tend greatly to strengthen and intensify the war feeling, and will rally all classes to a more cordial support of the government. And, although our position is well known, as demanding only to be let alone, yet it seems to me that for the sake of humanity, without having any weak or improper motives attributed to us, we might with propriety constantly tender negotiations. In doing so we would keep conspicuously before the world a disclaimer of our responsibility for the great slaughter of our race, and convince the humblest of our citizens- who sometimes forget the actual situation- that the government is tender of their lives and happiness, and would not prolong their sufferings unnecessarily one moment. Though statesmen might regard this as useless, the people will not, and I think our cause will be strengthened thereby. I have not suggested the method of these negotiations or their terms, the *effort* to obtain peace is the principal matter. Allow me to beg your earnest consideration of this suggestion.

Very respectfully yours,   Z.B. VANCE.

STATE OF NORTH CAROLINA, EXECUTIVE DEPARTMENT,
RALEIGH, DECEMBER 31ST, 1863.

Honorable James A. Seddon, Secretary of War, Richmond, Va.

MY DEAR SIR: I learn that large distilleries are in operation at Charlotte and Salisbury in this State, making spirits of the tithe grain by order of the War Department. Upon application to the office of Maj. Badham, chief collector of tithe for this State, I learn that he has orders to deliver 30,000 bushels of grain to the distilleries for this purpose. In addition to the many and weighty reasons which could be urged against the abstraction of this much bread from the army of the poor, I beg to inform you that the laws of this State positively forbid the distillation of any kind of grain within its borders under heavy penalties. It will, therefore, be my duty to interpose the arm of civil law to prevent and punish this violation thereof, unless you will order it to cease. It seems to me if spirits are so absolutely requisite to the Medical Department, that grain sufficient might be found in remote and plentiful districts, and leave for the use of the people every grain which is accessible. Be this as it may, I am sure you will agree with me in saying that no person can under authority of the Confederate Government violate State laws with impunity.

Very respectfully, your obedient servant,   Z.B. VANCE.

N. CAROLINA GOVERNOR
ZEBULON BAIRD VANCE

Photo by Julian Vannerson, published 1859, U.S. Library of Congress. Text is from "Life of Zebulon B. Vance," by Clement Dowd, published 1897.

Camp near Orange C.H. Va.
April the 11th 1864
Miss R.L. Proffit

Esteemed Cousin,

    Having an opportunity of droping you a few lines in answer to your very kind and interesting letter which came to hand some time ago and not having an opportunity of responding to your kind letter until the present, I hope you will excuse me for the same. Although, being the weather so unfavorable and we being on picket, taking the weather you may know it has been a bad chance.

    I have no news worth your attention at this time. We are expecting a hard fight here soon, and I do hope it will end the war and what is left alive can return home to live free from the loud roaring of the enemy's cannon which has so long been heard in our land trying to force us to live as the colored race of our land but, thank God, if we are on a just cause, the flag of our country in triumph shall wave over the graves of so many of our dear friends and relations who have already fought and sacrificed their lives for the true flag of their country.

    I can inform you that I received a letter from J.F. Lipps.[1] He is now garding the small pox in Gordonsville, Va. He stated he was expecting to take it ever day. He only had a few more days to stay if he did not take the small pox, &c.

    J.H. Cardwell[2] has joined the Navy and left us. He was ordered to report to Richmond and I do not where from there. As I have no news to write, I will close. You must write to me soon and give me the news for I haven't received a line from home in a month. Harvey and William Jesse Miller and all the buoys are well. Let my folks know I am all write. My love to Unkle Wm. and Aunt Mary. Tell Unkle Wm. I must come home and see his slave. I am very respectfully yours,

Samuel Walsh

---

1 *John F. Lipps, Co. K, 53rd N.C. Infantry*
2 *John H. Cardwell, Co. K, 53rd N.C. Infantry*

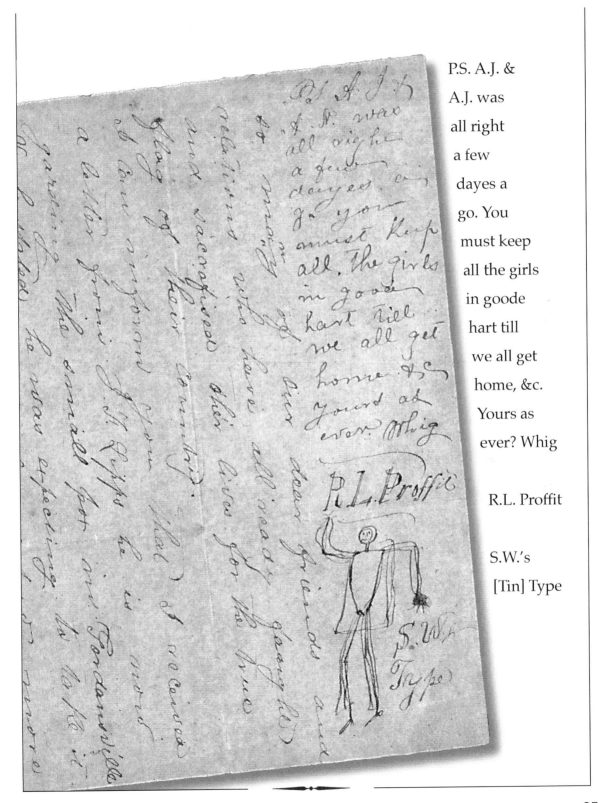

P.S. A.J. & A.J. was all right a few dayes a go. You must keep all the girls in goode hart till we all get home, &c. Yours as ever? Whig

R.L. Proffit

S.W.'s [Tin] Type

Near Orange C.H., Va.
Camp of the 53 Reg. N.C. T.
Apr. the 14th 1864
Miss R. L. Proffit

Dear Cousin,

I take up my pen in hand in order to drop you a few lines which will inform you that I am well, hoping these lines may find you all well. I have nothing mutch important to write you at present.

We are yet in camp near Orang, the wether has been so bad that we could not have moved, even if we had desired to do so. From what I can find out, some move is expect as soon as the roads will permit. I think that if the wether keep good for a few days, the bull will be opened without any doubt.

There is nothing between our forces and the forces of Old Grant but the Rapidan and it can be waded any whar. I should not be surprised for a fight to commence any time. It is not going to be a small matter when it does commence. I think Grant will make one of the most desperate efforts that has been made since the war commenced, to gain a victory over Lee but I have no fears of his being able to do any such thing unless he brings ten to one.

I think this army was never in better condition to receive him than at the present time. They have been mutch stronger, the health of the army was never better than at this time, & if all reports are true we will soon be abundantly supplied with reinforcements. But all there will not prevent many who are here living & in good health today from being hurlde [hurled] from time into eternity & no one can tell who they will be but we must all await its results & submit to our fate, be it what it may, the best we can. Thousands are now dreading the consequences of the bloody day which seems to be so near at hand & from which it seems ther is no means of escape. It may not be as dreadful as we anticipate.

I am vary sure it can't be mutch worse than I am looking for. I believe if we can whip the yankees right badly, here, this time, that we will have peace before a great while. They yankees are in fine spirits, now. They think they have the rebellion vary near crushed while a defeat under such circumstances would intirely change their notions on that point & perhaps make them become willing to let us a lone. Let us hope for the better the worse can but come. I will say no more on the subject at this time.

I can inform you that Finley Walsh[1] & John Wm. Church and several other Wilkes boys have been received into the 13th Reg. I have not seen nor heard from A.J., A.N. nor Phillip in some time. They wer well the last time I heard from them. I can inform you that Jack Cox[2] is dead- he died in the Hospital at Gordonsville. Ther is no sickness in the Companey, now.

You can tell Lilley I hope she will continue to beg for peace & not be discouraged by any means but just keep right on begging without ceasing till peace is made. That's the way for her to act if she does her duty. I did want to come home powerful bad & see you all this Spring, but ther is no chance now, & I have contacted you myself the best I can. I understood Uncle Wm. has bought a negro [illegible] Well, I hope you will not get to thinking yourself above the rest of us, as long as you have got rich.

Harvy, Whig and Jesse Miller are all well. John Cardwell has left us and gone to the Navy. Write soon & giveme all the news. Give my respects to Uncle Wm. and Aunt Ninny and all enquiring friends. No more at present, but remains, your cousin, till death,

Wm. Walsh

---

1 *Thomas Finley Walsh, Co. F, 13th N.C. Infantry, double first cousin to the Brothers*
2 *Smith Cox, Co. H, 13th N.C. Infantry, wounded, May 20, 1864, Spotsylvania Court House, d. May 27, 1864, at Hospital, Gordonsville, Va.*

Liberty Mills, Va.
Apr the 30th/'64

Affectionate Father & Mother,

After my best respects I write you a few lines which will inform you that I am in moderate health at present, hoping that my note may find you all in good health. I have nothing strange or particular to write . It is thought that we will not remain in camp much longer, though we are always expecting to march, so I do not know where we will go or how long we may stay. There has been a little cavalry rip near here, though it did not amount to much.

I can inform you that a great many soldiers has joined the Church, here, of late. The officers join the Prebyterians and the privates join the "mudheads." There has been a good many in my Co. joined and they have not stoled any of my rations since & I am in hopes that they will not ever be guilty of such a trick again, for they know that it is wrong. As I have no news, I will close. I have written you two letters since I had one from you. Give my respects to all my friends and relatives & all who may enquire for me. Write soon and give me the news- how you are getting a long with your work. I remain with the greatest respect, your old yellow boy &c.

A.J. Proffit

Camp of the 18 N.C.T.
Apr. 30, 64
R.L. Proffit

Beloved Cister,

I, again, write you, not in ansur to a letter from you, but to let you know that A.J. and my self are still survivors of the earth and are in moderate health at present and I hope when these lines comes to hand they may find you, with others of my friends, well. We are still in camp but expecting to leave soon. The cavalry had a skirmish yesterday- the enemy was driven back. We expect an early attact some whare between hear and Fredericksburg soon. Our notions are the same as when I last wrote.

Cis I have written home onse or twist cince I have had a letter. When we got any, they all came in a pile. We reciepted a letter from Betty a few days ago- she said she was doing tolerably well. In form me in your next what Pap has don with Jack- his age and how he and you are all satisfied, &c.

Tell Pap to do as he thinks best but if I was in his place, I should keep him. As I am out of news, I will soon close. Write soon and give me the news. I hear deserters are doing so bad as ever. Write me th[e] full account of it. Give my love to P. [&] M., Cis,

Your brother till death.

A.N.P.

Orang C.H. Va.
May 8th 1864
R.L. Proffit

Dear Sister,

    I attempt to write you in ansur to yours of 3d April. I think I was vary glad to recieve it and to learn that you ware all well, &c. It found me and A.J. well but on the road to the battlefield.

    We left camp (Wednesday) 5th. We reached the field in time to go in to it the next day (6). Thare was hard fighting all day- the yankes held thare position vary well. The next day- by then it was light enough to see- the[y] fired a signal gun and they, then charged and the first fire the infernal rascals fired, the[y] put it to me. I was struck just above the right eye. It split me to the skul a bout three inches, and you can guess if I didn't git away from thare. I left A.J. thare- I have not heard from him cince.

    I am now at the hospittal at Orange. My wound does not pain me any, all tho my eye is swollen and black. I have not heard from any of the relations.

    The fight is still raging. We commenst fighting between Mine Run and Chancellorsville. The[y] keep mooveing down nearer Fredericksburg- I understand fighting is going on at Drewry's Bluff and near Petersburg. A.P. Hill's, Ewel's and a part of Longstreet's Corps are hear- Boregard and Johnson below Fredericksburg.

    I will close. These lines leaves me well as for health.

Don't write untill I write again,

A.N. Proffit

Staunton, Va.
May 12, 64

Beloved Father and Mother,

I write you a few lines for your information concerning me and my health. My health is good, all though I have a slight wound. I will now give you some of the partickalers [particulars] of what we have just passed through.

We left camp last Wednesday- marched down the plank road to Mine Run where we made breast works last Winter. The next morning a little below thare, Ewel's Corps commenst fighting them and before night, it become regular all along the line. The yankees fought bravely. The[y] held thare ground. the fight begun the next morning by day light. The yankees got a cross fire on us. I was wounded- the first fire cut to the skull about 3 inches. I then left the field. Thare was not many gifting wounded at that time. The fight continued to rage all day. The enemy give way some, but slow. The[y] had thare great Gen. Grant thare but the rebals drove them back- taken a great many prisoners.

They have been fighting evry day cince it begun, I haven't heard any thing official for sometime. As for the rest of the buoys, I can't say any thing about them for I don't know anything.

Staunton Hospital
May 18th, 1864
R.L. Proffit

Dear Sister,

I, again, write you afew lines to lit you know that I am still living and doing vary well and I truly hope thse lines may find you and Father & Mother injoying the best of health. News of interest is scarse with me concerning the recint fight.

I hear no reliable news from the figh[t], annaway. I hear lots of news evry day but I put no confidence in it. I suppose the armys are a bout the same place as when the fight girst commenst. The yankees have give back some, I suppose. Boath we and the yankees are concentrating all the forces to Richmond from the West and the valley, &c.

It is reported that Jeneral Bankes has surrenderd to Taylor. Troops passed hear this morning from Richmond. Jonson's army is on the way to Richmond. It is the jeneral opinion this fight will end the war. Jen Lee is calling for horses- he sais he can't make the victory compleat without more.

I should love to come home on furlough and see you all the best kind, but my wound is not bad enough for 60 dayes and that is the shortest time they give now. My wound is gitting a long vary well- I think it will be well enough for me to go back in 10 or 12 dayes, &c.

I have not heard anything from A.J. nor has any of the rest of the buoyes, yet. I am now in Ward (N) at the Jen Hospital, No.1. My far[e] is as good as I could expect at sutch a time- I have a good tent and bunk to ly on and a good straw bed and tolerably good rashions [rations].

I will close. Give my love to all my friends, &c. I remain, as ever, yours.

A.N.P.

Sis, cince I came hear, I bought a button for $3.00 and made the prettist [prettiest] finger ring you ever saw, &c. I would love to have a letter from you the best kind, but I will wait until I go to the Regt. I expect thare has come some that I would like to have seen. I will send you a pretty, &c.

Yours, &c.

A.N. Proffit

June 2nd 1864
Staunton Hospital

R.L. Proffit

These lines are to inform you that I still exist and truly hope these lines may find you all well. I am in good health and a nurse in jeneral hospital, Ward 'H'- I have a heap to do. We have a heap of bad wounded men and lots of them are dying.

I wrote to A.J. a few days ago, but when it was ansurd, it came from the Sergt. of my Co., A.E. Floid,[1] informing me that a bout half of our Regt. was taken prisners cince I left- A.J. with the rest, &c.

Our forces are still in line of battle near Richmond, Va., but not mutch fighting going on. John Walsh was sent to the hospital be fore the fight with the meacels [measles]. As for the rest of the buoys, I can't say- I have not heard from any but A.J. and John. Thare is but six of my Co. left. I shall have a small Co. when I go back. I am doing vary well at presant. I have lots to eat and a good stomache.

I will close- perhaps you will never git it anyway- but if you do, write as soon as you git it and direct:

A.N. Proffit

Jeneral Hospital

Ward (H)

Staunton Va.

My love to my friends, &c., Yours, &c., writ soon

---

1 *Augustus Evander Floyd, Robeson County, Sergeant, Co. D, 18th N.C. Infantry*

> Richmond, Va.
> June the 11th '64
> Miss R.L. Proffit

Dare Cousin,

I drope you a fue lines to let you no I am yet livin an in ansee to your of some time paste an I have not hade time to ansee it. I am well as to helth an I hope this fue lines will fin alle you all well. I have no nuse to rite, more then we are in line of batle yet, but has not binn no regle in gagement in a week, but scrimish ever day an has binn evr sense the 4 of May an we have had some hevee fits, you ma bee shore. But God has binn with me an has brote me thru safe. I recon you hafe hard of you brothers before now- I rote it home twise, but I will rite to you. A.N. was wounde an I hope he is at home. He was wound in the head. A.J. is a prisner- I recon his Compine [Company] is all gon, but [illegible] an thay did not no what become of him.

I wante you to rite as soon as you git this.

Thomas [L?] is well, W. Church is missin. The rest of hour Cousin was all rite where I saw them and I saw all of them sens th 4 of May. We are in 10 milse of Richmond an in alyne of batle on parte of the olde batlefeld an I can'te tell you how longe we will stay here. Siss, give my love to all my friends an I wante you to Pray fore me. I hafe binn gratly blest in this ware. I have wente thrw shours of lede [illegible] ofton an has saw the young solgers fall all around me an has not binn hurte ther fore I thank God fore his goodnes.

So I will soone close, hopin to hare from you soone all tho I have not the promas of. To more no more,
                   Phillip Walsh

A few lines from L. F. Walsh:

As I have the chanc to inform you that I am well, I will say to you that I want to hear from you vary bad.

                       L.F. Walsh

Lynchburg, Va.
June 12th 1864

Est. Father & Mother,

I, again, write you to let you know that I am in the best of health and I trust these lines will find you the same. I am sorry to say the yankees run us away from Staunton. They whiped our forces out and taken the place but all that could walk got away. We had a long, hard march through the mountains- we all came to Lynchburg- we are now doing vary well. It is said the yankees are a going to try this place, soon. They have sent out all the men who ar able to fight to meat them, &c.

I am now in the kitchen cooking. I have plenty to eat and lots of work to do. I don't know how long I may stay hear- perhaps a good while and perhaps not long.

I have written home several times cince I was wounded but I don't know wheather you got them or not. I wrote for you to write me while at Staunton, but if you did, I left before it came. I have not heard a word from home cince the fight, I begin to want to hear from you all vary bad again, but it is no youse to write me unless I know how long I would stay hear. I suppose you know that A.J. is a prisnor as I have wrote it before. I know nothing about any of the rest of the buoys but John Walsh. He went to the Hospt. before the fight withe the Meazles.

I wrote to Wm. Whig and Harve but lef[t] be fore I got any ansur, &c.

Thare is not mutch fighting going on now. They had a battle near Peetersburg a few days ago. The yankees like to have got her- I understand they got in sight. They ware then whiped and sent back.

I will close for want of news. These lines leaves me in the best of health and I hope they may find you and all my friends well, &c.

Don't write me unitll I write again.

I close by saying I remain, as ever, your most obediant son untill death.

A.N. Proffit

Staunton, Va.
June the 27th 1864
Mrs. Elizabeth Miller

Esteemed Companion and Child,

I thru the merces of God drop you a short note to let you know whar I am, I left Gains Farm ten miles be low Richmond on the 13th at 2 o'clock in the morning and has bin apon a forst march ever since.

We went by the way Lieueasey [Louisa] C.H. then from thar to Charlottsville then Earlea's & Johnson's Divisions got on the cars and road to Linchburg. Marcht one hard day's march to Medder Station and got on the cars and arived at Linchburg at 3 o'clock in the evening.

Earley's & Johnson's Divisions had been fiting all day. We marcht out near the line of battle and struk up camp. Next morning we was marcht out afor to go in to the fite but when day came on, we soon learnt the yankees was all gone. Then we pursued them 3 days- the hardest marching I ever saw in my life. The yankees went rite along the rail road that leades to Tennessee and burnt some goverment shops and factreys and taken cattle, sheep and chickens & horses, &c. We persued them to Salem but with little afect.

I think it a por excuse for infantry to follow cavelry & we arrived here to day & I want for to see you and the children just as bad as a man can & these lines leaves me all most intierly broak down. I grately when tha come to hand you all may be in good helth & I remain yours, as ever,

Jesse Miller

P.S. Write soon and ofton as I want to here [from you]

Jenral Hospital No. 3 Lynchburg, Va.
Sunday, July 3rd 1864
R.L. Proffit

Esteemed Sister,

On the account of the late fighting round Peetersburg, knowing that the yankees had cut the railroad between thare and Weldon, it has caused me to neglect writing for some time, but I will give you another short note. I am still at the hospital, assisting in cooking for the sick and wounded.

My far[e] is vary good, I guess, I have plenty to eat and will if any boddy has any, &c.

The yankes has made a raid on this place cince I came hear. They came vary near taking it, but we got troops in time to give them a nice thrashing. They had to leave all their wounded in our hands.

We have a bout one hundred in this hospital. They are the worst wounded men I ever saw- a good many have died.

Times are tolerably still a bout Richmond and Pesters [Petersburg] but it is supposed that some of our forces are going to cross the Potomac as Ewel's & A.P. Hill's Corps and others are now in the valley.

As I have no news, I will close. These lines leave me well, &c.

A.N. Proffit

Lynchburg, Va.
July 10, 1864

R.L. Proffit

Having a good chance to send you a letter, I take these few lashure [leisure] moment in addressing you. I wrote you a letter by mail, yesterday, but as it is unseartain a bout its going, I will send one by Mr. Parsons.

I have nothing strange to write- I am still at the hospital, not because I am not able for duty- I am at hard work cooking for the sick and wounded. Times are vary good hear- we have lots to eat.

I would have wrote you but the railroad has been torn up by the yankees, so the mail could not pass. I suppose you have been vary uneasy about me, if you are a mind to be flustrated a bout sutch a beeing as I am but I am proud to tell you that I am all right on the goose.

I am thinking long of the time cince I heard from you and the rest of my friends if any in the old North State, which I hope I have. If I knew I was destitute of friends thare, I don't think I should bee so keen to return as I am. I want you to write me a long letter as soon as you git this. Give me a full account of our affars at home- the small grain, the corn crop, the fruit- and in form me how those trees don[e] that I hafe set out, &c. &c.

In form me how Betty[1] is doing- if she has plenty, &c. Give me some intelligence of A.J., P.W., S.W., H.W., and W.W. & J. Miller[2] as I have not heard from any of them cince the fight- except A.J. and nothing from him- only that he was captured.

Write me in ansur to all this, soon. Sis, we have women hear in the hospital attend to the men who call them selvs, Sisters of Charity, belonging to the Catholick Church and they will not marry. It is a gainst their profession to marry. They dress in a different way from any other woman. I wish you could see one of their bonnets.

---

1 sister, Elizabeth
2 Andrew J. Proffit, Phillip Walsh, Samuel Walsh, Harvey Walsh, William Walsh & Jesse Miller, probably.

SISTER
OF
CHARITY

I just think you would lauf till you could not stand.

I wish I could describe them to you, but I can't. I don't think any other person on earth could. They remind me more of some great fowl with its wings spread in the air to some a loft in the skise then any thing else.

As I have no more news, I will close by requesting you to write soon. Tell Unkle Sam's folks and McAlpin's and Thomas that I am all rite and would like to see them, &c.

These lines leaves me well, hoping they may find you fat and stout. Yours, as ever,

A.N. Proffit

P.S. Aunt Lovina Foster's John[1] is hear. He is on the mend, &c.

*When this you see, think of me,
for in Lynchburg I bee*

A.N.P.

---

1 John Thomas Foster, Son of Achilles Foster and Lavinia Goforth, Co. F, 52nd N.C. Infantry

Chester Station
July 27, '64

R.L. Proffit

I again write you to let you know whare I am and what I am doing. I am now at Chester Station, waiting for the train. I left Lynchburg 6 of this inst. for my Regt. I staid in Richmond last knight. I taken the train this morning to Petersburg- came hear and found my Regt. was at Clason's [Chafin's?] Farm below Richmond. I have stoped hear untill the train comes back again. I shall go to Richmond to knight, then take the boat down the James River to Drewry's Bluff, &c. I have had quite a long rest from the field but I shall reach it tomorrow if no bad luck.

Thare is no strange news- times are tolerably still along the lines. Some canonadeing and skirmishing along the lines- nothing serious, &c.

I left Lewis Waters[1] at Lynchburg. He was not vary bad of[f]. Wm. W., Whig and Harve was all rite when th[e]y started to Maryland & H.H. Baker, John Boman,[2] Franklin McNill[3] ware killed & I am well, &c.

I would rite more, but I don't know wheather you will git it or not. If you do, I don't know wheather you will ansur it or not- I have not heard from home cince April, &c.

I will close. Thes lines leaves me well, &c.

A.N.P.

---

1 Lewis Waters, Co. K, 53rd N.C. Infantry
2 John W. Bowman, Co. K, 53rd N.C. Infantry d. May 16, 1864, at Spotsylvania Court House, Virginia.
3 Franklin McNeil, Co. K, 53rd N.C. Infantry d. May 10, 1864, at Spotsylvania Court House, Virginia.

> Ten Miles below Richmond
> near Frasur's Farm, Va.
> July 29, '64
> William and Mary Proffit

Dear Father & Mother,

I again write you to let you know I have returned to my command, safe and sound. My health is fine.

The brigade was ingaged in a contacked with the enemy when I got in hearin of them. We drove them back some distance, but in the charge, our line got scattered so then we had to fall back and the yankees held the field- loss small on both sides. We are still in line but the[y] have not renewed the contacked, today. Thare is skirmishing and canonadeing along the lines evry day.

I saw P. Walsh, yesterday- he had received a slight wound in the side, but not ciriuous. It broosed mor than anything else. I think he will he will return in 6 or 8 dayes, &c.

Finly was well a few dayes ago. Wm. Whig, Harvy and Jesse Miller ware well when the[y] started to Maryland, &c.

As I have no news, I will close. Write soon and give me all the news from home and Wilkes & give my love to R.L. Tell her to writ soon. Inform one of L. Land's and J. Miller's folkes.

These lines leaves me well. I am yours, as ever,

A.N. Proffit

> 8 miles below Richmond, Va.
> in line of battle
> August 3rd 1864
> R.L. Proffit

Dear Sister,

I, again, write you, not in ansur to a letter from you for I have not seen a letter from you or any other friend in Wilkes in 8 months and you can guess wheather I want to hear or not. I know I wrote for you not to start a letter to me sevrel times and wrote to start some. If they ware started, I never got any of them.

But I hope to git one soon. When I got to the Regt. they ware ingaged in a heavy skirmish, which turned out to be a charge. We drove them back with a vary small loss, &c. &c.

We are now on the line injoying ourselves fine- we draw plenty to eat and have nuthing to do but cook and eat. I, of course, don't git as good things hear as at the hospt. but I have plenty sutch as it is. John Carlton is hear. Linzy is gon to the hospt. Rufus Robbends and Jesse Lewther are prisnors. P.W. was slight[l]y wounded and sent to the hospt.

I have not heard from any of the rest of the buoys.

Write soon and let your letter contain about 7 sheets for loss time, in full of crops, fruit, garden, health, &c. of Elizabeth, &c. Tell the Walshes to writ me if they are my friends, &c. In good health, I am yours, as ever,

> A.N. Proffit

Camp Near Bunker Hill, Va.
August the 7th 1864
Miss R.L. Proffit

Esteemed Cousin,

After a long delay of time, I drop you a few lines which will inform you that I am well at this time and I hope this note may find you all well, &c. I received a letter from you a long time ago, but I do not think you will think hard of me for not writing you sooner for I have had to fight the yankees nearly ever day all summer and they have tried verry hard to kill me, but my life has yet been spared though I have been, so many times, where it look like no man can live but we can only put our trust in a kind protector who is able to save us. You may think I am verry lonesome since Harvy and William is gone.

Well, indeed I am, but I have some of as good fellows as ever was to stay with. I do not know any thing of A.J. or A.N. any more than A.J. was a prisionner and A.N. was at Lynchburg the last I heard of him. Please write soon and inform me concerning them and P.W. and all the connection, &c. Give my love to Unkle Wm. and Aunt. Jesse Miller, J.F. Lipps[1] and all the Co. is well. Corpl. G.W. Murray[2] sends you his best respects. He is a verry good and accomadating fellow and no better a soldier than he.

I must close. Write soon and give me all the news. Yours, with great respect,

Whig

---

1 *John F. Lipps, Co. K, 53rd N.C. Infantry.*
2 *George W. Marley, Corporal, Co. K, 53rd N.C. Infantry, Promoted to Sergeant in 1865.*

Petersburg, Va.
September 1st, 1864
R.L.P. & S.R. Walsh

Esteemed Sister and Cousin,

Yours of the 22nd is at hand and it did not fail to interest me vary mutch to learn that you war all well.

I am glad to hear from those fine revivals in Wilkes. Also your fine crops- wheat turnips, corn, &c. I should love to be thare to help you eat some vegitables as they and so dear here, I can hardly by them. I will give you the prices of a few artickels:

> Apples from 2 to 5 dollars per dosin
> Peeaches the same
> Onions $3 a per quart
> Watermellons from 3 to 10 dollars a peace
> Butter $15 per lbs.
> Small loves of bread $2.00 a lofe
> Milck $4.00 per quart

other things according. I am glad to hear of your good prospect for potatoes for I just paid one dollar for 4 little things, &c.

I give you some account of our fight on the 23 inst. so I will sa[y] no more about it.

We are now in our breast works, two miles southwest of Petersburg. Thare are no yankees in our front near then one mile and a half but the pickett duty is vary hard as our brigade is vary small. We are drawing vary good rations- we all have as mutch bread and meat as we want- old strong bacon, but we got some beeaf today, &c.

Sarah,[1] inform me in your next of Unkle Andrew[2] and Ant Mary[3] and all the family, of the buoy[s] and what Regts. do the[y] belong- the health of Cousin Riley's[4] health, &c. Inform me how you like to live in Wilkes, what the prospect is for Marages, &c.

---

1 *Sarah Rebecca Walsh, b. 1838, Daughter of Andrew Walsh and Mary Blanchard*
2 *Andrew John Walsh, Jr., 1788 - 1870*
3 *Mary Ann Blanchard 1802 - 1870*
4 *Isaac Riley Walsh, b. 1821, Son of Andrew Walsh and Mary Blanchard*

Write me soon and excuse me for my imposition by asking you so many questions, &c. I hope you will excuse me for not recollecting your name when you first wrote me.

Tell Davy I shall be proud to see her and have a long talke with her for I could tell her some rich jokes. We have lots of fun along the lines.

Sis and Sarah, give my love and best wishes to all my friends and consider your selves two of them.

I am vary glad that you have formed the resolution to give me a letter once a week, for I have looked, in vain, a many a long day. Don't brake your intentioun, Sis. I send Julyan Miller a wring. Tell the rest I have no more, now, but if I have the chance, I will make them all one. Give her it as soon as you can- if it is two small, tell her to give it to one of the rest and I will make her another.

These lines leaves me in the best of health, hoping they may find you the same.

Yours, as ever,

A.N. Proffit

Petersburg, Va.
September 16, 1864
R.L.P. & S.R. Walsh

Yours of 5th inst. came to hand in due time and found me in the best of health. We are still in the trenches around Petersburg, but I can't say how long we will remain hear. We have marching orders now. The yankees are moving some way and we haft to move as they do. It is thought they are advancing on the South Side rail-road but I guess they will have some Rebbells to contend with before they git that as it is the only railroad to the old North State. We have a strong force yon to stop the raid.

Skirmishing and shelling is going on all the time.

We ar drawing flower all the time and it don't hold out so well as corn meal, but we are not suffering any yet. I saw Jesse Foster, yesterday. He sent you all his respeckes. I allso saw W.P. Walsh, J.D. Hall [and] Lafayett Prior- they are all well.

I was vary sorry to hear that Wm. and Harvy wore in yanks [illegible].

Buck Walsh of Elk is a prisnor.

No news from A.J.

I suppose P.W. has had his furlough extended 30 days longer and I have been looking for him for a long time. Tell him to hurry back for I am vary lonsome- noboddy to talk with but Dadburned Sandlappers who has been raised on yam potatoes. Girls, you must excuse a short and uninteresting letter for I can't think of anything to write. Pleas write soon and give me all the news. No more, I still remain yours, &c.

A.N. Proffit

>Petersburg, Va.
>Sept. 26th '64
>R.L. and S.R. Walsh

Esteemed Cousin and Sister.

Your vary kind and interesting letters of the 16th came to hand a few moments ago. They found me cooking dinner- I could not finish until I read them, after which I finished my dinner and ate vary harty of rice and grated corn bread and the corn was stolen- that made it a good deal better. Our bread rations are not vary good and the buoys of 18th flank anything they run up with. We take corn, pumpkins, shugar cane or anything we can eat, anywhare we finde it. I am glad to hear you are gitting along so well with your work. Tell Jack I say he must go ahead and wash his best.

You spoke of waning to see me vary bad. I think it impossabil for you to want to see me any more than I do you and I hope to soon. Sis, I think the war will close soon- in what way I nead not say- I leave that for you to guess at.

I am vary sorry I can't interest you with some good news, but I have none so you must excuse this short note. I give you all the news a few days ago. I am vary glad to hear from A.J. I hope he is all right at Point Lookout. Excuse me for I can't think of anything to write. These lines leaves me well and stout.

>I must close. Write soon,
>Yours, as ever,
>A.N. Profitt

Petersburg, Va.
Oct. the 8th 1864
Miss R.L. Proffitt

Dare Cousin,

I am hapy to say to you I am well and to drope you a few lines which I hope will find you an all the rest well. I have no good nuse to rite you. We are still in the wars an I see no chanse of bee inerwhare els[e]. I had to gor an afite the same day I gote back to my Compane an the nex day all so, but all is still, now. But I can'te say how longe they will stay so we haft to drink bad water. I wish I was at home to gor with you all to the santuary, but I no not when I will ever gite to come home againe. Give Cousin Rebecky my love an tell her to take good care of her little ba[b]e and keep him at home an not let him goe to the ware. Give Unkile an Ante my love an all inquirin frense, if eny, an recive a good parte, you[r]self.

Give Davie [Sole Erow Jane?] all my best respeck and tell them I wante to see them an goe with them to the mudehade metin [mudhead meeting] again an tell them I will rite to them before longe. A.N. Proffit as well. I have not saw none of hour kind [kin] but then I have no chance to goe no whare to see none of hour kind [kin].

So as I have not much to rite, I shall soone close, hopin to hare from you all soone. You can direck you letter as you all wase have to Richmond, Co. F, 37 Regt. Cournel Barber[1] is ded. He dide with the wound he recive the day I gote back, I hope you will excuse me for not ritin no more an for such bad ritin an speling. You no I no [caler?], so no more. You cousin an fren till deth,

P. Walsh

---

1 William M. Barbour, Colonel, Co. F, 37th N.C. Infantry, d. October 3, 1864, at Petersburg, Virginia.

Two miles west of Petersburg
Oct. 14, 1864

Sis,

Thes lines are to inform you that I have just eaten a harty brakefast beaf staek, soda bred, pure coffee, well sweetened- honey, &c. You may guess how my health is.

I have not rec'd. a letter from you for some tim[e], but I look for one Mondy. If it don't come, I will think you failed to write evry week as you said you would.

I commense of writing you a day or so ago, but I did not feel like writing. I threw down my pen and quill. So I expect you have failed to git a letter from me as well as I have from you but let's do better, hereafter. I have no no news worth writing, so you will except [accept] a short not[e] and write soon.

I give you all the news in Father's letter a few days ago about the last fight we have had if you could read it. We are not on the line, now. We have been out resting for a few days but we have but little wood and the wind begins to blow pretty cool- no prospect of going in winter quarters, this winter. It looks like we would suffer with coold this winter. I fear we will haft to stay in the ditch this season out, but I hope not.

Sis, last knight I dreamed of you and many others of my friends whom I would love to see, but I can't say when I shall, but soon, I hope. Tell S.R. I have not heard from hear for some time. Your friends are all well that are hear. No more from your friend till death,

A.N. Proffit

[At the top of page 1:]

P.S. The army is [recruiting] fast, now. All the stout men that are on details are called in to take the gun with the rest of us and I am glad of it.

[At the top of page 2:]

Wm. Church is dead, He died at the hospital in Richmond, some time ago. I don't know the disease.

Sunday, Nov. 20th 1864

Mutch Esteemed Sister,

This is in ansur to yours of 7th inst. which reached me in due time and found me well. We are still on the lines, three miles west of Petersburg. We don't anticipate another ingagement with the yankees, soone, for we have been building winter quarters for the last few days with great rapidity. We are building just in rear of our works. Today it is raining and I have my house up and the ruff on it and I guess A.N. is citting in it writing his little Sis a letter.

I have two men in my shanty- vary good fellows- but I can't git mutch fun out of them. They are from Robertson[1] Core [Corps].

Sis, we have just drawn a full suit of cloathing. Some of the prettiest kind. All I lack is my overcoat. If you can send it, I would bee glad. I do not want my blanket if you send any clothing but my coat with a par of sockes, &c.

Give my respecks to T.C. Land, T.C. Hill [and] G.J. Ball. Tell them I would be hapy in seeing them.

Inform me what States Troops, the No. of Regt. &c. G.J. belongs to.

I suppose you have not had a letter from me for some time- the cause of which I have not wrote it was three weeks that I was an had [illegible] its got any letters from Wilkes and I conclude the [illegible] stoped the mail so I quit writing.

These lines leaves me in good health and I trust they will find you all well and stout.

Yours, as ever,

A.N. Proffit

R.L. Proffit

P.S. Our friends in the 37th is well.

When this you see, remember me,
tho on the battlefield I be,
[illegible] at war we will bee free
yet soon I hope to be with th[ee]

---

1 *Brigadier General Jerome Bonaparte Robertson*

Camp of the 18th N.C.T.
Nov 27th 1864

Dear T.M. & Sister

Yours of Nov 13th is at hand. It found me in fine health and vary good spirits for I had my house vary nearly accomplished.

And I now have it entirly done. I have a splinded chimney and but two besides A.N. to enjoy its nourishing comforts if sutch a thing in camp like as comfort. I gave you a sketch in my last whare we had put up our quarters.

If no desterbence, we can enjoy our selves for the winter- so far as houses are consearned, but I fear rations are going to be short. I should love for L. Land to come out and bring me a box if he has the chance, but if not I suppose I can make out as well as common.

T.H. Walsh has returned safe. P. Walsh has just lef[t] her[e]. He toled me the painful news of the death of our mutch esteemed and beloved William Walsh who is said to have died at Point Lookout in prisoned by those mutch despisd invaders, &c.

I can deeply cimpacise [sympathize] with his dear father, mother, brother and sisters as well as many other kind friends & relations that ar lef[t] to mourn their loss for we all have the same troubls to bar[e], &c.

As I have no news to write, I will close for the present by requesting you to write me soon and give the interesting news of the times in that vicinity. Write the particulars of our private home affairs & how Elizabeth and family are doing, the prospect for provisions for another year, &c. &c.

I hope this will reach and find you all well. It leaves P.W. and I vary well

Yours, as ever,

A.N. Proffit

Petersburg, Va.
January 1st 1865

R.L. Proffit

You will see by these lines that my health is yet good and I hope the same of you and all my friends. Sis, Christmass has past and vary near in cilence hear- no fun- nothing to drink and but little to eat, therefore I think it a day [illegible] alltho I hope it has not been the case with you. I could but think of the times we youst [used] to have with sorrow and of the condition in which we are now plased, &c. Today is Sunday, the 1st of the year and I should love to be at home to go with you to Lewis Fork to church, but if as cold thare as hear, it would not be plesant. Thare is snow on the ground and the wind is vary sharp. Sis, it is said we are to have a great dinner for the hold [whole] army but I don't expect mutch, for if I was to get mutch, it would be more than I have don[e] lately. We have not drawn but two days rations of meat for five or six and one of them was spoilt, so I could not eat it but I don't wish to dis harten or make you uneasy. We have not been paid of yet- the talk is we will get it this week, but I can't say. I saw P.W., Dink W., T.D. Hall[1] and others, &c. a few days ago- they are all well. T.D. Hall will be home in a few days. He said he would bring me a box, provided it was taken to the railroad. I should love to have one of any chance. He is going to take the train at Hickry Station.

P.W. wants and I think Unkle Thomas and Pap could take us a box to the train. If you send me one, let it be the most meal, peas and beans, meat and as many other things as you all think proper to send. I should love to have some butter and molasses if you have them. Something good- a chicken, anything you have- anything is good to me. I want you to be shure to send it if any chance. If you do, tell Pap to nail a good loop around each end of the box.

If you don't send by Hall, send by the first chans. Send me some gloves and sockes. Don't send my blanket. If you fail to send it by Hall, thare will be others home some time before long.

I am vary anxious to get a letter from you for I have not got one from home for one month. Pleas write soon to your friend, A.N.P. if you please.

Tell Father and Mother I am not starving, but would love to have something good from home. Perhaps you could send by T.C. Land. I wrote to you last week, but did not send the letter off, &c.

Yours, &c. A.N.P.

---

1 *T. David Hall, Co. C, 26th N.C. Infantry*

Camp 18th N.C.T.
February 15, 1865
R.L. Proffit

Dear Sister,

Thes lines are to inform you that I am still in good health and truly hope they may find you, Father, Mother and my friends, jenraly well.

I don't know that I can interest you with any news that is good. L.L. stayed one day longer on account of an expected ingagement on our write with the yankees, but he did not stay quite long enough. The same day he left, the fight came and our loss in killed and wounded was 600 hundred- that of the yankees, unknown. Lane's Brigade was not engaged. Times has been quite evry cinse.

The soldiers are going home and to the yankees stedy. Some go almost evry night. Amongst others that have gon, P._____ and T._____ went a few days ago- that is to the yankees. They rather surprised me. I did not think of sutch a thing, but lots go that you would not think of.

I hardly think I shod go, but if I ever run away from the Army, thare is whar I shall go. I would not pretend to come home. Thare are things that would make me go but it is not worth while to say what those things are at present.

Sis, we have been paid off at last. I drew 6 months wages, but it is worth but a little. Meal is $2.25 per quart, peas, three. That is about all we can by to eat.

I was vary sorry I had no money to pay L.L. for bringing my box as he was dear of money as he left. I want you to inform me if Pap paid him anything for coming. He did not say when he was here. I told him I would pay him when I drew my money, but don't know how to send it. Thare is a risk to me in sending it in a letter and he never said what he charged to give me some information about it.

I started Betty a letter a few days ago. Sis, it seams like I can't git no more news from home by male. The letter L.L. brought is the only one cinse Dec. 11th. I will send you some stamps as soon as I can get them. It is said thare is none in Petersburg. If you nead kneadles and pins, let me know it and I will try to send you some. You will have to pay the postage on one or two more letters until I get some stamps.

Give my love to Father, Mother, &c. Write soon to your brother.

Sis, inform me if Pap and Mother thinks hard of me for not writing to them. If so, let me know it.

A.N. Proffit

Camp 18th N.C.T.
March 4, 1865

Father, Mother & Sister,

These lines are to inform you that I am still yet living and enjoying the finest health and hope these few lines may reach and find you all well. I have no straing news to rite, we are still in our quarters doing the best we can altho our duty is vary hard. We have lots of pickett duty to do and what makes it worse is so many desearting, the like has never been known. I don't know which takes the day, the yankees or the woods. They are going to the yankees evry night. We lost 16 out of it. 18 a few nites ago at one time- a squad start home evry few days.

I saw two shot a few minutes ago for deseartion. They belong to the 7th Reg. It is not our brigades alone for it is all the army. I suppose you have heard P._____ and T._____ went to the yankees - also N._____ of New Hope. I am in hopes A.J. will get home before long as our prisoners are being paroled I rather think A.J., Whig [and] Harve will get home this spring, &c.

Pap, I want you to write me a long letter, and do give me your ideas about the war, how you think it is going to terminate, the general opinion of all the citizens of Wilkes, &c.

I am vary sorry to inform you that I get no mail from home. The vary place I want items from. I have not had a letter from home by mail for near three months and I fear you do not get my letters. Thare is something the matter- you seartainly start them. I think if you do not, I want to find it out. Then I shall know you think nothing of me and I will follow P._____ to yankedom. I fear you don't start as many as you should for I get some from other sources. Perhaps you don't have these backed plain enough.

I have got no letter from L.L. cinse he left. I will send you some stamps and I would love to send sevral little things but Finly is not able to take them. My box is gon up the spout, but it don me a lot of good. If you have a good chance, send me a little more meal but don't put yourselves to any trouble for I have already troubled you a lot. I hear meal is selling for five dollars per quart in Petersburg. My money will not reach mutch at that note. The highest I have pate yet was three dollars per quart. I have drawn my money at last and promist to pay L.L. for his trouble and expense of my box, but I can't do it now for evrything is so hy it has taken the most of it. I will close by asking you to write soon.

Yours, &c. Joseph Jones A.N.P.

P.S. Inform Betty I have wrote her and had no ansur.

> Camp of the 37th Regt. N.C.T.
> March 11, '65
> Miss R.L. Proffit

Dare Cousin,

I seete my self to drope you a fue lines in ansur to your letter of 20 of Feb. an it come to hande an founde me well an I wase glade to hare from you. I hade allmost believe you done forgote to rite to me, but I cod not acounte fore it, but I hade not gote no letter frome Wilkes in a month. I sente some by hande and some by male, but I hope the male will goe thru study [steady] now. Well Cousin, I have no goode nuse to write to you at this time. I wish I code see you an all the rest of my freands. If I code bee with you I code tell you many things. I can't rite so I hope this cruel ware will close soone, so we all cane come home in pase.

Well Cousin, I cane informe you that yesterday wase a day of fastin an pray to allmity God an I don'te thinke I evr saw a lonsme [lonesome] day in my life. It wase darke an foggy an rainy an evr thinge wase still all day. I [illegible] like you rote to me. I wod love to write you a long an good letter if I code but I am in no fix to rite, today, so you will haft to excuse me this time an I will try to doe beter nest time. Give Unkle an Ante my love. A.N. is well an wantes to see you vary bade. Thomas T. Walsh is comin home- he is at home by this time, I recone. I sente a letter by hime to you. I hope this fue lines will reach an finde you well an all the rest. My helth is goode at this time. You rote Cousin Mary wase to bee baptise- I wish I cod see it.

Well Cousin, I wante you to write as soone as you gite this bade rote letter an give me the nuse fore I will haft to close fore I can'te write hafe today as well as commone. Whene this you see, remember me tho in the trenchis of Va. I bee.

Long wase frome you all, but I hope the time will come when we will all bee to gether in pease. Write soone an oftin. So, no more, you frend an Cousin till Deth.

> *Remember well an bee in minde,*
> *a fafule [faithful] frend is harde to finde*

> P. Walsh

Richmond, Va.
March 15th 1865

Dear Father,

    I drop you a short note which will inform you that I am in Howard's Grove hospitle. My health is quite bad though I do not think I am dangerous, for I am improving. I can get a furlough to come home if I was able to come, though I do not know when that will be. I have been sick so long- ever since the middle of Nov. I can walk about the ward & set up a little. I hope to be at home in a few weeks. Tell mother that I shall want some fine beer & a great many nice little things to eat, such as eggs, pickles, &c.

    If there is any brandy in the country, I want you to try to procure me a little. As I am quite weak, I will close. Please write as soon as this comes to hand & direct thus:

        General Hospitle

        Howard's Grove

        Second Division

        Ward 'F'

        Richmond, Va.

Yours truly,
A.J. Prophet

Sis, I recieved your vary kind and interesting letter which was a sourse of of the greatest pleashure to hear from you and the rest of the family. I want to hear from you oftimes if I can't see you.

I want to see you all the worst of all things. Tell Pap and Mother I dream of seeing them evry few knights and hope the time not distant when I shall have the pleashure of doing so. These lines leaves me well. I suppose A.J. has give you the news. I will close, hopeing to hear from you soon.

A.N. Proffit

[May 1864, Possibly from Staunton Hospital]

R.L.

I can inform you since I began to write you, P. Walsh has come to see us and brought us those things which you sent us and he is well. Also, James Howe and Lihew Lewther[1] is on the mend. I am quite glad to recieve those things. P.W. told us all about the affors [efforts] at home, but you must write soon and tell us all about your business. Write frequently. I will close, no more but remains, yours as ever,

A.N. Proffit

---

1 *Jesse Elihu Luther, Co. F, 37th N.C. Infantry*

As I missed getting to send it by Mr. Parsons, I will risk it by mail. If you git it ansur it immediately for I may not stay hear long. But you will recollect I am in good health andenjoying myself fine. Direct to:

A.N.P.

Collige Hospt.

Ward No.1

Lynchburg, Va.

Send me a spessaman [specimen] of your gardon flowers in your next &c. Tell Manervy Ellen to send me some pretty flowers.

My love to all my friends,

A.N. Proffit

P.S. I sent out the blackist shirt this morning to wash, you ever saw. I have a nice clean shirt but I can't say how long it will remain so.

[May 1864?]

Give my love to Father & Mother and all my friends. Inform me of my soldier friends for I have not heard from any of them. Inform me of A.J.. &c. Write soon and fail not. I have not heard from you cince April,

A.N. Proffit

Write soon and driect to:

A.N. Proffit

Colliege Hospital

1st Ward

Lynchburg, Va.

On yesterday, we captured some yankees and lost som rebels. We taken 2 or 3 peaces of canon and a few horses. My Co. consists of about 12 men and the rest of them are as bad or worse, &c.

Write as soon as you can as I have not got a letter cince April. I heard by P.W.'s letter that he got from you a few dayes ago. Direct as hear to fore.

I am your most obediant, until death,

A.N. Proffit

R.L.,

We have been vary hungry since this fight commenced. On yesterday, we ware vary hungry and went out to flank something, aiming to kill a sheap, but did not. We returned to camp and someboddy had killed a vary fat cow, not far from our camp, and taken the hind quarters and left the rest. And our buoys went and got what they wanted and I tell you, we had a fine mess and has not had a smart chance, yet.

I recieved those sockes you sent by Wm. Brown. I have wrote you, before, concerning them. You don't get all my letters, surly, and I know I don't git all yours, if you send any. Last night was the first I have got since P. Walsh came. Please write often and let me know how you are all getting along. I will close. I remain yours, &c.

A.N.P.

Don't write, for I think my wound will be well and me at my redgment in 10 or 12 days. I am now at Staunton Hospital. My far[e] is not as good as I want. The cause is thare are so many hear.

I will close for this time and write again in a few dayes. These lines leaves me well with the excepteance of my wound and when it gits well, I will try them again.

Yours, as ever,
A.N. Proffit

Sis, you wrot you had one of the smartest fishes I ever saw informin me whar he came from and his name, &c.

Inform me how you got the news about John Walsh. His Capt. has never heard it yet. Inform me if you have your kitchen don, how Pap swapt Jo for Jack, if Jack workes well.

I got letters today from L. Land,[1] Clarrinda Proffit[2] [and] T.F. Walsh. I shall ansur them when I git readdy. If you can't read this writeing good, I will do better as this is not the best I can do. Whar will the as-sotatioun [association?] be this year?

S.R., I am vary much obliged to you for ansuring my questions. I will ask som[e] mor[e] as soon as I can think of them, &c.

Yours, A.N. Proffit

---

1 *Linville Land*
2 *Clarinda Proffit was daughter of Thornton Profit, Andrew's uncle*

I think we will whip them. As you al tell P.& M. I am all right. The rascals only made an other horse kick on my head. When it gits well I will fight them again. Thare is a good many of my friends missing slightly wounded, &c. &c.

A.N.P.

R.L.P.

Sis excuse this bad wro[te] letter my hand is not steddy I will write you again when I hear from the last of the fight.

R.L. Proffit,

Esteemed sister, These lines are to inform you that I, with the rest of yor brothers, are all well and hope these few lines may reach and find you all well. I have no interesting news to communicate to you that would interest you in the least. I have written pretty mutch all I new to Pap and Mother. I suppose Elizabeth has you back home again. I recommend her for...[cut off sheet]

...so doing, I think she can do better thare than she can any whare else, this summer. Sis, when you git mooved, let me know, and I will come out and stay all night. I must soon come home and see all the girles in that cuntry, or they will forget me. Give them my love and respecks. Give my love to all my friends and except [accept] for yourself. Sis, excuse this short note and write soon. So no more but ever remains, yours,

A.N.P.

Part Four

Regiments & Battles

HISTORY OF COMPANY B, FIRST NORTH CAROLINA REGIMENT
BY R. A. SPAINHOUR

a diary, which was copied by his daughter, Mrs. F. G. Holman:

In the spring of 1861 Col. Sidney Stokes began to organize a company of Wilkes County men to join the war which seemed near at hand. They were called the Wilkes Valley Guards from which the U.D. Co's of Wilkesboro and North Wilkesboro have taken their name.

Young men from other counties joined this company. Col. Stokes drilled them until about the 27th of May. On this day they left Wilkesboro with Sidney Stokes, Captain, J.B. Gordon, 1st Lieutenant, Marcas A. Parks, 2nd Lieutenant, Thomas Bouchelle, 3rd Lieutenant.

The company on that day numbered 110 and nearly every man was over six feet tall. They first marched to Statesville via Taylorsville. We boarded the train at Statesville and went to Raleigh. The company there was located in what was then called the Old Baptist Grove. There Vance's company with others was also located. Up to this time our men had enlisted for only one year. Here the officers desired the company to re-enlist for the entire war. Some ten or twelve of the company came home- the others re-enlisted. Sidney Stokes was appointed colonel; Mat W. Ransom lieutenant colonel. We were then ordered to the Race Path near Warrenton for the purpose of forming a full regiment. Here we were joined by nine other companies. Ours was called Company B. After drilling at Warrenton some time we were ordered to Richmond. From there we went to Brook's station beyond Fredericksburg. Company B was here detached and sent to Aquia Creek to man heavy artillery on the river.

J.H. Spainhour was made chaplain of this First North Carolina Regiment on the 19th day of June, 1861. He only lived until October of the same year, having contracted pneumonia, and gave his brave young life for his country.

J.K. Howell was made chaplain after Chaplain Spainhour's death. He only served a short while. After him came the well known minister of western North Carolina, W.R. Gwaltney. He served until the close of the war and was much loved by the men in his charge.

During the fall and winter of '61 our regiment lost a good number of men from measles and pneumonia. During this fall J.B. Gordon was appointed cavalry officer. Matt W. Ransom was made colonel of another regiment. Allen Brown was then made captain of Company B. Marcus Parks came back to Wilkes and made up another company. He was made colonel of the regiment in which his company was placed.

John Hampton was Lieutenant in Company B. Also W.W. Vannoy.

We were ordered out on Mechanicsville pike June 26. Here we met McClellan's forces and an exceedingly severe engagement took place.

Col. Stokes was badly wounded in this fight and died a few days later. Many of the N.C. boys were killed here also. Maj. Skimer of our regiment was also killed here.

Next morning McClellan's troops fell back. We followed them until we overtook them at Cold Harbor and fought there until after the night came on.

Our regiment was badly wounded, Judson Curtis and Sid Weatherspoon were wounded in this fight. Few fields were so bloody as that of Cold Harbor.

In a few days followed the battle of Malvern Hill, a desperate fight. During July of '62 the second battle of Manassas was fought. The dead soldiers were thickly strewn over all the ground. Heavy fighting kept up all the year of '62 and oftentimes we cooked for our men just on stones and barbecued the beef. Camps were not settled long enough to do much cooking. The men suffered much through the winter of '62 from hard marching and lack of clothes- many were without shoes.

Lieutenant Vannoy of Wilkes lost his eye in a battle about the 12th of December.

January 1, 1863: Another year has passed and no peace yet. The monster war seems to be still active in his preparations to destroy more human beings. I hope he may be disappointed. February was quiet. During the month we have had some revival interest, our chaplain is W.R. Gwaltney,[1] a fine little man. I am tenting with him this winter.

---

1 See note on page 185.

March has been another month of snow, rain and wind. Fitz Hugh Lee whipped the Yankees on the upper Rappahannock River. On May 2, 1863, Gen. Jackson moved to left of U.S. force. This day he captured many prisoners by flank movement. On the next day a general engagement took place and was quite a bloody affair.

Lost many from Company B- T.J. Eller, John and Sam Pennel and several others, besides Clark, Whittington and others who died of wounds.

My youngest brother, W.M. Spainhour was wounded in hand and wrist, losing use of it for life. During this engagement Gen. Jackson was wounded and died of wounds received in the bloody battle of Chancellorsville.

The noted hero of our land, fell there among that noble band,
He led them on to victory's door, but fell before he could do more.

On the 1st and 2nd and 3rd of July our troops engaged the enemy at Gettysburg situated on a mountain in rear of Gettysburg, and after repeated attempts to drive them, our troops were forced to desist, though not till the hardest fighting I ever heard had taken place. On the third it was one continual roar of artillery and small arms. I suppose more than 200 pieces of artillery were in use at the same time. The slaughter on both sides was terrific. On July 4th we remained on the field all day, began to retreat that night but the mud was so deep we made little progress. At last we reached Williamsport but found the river so swollen we could not cross. We remained in line of battle for several days till pontoons were constructed. We then crossed and moved up the valley and across the Blue Ridge without further molestation.

A bloody year has just closed, scenes the bloodiest our country has ever witnessed have transpired.

1864 was ushered in with snow and very cold weather. Hard picket duty was our portion during January and February. The boys completed a church for worship and also had a school for those who could not read and write.

On the 22nd of March, 1864, a deep snow fell and the soldiers engaged in a sham fight. First and Third North Carolina against 10th, 23rd and 37th Virginia Regiments. It was as stubbornly contested as almost any fight. These sham battles were in progress over all the army.

Four Brothers in Gray

About the 1st of May the troops were moved from former picket line. Our men engaged the enemy above the Old Wilderness Tavern. We lost considerably. Faw, Gennings and Stockard were wounded. On May 8th, we moved about 20 miles in the direction of Fredericksburg until our right rested against Spotsylvania Court House. This has been a very hot day and the whole wilderness almost was on fire, as the fire, dust, smoke and heat of the sun all added to a very hard day's march made it quite oppressive. Many of the men gave out but most of them came up in the night. On the 10th of May, the 1st Regiment lost one of their bravest officers, Lieut. Larkin J. Curtis. He was ever at his post an indulgent officer and brave in battle.

On the 12th of May LaFayette Hemphill, father of our townsman, J.L. Hemphill, was killed instantly. He might have remained out of the battle freed by doctors' orders but he would not. His bravery was beautiful.

Here at Spotsylvania C.H., Col. Brown received three bad wounds. D.M. Carlton too fell here, from our Regiment. Few nobler hearted men than the three, that Company B lost on the 10th, 12th, and 14th of May, fell during the war. '64 saw many hard fought battles. January of '65 came- our hopes for our Southland, dim and uncertain after the weary days dragged by. Petersburg was burned and only loss of men and property seemed our portion. Gen. Lee felt that he could not ask more of his people and surrendered to the north.

From the diary we copy the closing words written after Spainhour's return from the four years of bloody war:

"The ladies in and around Wilkesboro gave the returned soldiers a fine dinner. The remembrance of the many who left there with us 4 years before, but who now sleep the last long sleep, some in unnamed and unhonored graves, made sad the day even though every kindness was shown us.

"Wilkes County nobly responded to her country's call, and no Company sent more men to the front than did Company B, 1st North Carolina Regiment."[1]

---

[1] From "The Land of Wilkes" Published by Wilkes County Historical Society, Copyright ©1962. Originally published in August 1913 issue of "The Southern Cross." Used by Permission.

1st Regiment
North Carolina Infantry

William Harrison Proffit joined the 1st NC Infantry, Company B, the *Wilkes Valley Guards*, as a Musician, May 27, 1861, at Camp Edwards in North Carolina. **Alfred Walsh**, son of Sanford Samuel; **William Walsh**, son of Kalip McAlpen Walsh; and **T.C. Land**, brother of Linville, all also joined the 1st NC Infantry, Company B.

The 1st Infantry Regiment was organized at the race track near Warrenton, North Carolina, during the spring of 1861. Its members were recruited in the counties of Chowan, Wilkes, New Hanover, Orange, Lincoln, Hertford, Northampton, Washington, Martin, Wake and Halifax.

In July it was mustered into Confederate service with more than 1,500 officers and men and ordered to Virginia. The regiment was brigaded under General Ripley, Colston, Stuart and Cox. It participated in the campaigns of the army from the Seven Days' Battles to Cold Harbor, was with Early in the Shenandoah Valley, and shared in the Appomattox operations.

This unit reported 142 casualties at Mechanicsville, 75 at Malvern Hill, 160 at South Mountain and Sharpsburg and 15 at Fredericksburg. It lost 34 killed and 83 wounded at Chancellorsville and forty percent of the 377 at Gettysburg. It surrendered 10 officers and 61 men in April, 1865.

The field officers were Colonels Hamilton A. Brown, John A. McDowell and Montfort S. Stokes; Lieutenant Colonels Jarrett N. Harrell and Matthew W. Ransom; and Majors James S. Hines, L.C. Latham and Tristim L. Skinner.

Information from the U.S. National Park Service.

13TH REGIMENT
NORTH CAROLINA INFANTRY

Calvin Luther Proffit joined the 13th NC Infantry, Company H, September 27, 1862, in Wake County, North Carolina. **Thomas Walsh**, son of Kalip McAlpen Walsh joined Company H and **Thomas Finley**, son of Thomas Walsh joined Company F of the 13th N.C.T.

The 13th Infantry Regiment, formerly the 3rd Volunteers, was organized at Garysburg, North Carolina, in May, 1861, with 1,100 men. Its members were recruited in Caswell, Mecklenburg, Davie, Edgecombe and Rockingham counties.

Ordered to Virginia, the unit was assigned to General Colston's, Garland's, Pender's and Scales' Brigade. It shared in the many campaigns of the Army of Northern Virginia from Williamsburg to Cold Harbor, endured the battles and hardships of the Petersburg trenches south of the James River and took part in the Appomattox operations.

This regiment totalled 575 effectives in April, 1862, lost 29 killed and 80 wounded during the Seven Days' Battles, and had 41 killed and 149 wounded in the Maryland Campaign. It reported 37 casualties at Fredericksburg and 216 at Chancellorsville. Of the 232 engaged at Gettysburg, more than seventy-five percent were disabled. It surrendered 22 officers and 193 men.

The field officers were Colonels Joseph H. Hyman, William D. Pender and Alfred M. Scales; Lieutenant Colonels W.S. Guy, Henry A. Rogers, Thomas Ruffin, Jr. and E. Benton Withers; and Majors John T. Hambrick, D.H. Hamilton, Jr. and T.A. Martin.

Information from the U.S. National Park Service.

18th Regiment
North Carolina Infantry

Andrew J. Proffit and **Alfred Newton Proffit** joined the 18th NC Infantry, Company D, August 22, 1862, at Camp Hill in North Carolina. **T.C. Walsh** joined Company G of the 18th N.C.T.

The 18th Infantry Regiment, formerly the 8th Volunteers, was organized at Camp Wyatt, near Carolina Beach, North Carolina, in July, 1861. Its members were from Wilmington and the counties of Robeson, New Hanover, Bladen, Columbus and Richmond.

It moved to South Carolina, returned to North Carolina, then in the spring of 1862 proceeded to Virginia. The 18th served in General Branch's and Lane's Brigade, Army of Northern Virginia. After fighting at Hanover Court House, it participated in various conflicts of the army from the Seven Days' Battles to Cold Harbor. It continued the fight in the trenches of Petersburg south of the James River and ended the war at Appomattox.

This unit was organized with 1,100 men, lost fifty-seven percent of the 396 engaged during the Seven Days' Battles, and reported 14 casualties at Cedar Mountain and 12 at Second Manassas. There were 13 killed and 77 wounded at Fredericksburg and 30 killed and 96 wounded at Chancellorsville. Of the 346 in action at Gettysburg, about twenty-five percent were disabled. It surrendered 12 officers and 81 men.

The field officers were Colonels John D. Barry, Robert H. Cowan, Thomas J. Purdie and James D. Radcliffe; Lieutenant Colonels Forney George, John W. McGill and Oliver P. Meares; and Majors George Tait and Thomas J. Wooten.

Information from the U.S. National Park Service.

37th Regiment
North Carolina Infantry

Phillip Walsh son of Thomas Walsh joined the 37th NC Infantry, Company F, November 20, 1861.

The 37th Infantry Regiment, organized by Colonel C.C. Lee, was assembled at High Point, North Carolina, in November, 1861.

The men were raised in the counties of Buncombe, Watauga, Mecklenburg, Wake, Ashe, Alexander and Gaston.

The unit fought at New Bern, then moved to Virginia in the spring of 1862. It was assigned to General Branch's and Lane's Brigade, Army of Northern Virginia. The 37th saw action at Hanover Court House and particpated in many campaigns of the army from the Seven Days' Battles to Cold Harbor. It continued the fight in the Petersburg trenches and around Appomattox.

This regiment reported 125 casualties during the Seven Days' Battles, 15 at Cedar Mountain, 81 at Second Manassas, 93 at Fredericksburg and 235 at Chancellorsville. Of the 379 engaged at Gettysburg, more than thirty percent were disabled. It surrendered 10 officers and 98 men.

The field officers were Colonels William M. Barbour and Charles C. Lee; Lieutenant Colonel John B. Ashcraft, Charles N. Hickerson and William G. Morris; and Majors Jackson L. Bost, Owen N. Brown, John G. Bryan, Rufus M. Rankin and William R. Rankin.

Information from the U.S. National Park Service.

53rd Regiment
North Carolina Infantry

Harvey and **Samuel Wals**h, both sons of Sanford Samuel Walsh; **William Leander Walsh** son of Thomas Walsh and **Jesse Miller** husband of Elizabeth Proffit, all joined the 53rd NC Infantry, Company K. **T.C. Land** also, later, joined Company K in the 53rd.

The 53rd Infantry Regiment was organized in April, 1862, at Camp Mangum, near Raleigh, North Carolina. Its members were recruited in Guilford, Mecklenburg, Johnston, Stokes, Forsyth, Surry, Alamance, Chatham, Union and Wilkes counties.

It served in the Department of North Carolina and then was assigned to General Daniel's and Grimes' Brigade, Army of Northern Virginia. The 53rd fought in many conflicts including Gettysburg, Wilderness, Spotsylvania and Cold Harbor. It participated in all the battles in the Shenandoah Valley, and was active in the Appomattox Campaign.

It totalled about 900 effectives in November, 1864. It lost thirty-six percent of the 322 engaged at Gettysburg, had 1 wounded at Bristoe and 2 killed at Mine Run. The unit surrendered 6 officers and 81 men. It surrendered at Appomatox Court House, Virginia, a force of nearly 250 on April 26, 1865.

The field officers were Colonels James T. Morehead and William A. Owens, and Majors James J. Iredell and John W. Rierson.

Information from the U.S. National Park Service.

RETURN TO THE TENTED FIELD
by Thomas Charles Land

When first the bugle sounded, to call us forth to arms,
I left my native country and its endearing charms.

And hastened to Virginia, the land of brave and free,
to fight for independence for rights and liberty.

'Twas on a little river called the Chickahominy,
there I first met the Yankees and fought for liberty.

For seven days we fought them, our victory was complete;
we made the great McClellan and his big gun-boats retreat.

Whilst in this mighty struggle a wound I did receive,
which caused me for a season my friends in arms to leave.

To friends and home I hastened and when my wounds were healed,
again I joined my comrades upon that "tented field."

Then soon to North Carolina we went to meet the foe;
but Foster would not fight us, so there it was no go.

Again to old Virginia we went to meet old Meade,
who tried to capture Richmond, though he never did succeed.

'Twas the first month of summer near Fredericksburg that we,
set out for Pennsylvania, Billy Yank again to see.

At Gettysburg we met them, the struggle was severe.
My friends fell thick around me, among them a nephew dear.

He gallantly was leading his band of soldiers brave,
but on that July evening sank into a hero's grave.

Here in the din of battle, mid shrapnel, ball and shell,
we charged and drove the Federals, though many heroes fell.

Then back to old Virginia went officers and men,
and spent the dreary winter upon the Rapidan.

And when that dreary winter had fully passed away,
again we met the enemy, 'twas on the fifth of May.

There Grant with all his forces, in the Wilderness we met,
we gave them such a scourging they never will forget.

Then we to Spotsylvania quite speedily did go,
once more to meet the Yankee, our cruel northern foe.

Here many days we fought them, the battle raging sore,
we gave them the worst thrashing they ever had before.

Yet here some noble soldiers, heroically they fell,
among who was our brave General we all did love so well.

Next at Hanover Junction we met Ulysses' host,
but here he failed to charge us, although he made the boast,

That he would rout our army and straight to Richmond go
in spite of all the efforts made by his Rebel foe.

Soon after this we left them and went to another place
and soon met up with Hunter and gave him such a chase.

That he will oft remember till time shall be no more,
till Yankees cease from fighting and cannon cease to roar.

So fleet was "Black Dave" Hunter, we could not him overtake,
so down the Shenandoah a pleasant trip we made.

Whilst in this lovely valley kind friends we daily met,
and though I'm from them parted, I will not them forget.

We went to Harper's Ferry, Yankee Bill to see,
and scared them as completely as Yankee Bill could be.

We got their pork and bacon, their beef and flour, too,
and sugar by the bushel we for our rations drew.

We also drew much coffee, molasses candy, too,
spice, ginger, salt and pepper and dainties not a few.

Here each poor ragged Rebel had plenty of the best;
each ate and drank aplenty, and calmly took a rest.

Our feasting over, we hastened as soon you'll understand,
to wade the green Potomac and go to Maryland.

Here we found many cattle, fat mules and horses, too
and friends both kind and clever to their southern country true.

We went to Frederick City, near which we met the Yanks,
and routed them completely near Monocacy's banks.

Then we in best of spirits did haste near Washington
that scared old Abe so badly that from his home he run.

I guess he thought he'd rather be back in Illinois,
where he was a rail-splinter when he was but a boy.

Then Jubal E. retired to old Virginia's shore,
and near the Shenandoah we rested one time more.

But old Sheridan quite angry, resolved to set a trap
for General Jubal Early, it was there at Snicker's Gap.

But Early was not sleeping and soon this trap did see,
there he met the Union forces and gained the victory.

Then up the Shenandoah to Fisher's Hill we went,
and in this pleasant valley some pleasant days were spent.

Old Sheridan advancing, the Valley we went down
and badly thrashed the Yankees one evening at Kernstown.

Through Winchester we drove them; the people did rejoice
to see the Yanks skedaddle before their Rebel boys.

To Bunker Hill we hastened, pursuit was not in vain,
we pressed the Yanks so closely they burned their wagon-train.

From Martinsburg we drove them, they could not make a stand;
We made them cross the river back into Maryland.

With Sheridan defeated, to Bunker Hill we go,
with friends both kind and generous, to rest a day or so.

Near this delightful station we bivouacked many days,
and feasted on nice apples, potatoes and green maize.

But in the mild September near Winchester we met,
the largest Yankee army seen in the Valley yet.

Though here they us outnumbered, at least four Yanks to one,
we made the boasting bluecoats in sad confusion run.

While we the Yanks were chasing, they fell upon our flanks;
and with their mighty numbers did quickly break our ranks.

Here in this mighty struggle, while friends were falling fast,
our General Rodes was wounded and quickly breathed his last.

Thus being overpowered, we slowly did retire,
exposed to grape and shrapnel, and to a galling fire.

Here I was badly wounded and left the battlefield,
on which we were outnumbered and therefore forced to yield.

Then I was sent to Lynchburg for treatment and for ease;
here friends made every effort my sufferings to appease.

Soon I obtained a furlough and soon did haste away,
to friends, to home and parents awhile with them to stay.

For many weeks I suffered, at length my wounds were healed,
and then again I hastened back to the "tented field."

We received this poem from Glenn Land, direct descendant of Thomas Land, T.C. Land's grandfather and namesake. According to Glenn:

"Thomas is believed to be the author of the words to the 'Ballad of Tom Dooley.' Either the version made famous by the Kingston Trio in the 1960's, or the version Doc Watson used to do. I rather think it was the latter. His brother, Reverend Linville Land (married to Rhoda Proffit) was also a carpenter. Oral family history says he made Tom Dooley's coffin and the coffin for the remains of his victim, Laura Foster.

"The 'dear nephew' he mentions being killed at Gettysburg was his Captain, William J. Miller."

William J. Miller was also nephew to Jesse Miller, husband of Elizabeth Proffit. Captain Miller and his two uncles all served in Company K, 53rd N.C. Infantry.

—PUBLISHERS.

Made in the USA
Columbia, SC
05 April 2025